'This book offers practical advice for anyor[...] ing their own business. The format is very [...] to reflect and think about the importance [...] jumping into the world of entrepreneurship. working [...] porter of SMEs, I am confident that many of our customers and other aspiring entrepreneurs will benefit from Bianca and Byron's personal experience.'

> *Gordon Merrylees – Head of Entrepreneurship, Royal Bank of Scotland, NatWest and Ulster Bank*

'Successful entrepreneurs learn fast. *Self Made* is a fantastic way to learn an incredible amount of hugely practical information very, very quickly.'

> *Dhiraj Mukherjee – co-founder of Shazam, investor and business consultant*

'Bianca and Byron have written an accessible and engaging route map for budding entrepreneurs. Not only do they take you through the process, they also offer their own perspective on the advantages and pitfalls associated with the many choices entrepreneurs have to make about funding, marketing and operations. *Self Made* will prove to be an excellent guide for many.'

> *Professor Steven McGuire – Professor of Business and Public Policy, and Head of School (School of Business, Management and Economics), University of Sussex*

'In *Self Made*, Bianca and Byron succeed in providing the necessary tools for young enterprising professionals. They meticulously construct their advice through four steps: Vision, Action, Reaction and Evolution, and by doing so craft a business mindset that is both daring and responsible. The book seamlessly integrates modern technology and social media tactics, making it a must-read for the new generation of entrepreneurs.

To climb any mountain, you need support. If starting a business is like climbing a mountain, *Self Made* is the support rope.'

> *Marc Adelman – media consultant, Los Angeles*

'For a business to survive in today's challenging economic climate, you need drive, passion, knowledge and a pretty robust business network. Whether you are just starting a business or you're an established entrepreneur with many businesses, *Self Made* shows you both the pitfalls and the opportunities entrepreneurs will experience on their business journey. *Self Made* is the essential toolkit that you absolutely need by your side! To the social media savvy it's #mustreadselfmade.'

> *Heather P Melville OBE – Director of Strategic Partnerships & Head of Women in Business, RBS*

'Seriously this is the book entrepreneurs have been waiting for, it is truly excellent! *Self Made* is an absolute must-read for any budding entrepreneur. The book is full to the brim of practical tips and key insights in to exactly what it takes to start a business. Bianca and Byron write with such clarity and share their own experiences in an easy-to-consume format, including checklists and resources. You really could pick up this book and get to work setting up your business the moment you put it down! If there is one book you buy this year before expanding your business or taking that all important leap to start up, then this is one! I just wish this book had been around ten years ago! 10 out of 10 for *Self Made*.'

Vanessa Vallely – Managing Director, WeAreTheCity

'This book reads like a conversation between old friends. No matter what type of business you are launching, Bianca and Byron give you a step-by-step guide to the questions that every business owner needs to ask themselves when starting up, and they advise you on how to avoid the pitfalls. Many people want to be an entrepreneur, but this book breaks down the work that comes with that title in an easy-to-grasp format.

Compared to a lot of authors out there, Bianca and Byron have actually done it and they share their experiences in an easy-to-read, easy-to-apply format that will have you up and running your business in no time.'

Melanie Eusebe – entrepreneur and co-founder of the Black British Business Awards

'Ten years ago I started a charity to help young people from underserved communities to set up their own businesses. Over 270 businesses started as a result, yet we still see people confused about what business is all about. What Bianca and Byron have provided in their comprehensive guide to starting up a business, is an easy-to-follow but detailed roadmap of things that the aspiring business owner should consider. Additionally, for those who have already begun the journey the guide offers insights that can help their business go to the next stage. As the world continues to change, the need for helpful and sage advice increases. *Self Made: The definitive guide to business startup success* does what it says on the tin and adds to the much needed information for the next generation of successful business owners.'

Tim Campbell – entrepreneur and winner of The Apprentice, 2005

'I am very excited about this book. It is beyond brilliant and much needed as it covers absolutely everything you need to know when setting up a business – there is even a chapter on mindset which is so important. I really wish this book was around when I started my ventures.'

Emma Sexton – founder of Make Your Words Work™, co-founder of Flock Global™, broadcaster, Creative-in-Residence at King's College London

Self Made

Self Made

The Definitive Guide to Business Startup Success

BIANCA MILLER-COLE
BYRON COLE

JOHN
MURRAY
LEARNING

First published in Great Britain by John Murray Learning in 2017
An imprint of John Murray Press
A division of Hodder & Stoughton Ltd,
An Hachette UK company

This paperback edition published in 2022

1

Paperback ISBN 978 1 529 38227 3
Trade Paperback ISBN 978 1 473 65529 4
eBook ISBN 978 1 473 65530 0

Typeset by KnowledgeWorks Global Ltd.

Printed and bound in Great Britain by Clays Ltd, Elcograf S.p.A.

John Murray Press policy is to use papers that are natural, renewable and recyclable products
and made from wood grown in sustainable forests. The logging and manufacturing processes
are expected to conform to the environmental regulations of the country of origin.

John Murray Press   Nicholas Brealey Publishing
Carmelite House   Hachette Book Group
50 Victoria Embankment   Market Place, Center 53, State Street
London EC4Y 0DZ   Boston, MA 02109, USA

www.johnmurraypress.co.uk

Contents

Acknowledgements

We would both like to thank our family and friends for your continued love and support. You all play an important role in keeping us grounded and we love you unconditionally.

To our interviewees, industry experts, publisher, editor, Cheryl, Claude and everyone who helped put this book together, we want to extend a special 'thank you' to you all.

Byron: First and foremost, I would like to thank God. During my business journey I have realized that business is my gift. My dreams have long been accomplished and I now strive for accomplishments beyond my wildest dreams.

To my amazing wife for being my rock and being with me every step of the way both in business and in our lives. Thank you for your unquestioning belief in me despite my continual crazy business ideas. Our journey is amazing and I look forward to what the future holds.

To my mother and sister, I thank you for all of your support and endless positive attitude. You have no idea what a positive impact you both have on my life. You are my continued motivation and inspiration.

Bianca: To my parents, for always (ALWAYS) being supportive of everything I do and want to do (now and in the future) and for always pushing me to try harder and be better. You encouraged me to believe that the sky was not the limit and to find a partner who believed the same. That spirit of determination, the work ethic and my enthusiasm for life as well as entrepreneurship come from you both. Your ongoing wisdom, love and support have made me who I am today. Thank you.

To my husband, best friend, business partner and now co-author… what can I say? We talked about it and we did it! Thank you for always pushing me, supporting me and sometimes forcing me to reassess risk. I pray our risks and pursuits continue to be fruitful as we continue to build our lives together.

To all of you budding entrepreneurs out there, to each and every person who queued up after a talk to ask a question or reached out to get help with your business journey – you inspired us to write this book. Thank you for being an inspiration – I hope this book motivates and guides you as you strive to make your dreams a reality!

Foreword

As I begin this foreword it is only fair that I declare a strong bias in favour of Bianca Miller-Cole.

I first encountered Bianca when she successfully applied to be one of the candidates on *The Apprentice*. She excelled throughout the gruelling 12-week process and was hugely impressive during the interview episode with her calm manner, professionalism, well-structured business plan and an ability to articulate her proposal.

It was therefore no surprise to me when Bianca launched her business and it has been a pleasure to observe from afar how she developed and adjusted her business plan, overcame obstacles and now has a business that is going from strength to strength. I wish her and Byron continued success.

Self Made: The Definitive Guide to Business Startup Success is a pretty bold statement, and to embark on a book with that title is surely something of a stretch. I therefore read the manuscript with a certain degree of scepticism and a sense of foreboding that Bianca and Byron had taken leave of their senses!

After all, the only way to really understand about being your own boss and launching a business, is to actually go out and do it. In reading the book, I immediately warmed to it. I enjoyed the anecdotes and was able to relate to many of them; they were peppered with real-life experiences and frank advice. I began to find it compelling reading, and my thoughts turned to how much I might have benefited from such a book before embarking on my career in business; I would surely have avoided some of the more common mistakes.

The book is presented in a clear, logical, and very readable format, simplifying and explaining company and business jargon. There are some really valuable nuggets to help you map out your business, address the matter of gaining access to sources of finance, build your brand and use networking to the best advantage. Indeed, the book is so comprehensive and well researched that it leaves no stone unturned in its effort to live up to its title. In my opinion is does exactly what it says on the front cover!

Anyone who has started a business knows that it can be a tough and lonely existence. You need to be resilient, single-minded, adaptable and lucky! On the journey to becoming *Self Made* there is no-one to blame but yourself if things go 'off the rails'; however, the massive sense of satisfaction, and relief, when business picks up and you gain confidence is absolutely exhilarating.

The thing about business is that it is dynamic, and what has worked today, may not work tomorrow! *Self Made: The Definitive Guide to Business Startup Success* identifies the skills required no matter what the change in landscape: qualities such as being inquisitive, asking questions, listening to the answers, spotting trends and business opportunities, and learning from your own experience and from those of others.

I can now summarize my thoughts. **Read the book, you won't be disappointed.**

Claude Littner
Entrepreneur and advisor to Lord Sugar on *The Apprentice*

Introduction

In business, as in life, you don't know what you don't know. And so you make mistakes. And, whilst mistakes can be useful learning tools – showing you what not to do and what you should do differently next time – when you are starting a new business with a limited budget, there might not even be a next time, as mistakes can be crippling. If a mistake wipes out your vital capital, there might not be a second chance. As a startup, what you often lack is capital and time (as you will be juggling several roles and wearing all the hats). So you really need to carefully consider your time and your money and how you invest those two things. As such, it's incredibly helpful for new business owners to learn from those who have already made the mistakes and learned from them – which is where this book comes in.

As budding entrepreneurs, you all know why you want to be 'self-made': the flexibility, the higher earning potential, the limitations removed, the chance to fulfil a dream or passion. The million dollar question is how do you make it happen?

Self Made is a definitive guide to becoming a self-made business success. It is based on the experiences and frank opinions of me, Bianca Miller-Cole, entrepreneur, consultant and *The Apprentice* finalist, and my husband, serial-entrepreneur Byron Cole, as we fulfil our roles as owners and Chief Executive Officers of The Be Group/ Bianca Miller London and The BLC Group respectively. The book provides practical step-by-step advice on all aspects of business enterprise – from startup through growth to exit – and benefits from our insights into our achievements and the challenges we have faced.

For decades, the plethora of business books out there have advised you to develop a 'millionaire's mindset', create a 'circle of influence' and 'turn your dreams into reality'. Now it's time to really scratch under the surface to discover precisely how to start, sustain and sell your own enterprises and be successful.

Supported by anecdotal evidence at every tier of the business development process, this is a 'go-to' book for all entrepreneurs at any stage of business. Decoding the jargon that is prevalent in business circles today, our aim for this book is to provide straightforward advice on converting an innovative business concept into a commercially viable proposition.

Our story so far – Byron and Bianca

In pursuit of his childhood dream of becoming self made, Byron accumulated a wealth of knowledge from a vast reading list written by a 'who's who' in the international business community – past and present. Initially enamoured with the core principles governing business success, Byron eventually began to feel short-changed by the glaring lack of detail about how to become self made.

Moreover, Byron observed that, whilst their content was theoretically sound, the majority of published works he read were written by speakers and consultants – many of whom had never run their own business before. He set out to fill this gap and write a definitive 'how-to' guide to business success which includes the struggles, the hindsight 'hacks' and straightforward practical advice.

Having grown up in entrepreneurial household, I also shared Byron's childhood dream of running my own business. Having made that dream a reality at the age of 23, I witnessed first-hand the many pitfalls and potential mistakes that can be made in business. Conversely, I also saw the success that can come from areas often overlooked in business such as networking, personal branding and mentoring.

I chose to seek guidance from training programmes, books and mentors. In doing so, I discovered that it was often the experienced mentors and business people who were able to relay the most important, helpful and relevant information. In business, it is from experience that you learn what to do, and what not to do; although, notably, that experience doesn't always have to be your own! For me, it was financially more prudent to learn from other people's mistakes and successes when creating my own legacy. And so I did.

Now, together, Byron and I have used our experiences of riding the rollercoaster of running businesses, to produce an easy-to-read guide that provides budding entrepreneurs with all of the tools needed to achieve success.

From dreaming up an idea and bringing the vision to fruition, to being proactive and reactive and evolving, the book is split into four parts. You will learn how to:

- start up with an alternative to a business plan
- find information that really matters
- form a company and create a website on a budget
- stand out from the crowd
- build a personal brand
- communicate effectively with anyone
- find the best deals to save money
- find the best customers with only a computer and a phone
- make networking work for you
- convert social media into revenue
- source funding
- sell, grow and collaborate
- manage time to make the most of every minute
- value and sell the business on.

Self Made is intended to be a personal coaching manual that readers can dip in and out of and work through at their own pace. Both practical and inspirational, this book will show you how to overcome challenges, learn from those who have gone before you and run your best possible enterprise.

Part 1: The Vision

You've got your business idea: now you need to set about making it a reality. In Part 1, we'll look at how to get your new startup off the ground, covering subjects including business plans, market research, brand identity, marketing and finance. We'll also get an expert insight into legal requirements for business from solicitor Trevor Japal.

I

Business mapping

A clear vision of *where* you are heading on your business journey is the first and most vital imperative. You can't plan your route if you don't know where you are going, so your dreamed destination as you see it in your mind's eye, is critical. Every successful self-made person has a vision of what they are striving to achieve.

From Bill Gates' dream to 'put a computer on every desk',[1] and Sergey Brin and Larry Page's vision 'to organize the Internet,'[2] to Jason Vale's goal to 'juice the world':[3] they all started with the end in mind. Your own long-term objectives are what will drive you when the going gets tough and are what will help shape your business decisions. Your vision is your 'why' – it's your ultimate reason for doing this. Yes, you probably want to be self made because you want the flexibility that being self-employed affords you; you want to remove the earnings ceiling that being employed creates, and you want to be your own boss, but you should also have a vision of what you hope to do, and what problem you wish to solve.

You may also have a personal vision of what your self-made success will make possible, such as having a big house and nice car, but what we are talking about here is your ultimate business destination.

Once you are clear on what your destination is, you can begin mapping out your journey and start planning. First of all you need to decide on your business status and name so that you can notify the appropriate authorities.

Define who you are and where you'll be based

The status you choose to operate under will impact a number of things, including personal liability for debts, and how much paperwork you will have to do. There are three main options to choose from in the UK:

1 **Sole trader** – just one person owns the business and there is no need to register with Companies House (so no company registration fees). You must register with HMRC however, so that you can fill out an annual self-assessment income tax form. If anything goes wrong, you will be personally liable for any debts incurred by the company.

2 **Partnership** – a general partnership is run like a sole tradership but with two partners rather than one person (making you both liable for any debts). Alternatively, a limited liability partnership is run like a limited company.

3 **Limited company** – there is more paperwork involved but you have a level of personal protection, and have the credibility of being a legitimate company. You register your company with Companies House and, as the company owner, you have limited liability. This means that, should anything go wrong, the company is liable for debts, rather than you personally. You and the company are separate entities which means that money generated by the company belongs to the company, rather than the owner. You are a director and shareholder of the company and are paid dividends and/or a salary via a payroll system.

The majority of businesses tend to start up as sole traders due to the lack of complexity and the ability to get on and test the market. Registration and record-keeping is straightforward too. As a sole trader you can still use a business name but, when you fill out your tax return, for example, you'd be 'Joe Bloggs trading as Acme Floristry' rather than 'Acme Floristry Ltd'.

Sometimes a business needs to be established as a limited company from the start because of the kinds of customers it seeks. So, for example, a consultancy striving to win a contract with an organization which doesn't use sole traders has to set up as a limited company. It certainly lends credibility in some industries.

There are also some tax benefits to being paid dividends as a director of a company, rather than a salary or taking income from profits. However, as a limited company you have to pay corporation tax as well as income tax (whereas, a sole trader only pays income tax on their earnings). As well as your annual tax return you are required by law to file an annual company return. Furthermore, anyone can look at your company accounts, just as you can look at your competitors' accounts via Companies House, so there's less privacy.

Before you can register your new business with HMRC and Companies House you'll need a name for it, so make sure you choose something that's easy to spell and is memorable.

Before you commit to the name, it's also critical that you check its availability as a domain name via a domain name registry, such as GoDaddy or 123 Reg. Furthermore, you should search Companies House online register to check that your preferred name isn't already being used. As well as availability and uniqueness, it's important that your name fits with your brand persona. It may even feature your own name, especially if you have built up a strong profile. That's why we chose 'Bianca Miller London' for my new business, as during my time on *The Apprentice* I had become known as the 'tights lady', so it made sense to utilize my name for the brand. It was also a name that allowed me to diversify the offering in the future. Also consider how the business is likely to be perceived in the marketplace. For example, the name of another of my businesses, The Be Group, has the instant connotation of being a large company and, given its corporate clientele, this is important.

Define and understand your product or service

If you imagine your business as a map, your vision as your final destination and your strategy and associated actions as the stop-off points along the way, you need to first define what your product or service is (what problem is it solving and/or what benefits is it providing?) You also need to decide on the business model (how will your product/service generate revenue?) Once you know what you will be selling and via which model, you need to figure out your routes to market and plot those onto your map. However, before you can do that you need to go out into the market and gather as much information as you can.

Clarity around all of this is key.

So, let's take this one step at a time:

1 **What product or service do you aim to provide and why?** What do you intend to sell? What problem (if any) does your product or service solve, or what need does it fulfil?

2 **What benefits will your product or service provide for your customers?** For example, will it provide them with more choice? Will it help them to save time or money? Will it help them to perform a task better or faster or with less waste or more accuracy?

3 **What business model will you use in order to generate revenue and how will you reach your customers?** For example:

- Will you sell direct to your customers from your website or from a high street shop or market stall (retail), or will you sell to businesses who then sell those products on to the customer (wholesale)?
- Will you charge a monthly membership/subscription fee for your services (subscription model)?
- Will you ask for money up front and get your customers to vote on what you sell in order to pass on the savings of bulk buying (me-tail)?
- Or will you provide free versions of your product or service to generate significant awareness and package up a premium version to sell on the back of that widespread coverage (freemium)?
- You might set up a marketplace, charge fees and earn commission from each sale that is made on your platform, or maybe you want to join forces with another business that already has significant reach in your market and split the proceeds (revenue share model)?
- Will you sell the licence to your material and enable others to sell your product, service or software under their own brand name (licensing model)?
- Or will you set up a business that, once successful, can be duplicated across regions (franchise model)?

Once you have the basics in place and know who you are, what your status is and what you intend to sell via which business model, it's time to do your homework and dig deep into the market that you are about to enter.

Knowledge is power – research your market

Many businesses come to life because the entrepreneur has identified a problem and found a solution. Bianca Miller London came about when I couldn't find nude hosiery that complemented my skin tone, so the business idea was born out of a problem that I had personally. Similarly, when Byron and I got engaged we started going to wedding shows and realized how time-consuming and overwhelming they can be. We were given bags filled with leaflets which we then had to wade through, hindering rather than helping the planning stage. That feeling of 'surely there's got to be a better way' led Byron to set up the 'Happy Bride Guide', a one-stop-shop for couples getting married: essentially, an online wedding planning directory. However, he still needed to do his homework: assess viability and see what was already out there in the marketplace.

Before you sell anything to anyone you need to answer the following questions: who is most likely to want what you are selling? Why so? Where might they buy it from? And how much would they pay? You also need to have a good handle on who else offers similar alternatives.

Ultimately, you need to ensure that there is a demonstrable demand, and that you are not simply inventing a problem to solve. The good news is that, once you've found a real problem and have ascertained what solutions (if any) already exist, you can get out there and put your idea to the test to assess its viability with minimal funds. You need to consider how you are going to make your solution different and/or better than existing ones; the best way to do that is to get your hands dirty, get into the marketplace and ask lots of questions.

I learned a great deal from my experience on *The Apprentice*. Apart from the power of video editing and the importance of having a strong network, I learned the importance of focus groups and gathering feedback. For example, Bianca Miller London sells a range of hosiery designed to match women's natural skin tones; whichever way you look at it, it's a great concept. The issue we had on *The Apprentice* was the pricing which, according to focus group feedback, was too high. My plan had been to launch with a high-price item and then, a year later, launch a diffusion range at a lower price point for mass market appeal. My idea was to sell into both the luxury and mass markets. In fact, when I researched the most expensive brands I discovered a gap in the market, as they didn't offer the same colours, so I thought I could charge a premium on that basis. On paper, that works. However, in reality, perhaps it was too high. Were people going to pay £30 for a pair of tights? Some, perhaps, but not as many as I'd hoped. So the focus group and industry feedback from *The Apprentice* was very valuable; it gave me a powerful opportunity to test the market and see what it said. What came back was the absolute validation of the idea being a great one, but that the initial retail price would be too high. That feedback was consistent, and I was able to use it to refine and fine-tune my business prior to launch and develop it into what it has become today.

Establishing a new business and trying to stand out in a crowded market – that's really tough. But all of it is made easier if you get to know as much as you can about your chosen marketplace, so you can uncover how best to distinguish yourself from your competitors and persuade customers to buy from you rather than from them.

New entrants, disruptive game-changers, copycats – they will constantly enter into the marketplace in which you operate, that's a given. So you need to keep your ears to the ground and your eye on the ball from the outset. Furthermore, because trends can come and go, you can never know it all in business. So, if you factor in time to gain as much knowledge as you can about your market, current trends, customer needs, competitors and so on, you'll be well positioned to lead the way and to change course if necessary.

So, you know that you need to keep your finger on the pulse of your industry and equip yourself with knowledge. But where do you start? Wherever you like is the answer. It's best to gather information from multiple resources. So, go online, join relevant Facebook groups and participate in forums. Post questions and visit the library to read trade journals and research papers. Set up Google News alerts for terms you are researching. Dig out figures from the Office of National Statistics. Read white papers and government reports, visit trade shows, order competitors' products and download their brochures. Find out from suppliers what their best-selling items are and whether the market is rising or falling in terms of demand. All of this research will add to your knowledge of the marketplace and allow you to better position your brand.

Customers

Create a customer profile based on who your customers are. Do they fit into a niche? For example, Byron's wedding directory business has individual customers, all of whom have one thing in common – they are getting married. On the other side are the business customers, all of whom are suppliers within the wedding trade. But we can break these groups down further into customer segments; for example, suppliers might be florists and chauffeurs, and individual customers could be brides-to-be aged between 21 and 35. We could break the latter segment down even further to target professionals and city-dwellers who are planning a wedding. We then need to consider what they aspire to have, be and do. What problems are they facing? What is keeping them up at night? Then, if we picture an individual who is representative of our drilled-down target audience, we can find out where that person might go to source information and products such as ours, or uncover what someone with that profile is liking on Facebook or following on Twitter. We can then make our presence felt in those places, ask the right questions at the right time, and speak directly to that specific customer.

As you begin to consider the customer profile for your business you will also need to establish:

- How much money is spent in the industry you are about to enter?
- What is important to your target market? What do they spend their money on?
- Who are the key influencers on this target market (e.g. bloggers with large audiences)?

- What publications do your audience read and which websites do they frequent? Do they use social media much and, if so, do they prefer Facebook or Twitter, Instagram or LinkedIn?
- How much might they pay for a service such as yours? It's important to know what your competition charges.
- What do they like and dislike about what's already out there?
- What core benefits are they seeking and which problems do they need a solution for? Your goal is to determine demand.

You can plot all of this information into your business plan, and when you are ticking off your marketing mix checklist, later in the chapter.

Competitors

In business, being knowledgeable about other people in the market is crucial. As well as gathering information from potential customers about which benefits appeal to them most, what price they would expect to pay, where they currently shop for items/services such as yours, and so on, you also need to study your competitors and gain as much competitor intelligence as possible. You can then find windows of opportunity and turn competitors' weaknesses into your strengths.

- Dig deep to gather competitor intelligence. Find out who the market leaders are, the main players and the main suppliers, how much share of the market they possess and why? Examine their weaknesses as well as their strengths.
- List what they do and don't offer. Can you provide something not currently offered and find a gap in the market by serving an area currently underserved?
- What could you do to persuade their customers to switch to you? What are their best- and worst-selling items? What channels do they use and is there a gap in the distribution method that might be filled?
- What is your unique selling point? How exactly will you stand out from your competition?

Equipping yourself with this data is valuable because, whilst belief keeps you focused when a handful of people question or don't understand what you are trying do, it's far better to back up your own belief in your business idea with hard factual evidence. Because sometimes you may question: is belief enough?

That said, your belief enables you to focus on your end goal and, importantly, to tune into relevant findings, ignoring distracting side issues. A big problem in business is that there's a lot of 'noise'. Everyone wants to give you advice and suggestions but not always give you actionable ways of achieving your goal. So, whilst you should listen to your customers and focus groups, you need to be able to filter out the constructive feedback – some of which may be different from what you were expecting – and take that on board, leaving aside the less helpful feedback (for example, the one or two people who have a different opinion from the majority). You should be flexible enough to pivot if needs be, but carve a path through the noise, listening to the consistent findings from your most treasured target audience segments.

One way to make sure you have answered all the questions you need to answer before you enter data into your business plan, is to focus on the marketing mix, otherwise known as the 4 Ps.

The marketing mix – the 4 Ps: Product, Place, Price and Promotion

There is no point setting up your business if there is no demand and, even if there is demand, there is still a lot of work to do to ensure that your product or service is in the right place (in front of the right people) at the right price at the right time. Furthermore, you need to be sure that, through your promotional activities, you will be able to notify those 'right people' of your existence.

It sounds simple enough – offer a product that a specific group of people have a need for, put it in front of those people in places that they visit regularly, price it at a level that makes them feel that they gain good value from it, and do all of this at the specific time that they are ready to buy.

Of course, in order to do this effectively you need to do significant groundwork to establish what customers actually want, where they go to find products and services such as yours, what their expectations are around price and ensure that this is all happening at the time they are ready to buy. Hence the importance of all of this research, because the more you know the more equipped you are to succeed.

If you get just one element of the 4 Ps wrong, it could be disastrous for your emerging enterprise. If nobody wants the product the way that you've created it, you won't get any sales. For example, if you produce a range of owl t-shirts in a country where owls are associated with the occult, you won't sell many. If you create some amazing pencil cases or schoolwear after the beginning of the new school year, you may not fare well. And if your product is priced too high or too low to attract your target market, again, you are likely to have few sales.

This all may sound rather daunting, but read on because, as well as defining key questions to ask to help you build up an accurate picture and develop a potentially successful marketing mix, you can also learn from a couple of mistakes that Byron and I made when we started businesses.

The 4 Ps – Product, Place, Price and Promotion – have been around for many decades, and were first introduced by E. J. McCarthy in 1960.[4] These four elements can be defined by the questions you should aim to answer during your market research.

For example, to ensure you have the optimum PRODUCT or service for your target customers, try to establish:

- What benefits does my customer want from my product/ service?
- What problems must it solve?
- Does it have any features that are unlikely to be used?
- Where and how will the customer use the product and why?
- Will the name/colours/size appeal to the customers and why?
- What makes it stand out from the competition?

When figuring out how best to PLACE your product or service, consider:

- Where do buyers go when they are seeking out products or services such as yours? Do they go online, use a catalogue, visit trade fairs, opt for specialist boutique shops, supermarkets or department stores?
- Is location important? Note: Do not just consider the location of your office or shop in terms of where your customers are, but also in terms of where the best staff are. In fact, here you can learn from something that Byron would do differently with the benefit of hindsight. Byron chose to open the Happy Bride Guide company in Blackpool for the following reasons: a key member of staff he had headhunted lived there, he would rarely need to be there, and establishing premises there would avoid the expense of recruitment and additional office space in London. He explains. 'In reality, when we needed more telesales staff to move forward, geographically we had a much smaller pool of suitable candidates. This has impacted the recruitment side of the business. So, if I could go back and make that decision again, I would have based the business in London. The lesson I've learned is that location is important both in terms of customers and in terms of staffing.'
- How might you be able to place your product into the correct distribution channels?
- Will you need to hire a sales team or send samples to catalogue companies? Will you sell primarily via a physical retail outlet or your own website? What other websites might you need to register with?

PRICE is often the hardest to get right. Try to find out:

- What is the value of the product or service to the buyer?
- What are the established price points for products and services in this area?
- How do your competitors price their products?

- Is your target market sensitive to pricing? Might a tiny decrease in price provide you with greater market share, or might a little increase in price go relatively unnoticed yet improve your profit margin?
- How might you discount your offering to trade (wholesale) customers or other segments of your market?
- Does the price point have enough margin in it to allow you to pay for the product and sell at a wholesale rate to stores?

Once you have determined these key components of the marketing mix, you need to ensure that you can shout about your offerings from the rooftops. So, in terms of PROMOTION, establish:

- How will you reach your audience? Which marketing channels are they most likely to respond to? Editorial in targeted magazines? Social media networks? Radio or TV? Direct marketing mailshots? Search engines? Networking face-to-face? Often, because you don't know where the majority of your business will come from until you are out there in the marketplace trying to drum up business, it can be a case of 'you don't know what you don't know'. For that reason, I advise not spending too much capital on any medium of promotion until you are really clear on which is generating the best results. I learned this the hard way, so you can learn from my mistake.

    When I started my business in 2012 I managed to secure investment; however, I spent too much of that money on the wrong types of marketing activity: SEO (Search Engine Optimization) and PPC (Pay Per Click). I had seen this work incredibly well for Byron, who had spent £30k per annum on Adwords and got an amazing return on his investment. I assumed these methods would work for me too. But, what works for one business doesn't always work so well for another. Once I understood my own industry better, I realized that more business was coming from my networking and building relationships with people. I gained a large number of referrals this way, and more business was coming from partnerships and networking than ever came from SEO or PPC. Evidently I would have got a much better return on my investment if I had focused on building relationships instead. So you need to have a keen understanding of the industry before investing heavily on promotion. Get to know where the majority of your business comes from and then concentrate your investment in that promotional activity.

- When should you promote? Are there any timing issues that dictate when is best to do so, such as seasonality or occurrences of certain events, or media coverage of certain topics?
- Where can you see your competitors' marketing messages?

The next stage is to forecast your finances: how much you will need to spend and how much you are likely to make.

Create financial forecasts

From a startup perspective what you often lack is the capital. So you really need to carefully consider your time and your money and how you invest those two things. People often forget that their time is worth money. However, if you are out there making connections with people and building relationships, that's time well spent, as I learned from my own marketing expenditure mistake.

And here's another lesson that you cannot know until you have launched your business and learned by running it: everything tends to cost more and take longer than you think it will. For that reason, whilst it is important to create financial forecasts, you must understand from the outset that there will be costs you have forgotten to include and there will be projects that run on for longer and cost more than you estimated. Plus, products that look great on paper may not sell as well as other products which you may have assumed would have a low return. So you need to be flexible.

Everything in a textbook looks quite straightforward and manageable, but in reality business isn't like that. You could write an astounding business plan but it doesn't mean that what you have forecast will actually happen. For example, our business degrees were useful for lending us credibility and giving us a good understanding of the foundations from a theoretical perspective, but real life teaches you what being in business is actually like – what it feels like to bring an idea to fruition and give it life. A business degree teaches you to research, forecast and create the plan. It doesn't tell you how to action that plan (that's what we aim to show you in the pages of this book).

In real life, a customer might tell you they love what you're doing and are going to book you tomorrow. But tomorrow in the business world sometimes means in two months' time. And, if you haven't forecast or allowed for that in your planning, then you could be in real trouble. What's more, many people doing their financial forecasts don't think about payment terms. For example, you might do a job in January but not get paid until March. And, when you start a business, it's unlikely you'll know that the bigger the company the longer they may take to pay. They don't teach that in business school! Taking these sorts of problems into account will help you when you do your financial planning.

'Projections are guesswork,' says 'Juice Master' Jason Vale who has turned his vision to write a book and 'juice the world' into a multi-million pound juice business empire. 'Intuitive business is the way forward,' he adds. Of course, it's easier to use your intuition when you know your customers and what they want, which comes down to market research and a passion for delivering what they need and exceeding their expectations. We'll focus on achieving that and hear a lot more from Jason later on.

What you DO need to include in your financial planning, however, is:

- **Startup capital.** How much you need to get the business off the ground. Remember to list expenses such as building a website, purchase of a domain name (web address), logo design, the cost of stock (once you know what minimum orders are likely to be), equipment, and so on.

- **Working capital.** How much you need to sustain the business. Remember to list costs such as UK and international postage and packaging (find out how much it will cost to post your items by packaging some up and taking them to the post office), staff payments, renting premises, stationery, web hosting, marketing, loan repayments, tax payments, accountancy fees, business travel and so on.

Furthermore, although you can send all of your financial records to an accountant to manage your books, you should understand the basics and, at the very least, know the difference between cash flow, and profit and loss.

Cash flow is the balance of all the money that flows in to and out of your business on a daily basis. It's not the amount you've invoiced which is owed *to* you, or money owed *by* you, it's the payments that are actually received by and paid out from the business. If you spend more than you are earning, a cash–flow crisis could be on the cards, even if you will be profitable once the invoices are paid. Essentially, you need to know that you have money in the bank to pay bills on an ongoing basis, even when invoiced amounts are not yet paid. Not staying on top of this is how even profitable businesses can go bust. If you are a service company which sells on credit so, for example, you do work upfront and invoice with payment terms of 60 days, you won't see the money in your account for at least two months; therefore, you need to be prepared for that and still be able to pay the bills in the meantime. By knowing your cash flow at any given moment you can ensure you have enough cash in the bank to cover your sales cycle (the period of time from when you secure an order to the time you receive payment for it).

A **profit and loss** account tells you whether your business is set to make a profit or a loss by giving you a snapshot of your trading performance over a given time/accounting period. So this shows when sales are invoiced, unlike cash flow accounts which show when invoiced sales are actually paid. Based on this snapshot you will know whether you need to boost your sales, sell assets or reduce costs, or seek finance to strive for a profitable account.

Once you have figured out who you are, what you will sell, why you will sell it and how (via which routes to market) you can plot this out on your route map, otherwise known as a business plan.

The business plan – your route map

To achieve great things, two things are needed:
a plan, and not quite enough time.

Leonard Bernstein, composer and conductor

As we've outlined above, in business, everything tends to cost more and take longer than you think it will. With that in mind, whilst a business plan is helpful in terms of setting out how you will operate and what you will sell, to whom and why, it is not written in stone and should therefore be flexible. Things change, goalposts move, strategies pivot; you need to have a healthy balance between FOCUS and FLEXIBILITY in order to move forward in the most effective and lucrative way that you can.

For example, when you're forecasting your income and expenditure it's worth adding 10 per cent to your expenditure figure and, strategy wise, to have a plan B. Some advisors suggest predicting three different outcomes – best-case scenario, worst-case scenario and likely-case scenario. Essentially it's up to you how you build that modicum of flexibility into your focused plan. The crucial part is that you DO plan. You'll have heard the quote by Alan Lakein, 'failing to plan is planning to fail', and this is true. There's a lot at stake when you invest your time and money (and often someone else's money too) into becoming self made and sustaining that way of living and working, so it's not worth taking the 'just wing it' attitude.

We suggest that you carve out some time each week to map out your goals and actions and, before you do anything further, create your overall route map – your business plan – so that you know which direction you are heading in and where you want to end up.

Direction and destination: plotting your route map

To get from where you are right now to where you want to be, you need some kind of map to follow. The most successful self-made people, be they in commerce or showbusiness, have a plan. They set goals, they visualize achieving them and they devote time to taking intentional actions towards bringing their dreams to fruition.

Take self-made woman, singer-songwriter and *Britain's Got Talent* Judge, Alesha Dixon, for example. We had the pleasure of speaking to Alesha about becoming self made and she told us that she has always set goals.

'As far back as I remember, when I was in school, I always had a plan,' she smiles. 'Now, that plan doesn't always pan out and things don't always go the way you planned them to, but I always had a vision and I always had an idea of what I wanted to do. There was a period of time when I wanted to be a teacher, so I had a plan for that. I did a B-Tech National Diploma in sports studies and I wanted to go to Loughborough University. However, somewhere in that plan, my love for music took over, and that became a new plan.'

Sometimes you might take a detour and other times the road is going to get bumpy, so much so that you might change direction altogether. This is what Richard Moross of MOO.com famously did when his original idea for 'social media contact cards' wasn't working.[5] He pivoted: dropped the social network side of the business completely and turned his business into a multi-million dollar one by targeting the creative community, including photographers and designers, who could use Moo's customization tool to showcase their work on their business cards. This helped him to create a market of 'sticky' customers (customers who would return time and time again).

Indeed, the ability to pivot is a critical part of being self made, because you will often find yourself going a certain route, adhering to your plan and then arriving at a dead end. Those who succeed are those who are able to shift direction and plot a new course. Many companies have done this based on market feedback and/or fresh opportunities presenting themselves, or simply by taking a decision to pursue a more authentic passion. Starbucks pivoted from selling coffee beans and espresso makers into a European-style coffee-house[6] and Twitter pivoted from its original business model (a podcast directory) into a status-updating micro-blogging platform.[7] Alesha pivoted from her plan of wanting to teach to wanting to make music, which then led her on to other opportunities, including being a judge on *Strictly Come Dancing* and *Britain's Got Talent*, and even launching her own fashion collection. She says,

'I've always liked the idea of being able to do things outside of the box and surprise people. The challenge for me is always to come up with the next thing; do something fresh and interesting, something that gets me excited and challenges me.'

A sound business plan helps you to get from where you are now to where you want to be – avoiding as many hurdles as possible along the way. Your route map isn't just something to hand over to bank managers and deep-pocketed investors (although it's worth considering when you write it that they may well ask to see it). It's for you. So, what information should you include?

- **Business and Contact Information**: your business name, address, email and contact numbers.
- **Contents Page:** including page numbers to help you or other readers find specific points of interest.
- **Executive Summary:** this is where you write your elevator pitch as it should summarize your business within around 30–60 seconds (as if you were stuck in a lift with an influential person and needed to communicate why your business is the best thing since sliced bread before they reach their floor and press the 'open doors' button). Ultimately, you need to communicate why you started this business, its unique selling points (i.e. what it does better or differently to any other business out there), what problems

it solves and what solutions it provides. For example, if your product gives parents peace of mind about safety, this is where you say so. Also, include any traction you already have. For example: 'We have already tested the product and have 50 pre-orders and a mailing list of 200.' The key is to demonstrate demand and showcase the opportunity as well as explaining concisely why this business is something you feel compelled to do, as this will communicate your passion for the enterprise.

- **The Proposition:**
  - What is your product?
  - Who is it intended for?
  - How did you come up with this idea?
  - What makes it different and/or better than the rest (i.e. what do you provide that others don't)?
  - What benefits will customers get by choosing to buy from you rather than from someone else? Will it make their lives/work easier, more enjoyable, safer? Will it enable them to save time or money or both?

- **The Vision and Purpose:**
  - Why does your business exist?
  - What is your long-term vision? Paint the bigger picture.
  - Where do you see the business in three years' time? Five years' time?

- **The Opportunity:**
  - How big is the opportunity (i.e. what is the size of the market and the share of the market segment that you intend to reach)?
  - Who are your main competitors and what are their strengths?
  - How can you make their weaknesses your strengths?
  - Who are the biggest customers of your competitors?
  - What trends are currently driving the market?
  - Are you able to demonstrate demand/proof of concept?

- **People:**
  - Who are you and why are you well positioned to run this business? What skills and experience do you have?
  - What are your strengths in terms of your capabilities?
  - How can you fill the gaps? Which people will do that? What skills/experience do they have?
  - Are any strategic alliances, joint ventures or partnerships in place or in the pipeline? Who with and why?

- **Plans:**
  - How will you develop, make or source your product or supply your service?
  - How will you sell it to people through marketing and promotion (e.g. PR, social media, TV/radio, email marketing, telesales, face-to-face, networking, attending exhibitions)?
  - Through which channels will you sell (e.g. online via your own website; via other websites such as Amazon, eBay or notonthehightstreet.com; via external distributors/stores; on the high street through your own shop; through a pop-up shop or market stall; mail order via a direct mail catalogue; and so on...)?

- **Operations and Financials:**
  - What is the price point? How much will you sell your product/service for?
  - How much does your product cost to make (including all manufacturing costs, staff, training and postage/packaging costs)?
  - How will you finance those costs?
  - How much money do you need to start up?
  - How much credit will suppliers provide, if any?
  - How much will you borrow and how will you repay loans, overdrafts or other credit facilities?
  - What machinery, premises or equipment do you need to buy or hire?

- What is your growth strategy?
- What are your best-case, worst-case and likely-case financial forecasts over the next three years?
- Make sure you know how many sales you need to break even and become profitable.

● **Investment:**
  - Are you likely to need external investment – startup capital/working capital?
  - If so, how much?
  - What will you spend the money on?
  - How and when will investors get a return on their investment?
  - What is the exit strategy for the business? Do you intend to sell the business or pass it down the family?

● **SWOT analysis:**
  - What are your existing Strengths (advantages), Weaknesses (disadvantages), Opportunities (favourable circumstances) and Threats (circumstances that may create difficulties)? Strengths and Weaknesses tend to be internal whilst Opportunities and Threats are often external.

● **Appendix:** include here market research statistics, CVs and other supporting documents.

Action plan

This is the core part of the route map as it plots out the actions you need to take *en route* to your destination: from sourcing suppliers and getting feedback from a focus group to sending out press releases and building your email list. Give each task a date and objective (for example, to prove the concept or to gather contacts). Break goals down into manageable chunks and evaluate regularly to see how much progress you've made.

Being clear about the steps you need to take to help you reach your goals is critical. Alesha Dixon advises:

'I think it's important for people to have an action plan, both a visualization [of what the end result will look like] and a written plan. I've always made a list of all the things I wanted to do. Some of those things have been ticked off, but some haven't and I think that's okay. It always gives you somewhere else to go. I still write lists now. A few days ago I wrote down my list of intentions, things that I still hope to do, and writing it all down helps focus me. It helps affirm something and it gives me something to keep referring back to. When you *are* your own business, even if you have people that work with you and help you, essentially you still have to drive it and be more focused than anyone else.'

Indeed, drive is the vital part of planning: figuring out your destination and your route so you can drive there. Creating a plan puts you in the driving seat towards your goals. Your plan is the map. By being diligent in your planning you give yourself and your team focus, and can start taking those steps towards achieving your goals and realizing your vision.

As you start and begin to grow, in addition to your business plan, you can create an alternative business plan, known as the Business Model Canvas.

The Business Model Canvas

This is a template which enables you to plot your business visually and showcase on one page your value proposition, infrastructure, finances and customers. It was invented by Alexander Osterwalder and involves listing:[8]

- **Key partners and suppliers** – who are they and what are your motivations for having those partnerships? Can your key partners be mapped to your key activities?
- **Key activities** – what does your value proposition require and which activities are most important in terms of your revenue streams, building and maintaining customer

relationships and distribution channels? For example, if selling your wares via third parties is part of your value proposition, key activities will include strong channel/contacts management. If you sell products to a niche audience, a key activity might include learning more about customers, gathering feedback about their needs, conducting focus groups, working on aftersales care, and so on. Consider how your key activities (and key resources, see below) actually drive your value propositions and whether they are absolutely focused?

- **Value proposition** – define the core value that you deliver to your customer and what customer needs your product/service fulfils. Why does your customer choose you over alternatives? Which customer needs are the most important? You might rank these in order of importance and even map them to fit specific customer segments (see below).
- **Customer relationships** – determine the kind of relationship that your customer expects you to maintain, and how you might integrate that into your business costs. How do you communicate your business proposition to your channels (e.g. via your website, via Adwords, via a market stall)? Strive to define how you interface/interact with your customers in terms of their journey. Where are the customer touch points during that journey, from initial awareness to final purchase and follow up and beyond? Do they deal with a specific person who is dedicated to their account or do they communicate with any number of people? How does the interaction take place – online, face-to-face or over the phone? How can you assess and improve each touch point?
- **Customer segments** – who are your most important customers demographically? If you could only choose one segment, which would you choose? Do you have one single market or a multi-sided market? For example if, like Google, you have service users on one side and advertisers on the other, that's a multi-sided market (a business with at least

two different types of customer). Are you able to split your customer segments into personas? Which value propositions do those customer segments care most about?

- **Key resources** – decide what key resources your value proposition needs and which are most important in terms of your revenue streams, building and maintaining customer relationships, and distribution channels. For example, specialists within critical areas of expertise could be a key resource, as might intellectual property that relates to your core offering.

- **Cost structure** – which key resources, costs and activities tend to be the most expensive? How do your key activities drive costs and are those costs aligned with your value propositions? Are they scalable or fixed?

- **Revenue streams** – what are your customers willing to pay for and how do they pay/would you prefer them to pay? What percentage of total revenue does each revenue stream contribute? Link all revenue streams to customer segments/ personas so that you can assess whether your revenue streams are aligned with your key focal points of business.

All of this information is vital to give your enterprise the best chance of success. In order to be able to see into the future you need to have a clear vision and equip yourself with as much knowledge as you can.

Fundamentally then, in order to achieve your vision of success, you need a route map so that you can plot the best course towards that destination. In order to guide you on your journey you need to put effort into doing your homework so that you know your market, know why customers will buy, have a firm understanding of how you will stand out, be clear on your own marketing mix and have well-defined action steps that will help you to reach each pit stop *en route* to your dream. The more information you can gather, the more complete your bigger picture and the more accurate your forecasting will be. Knowledge is most definitely power (and fuel) when it comes to starting up your engine and going on the self-made journey towards your ultimate destination – success.

Once you have all that knowledge and have plotted your route to your destination, it's time to get started, so here's a checklist to help you on your way.

Good luck!

Getting started: a checklist

1 Secure your domain name and social media profiles

As soon as you are sure about your name, have checked that nobody else is using it (by visiting the Companies House website and browsing the web) you should, as a priority, secure the domain name for it. Do this before registering with HMRC or Companies House, as it can be a nuisance to find out that the name is being used elsewhere and then have to notify the relevant authorities accordingly. So visit GoDaddy.com or 123-reg.co.uk to search for your domain name and secure it. Do the same with Twitter, Facebook and Instagram profiles. If your Twitter handle is taken, you may need to be creative. The main thing is to secure your chosen trading name as a domain name, as this will be your website address. In our opinion if you are a UK business it makes sense to purchase a UK domain as your primary domain and purchase the .com for brand protection.

2 Set up your company

If you are planning to set up as a sole trader, you simply need to notify HMRC so that they can send you relevant self-assessment forms. If you are planning to register as a limited company you can either hire a verified agent, such as Duport.co.uk, who can do so on your behalf, or simply follow the instructions on the Companies House website. It explains everything you need and precisely how to register your company. You can find the links you need and how to register on our resource page on www.selfmadebook.uk.

3 Hire an accountant or DIY

Accountants can save you money as they know what expenses are deductible/allowable for tax purposes; they can also save you the time it takes to fill out a tax return and avoid penalties that may arise from filing late. That said, you may prefer to do your own book-keeping, and use the associated financial records (invoices, receipts and monthly accounts, etc.) to fill out your own self-assessment and company returns forms. Either way, you need to keep this part of your business in order, not only to ensure that your enterprise is law-abiding, but also because, when it comes to selling or passing on your business, you will have all of your documentation ready to go.

4 Open a bank account

All businesses have one thing in common, and that is the need for a good business bank account. So it is important to shop around to see how closely you can match your needs with the offers from the different banks. Given that most business owners access their accounts online, and that most business accounts offer a free banking period and other incentives, it's worth finding out what each has to offer. Rather than checking out each bank individually, you can save time by visiting a comparison website where they've done the hard work for you.

5 Get business insurance

You need to protect your business and will need to explore which types of business insurance you must have as a legal requirement and which are advisable rather than compulsory. From public liability insurance, which covers you against claims made by third parties that your business comes into contact with (on your or their premises, or even on the street) to professional indemnity insurance, which covers claims made by anyone who suffers a 'business loss' as a result of your mistakes or misguidance (particularly worthwhile for advice/service providers), there are many types of insurance to consider. It is important to consider reading a guide on the best type of insurance for you or calling around and gaining an insight from insurers and brokers.

6 Register your business for VAT

In general, if your turnover exceeds a specific threshold in any 12-month period (£85,000 in 2017), registering for VAT is compulsory. As a startup, you may spend more than you earn at first so that turnover figure may not be applicable for a while. However you can register for VAT earlier if you think it would be beneficial for your business. For example, if you are selling to corporations or larger businesses who are VAT registered, it may be worth registering early to give you the added credibility of having a VAT registration number on your invoices. Some VAT-registered companies prefer to do business with other VAT-registered suppliers, as they can then claim back the VAT they've paid from HMRC. That is a clear benefit of registering: any VAT you pay can be reclaimed. So if you are likely to spend a lot on goods or services from VAT-registered suppliers, registering could be worthwhile. That said, it does increase the amount of paperwork that you have to do as monthly VAT returns are required.

If your customer base is more likely to comprise individual consumers, charging VAT on your prices could be off-putting and they may go somewhere where the price is VAT free. For more information on VAT registration visit your local government website or the *Self Made* website.

• •

Expert insight

*Law for business – getting it right. Q&A with Trevor Japal,
partner at Lex Sterling solicitors*

Business and commercial enterprise takes place within a legal context and is always governed and regulated by law. One of the problems facing an entrepreneur starting their own business, whether it be a sole trader or a limited company, is that business takes place within a general and wide-ranging legal environment but a businessman or woman is required to have more than a passing knowledge of the legal rules and procedures which impact on business activity.

However, when starting and growing a business it is important to realize that having an *adequate* knowledge of a few key areas of law which are important to your business is far more useful than having an in-depth knowledge of one or two areas of law that might not. When in doubt, it is always best to seek the assistance of a solicitor or legal professional but some key knowledge and research can really save you a lot of time and money as a new entrepreneur.

There is a lot to consider within the first three months of the life of a new business, from establishing a company and brand, to preparing to sell new products or services and employing staff to help the business succeed. Most entrepreneurs will be passionate about their product or service, but will probably have limited or no legal knowledge. It is important to get a few key decisions right at the beginning to prevent costly and stressful problems in the future and to ensure that you give your business the very best possible start, and the best chance for survival and growth.

Before going any further, if I could impart any one piece of advice that you should take away when making any major legal decision for your business, it is worthwhile asking three important questions:

1 What are the benefits?
2 What are the risks and disadvantages?
3 What are the alternatives?

When we consider the issues that will arise in the first three months of your business, it is always worth looking at all of the available options and analysing what is good about them, what problems or risks they may pose, and what other choices you may have. With that in mind, I have answered the following key questions regarding starting a business and beginning to trade.

Q: *Should I start as a sole trader or form a company structure?*

A: One of the first decisions you will make when starting trading, whether you are selling goods or services, is how to trade. Some of the smallest businesses have started from a bedroom, home office or garage and it may be that you can run a successful business as a sole trader for a long time. The decision as to whether to operate as a sole trader or form a company structure will very much depend on the nature and stage of your business, the size of it and those involved. It is always a good idea to appoint a suitable accountant at the beginning of every business venture who will be able to provide in-depth advice on such decisions. They will also advise you, based on your predicted turnover, whether or not to make an application to HMRC to be registered for VAT.

Many businessmen or women will start their business lives as a sole trader, which is very popular for a number of reasons. A sole proprietorship is a business owned by one person who has full control of the business and how it is run, and is suitable for a business startup. If you decide to be a sole trader you will own all of the assets of the business and any profit that it makes will be yours. However, you will also be liable for the debts and liabilities of the business. If you decide to commence as a sole trader, either you or an accountant of your choice will have to register you as self-employed with HM Revenue and Customs and you will be obliged to submit an annual self-assessment to determine how much tax you will pay.

Thinking about the three key questions raised earlier:

Q: *What are the benefits of being a sole trader?*

A:

- You will have full control of your business and will not have to account to anybody else when making decisions.
- Information about your business will be kept private and will not be in the public domain. Only you and those you choose to share it with will have access to your financial and other information.
- You will be able to retain all of the profits of the business.
- You will be able to make decisions more quickly.

Q: *What are the risks and disadvantages of being a sole trader?*

A:

- Whilst you will be able to retain all of the profits of the business you will also be responsible for all of the losses, if any. If you opt to be a sole trader, you become the business which means that you and the business are the same entity. If your business gets into financial hardship or debt, then you will be liable and you may be risking your savings, your home and any other assets.

- Whilst you may be able to make your own decisions and act on them swiftly, this can also be a disadvantage as the success and failure of your business will rest on the decisions that you make.
- Sole traders often find it difficult to raise finance for their business and may struggle with expansion or borrowing in the future.
- Sole traders may struggle with smaller economies of scale.

Q: *What is the alternative?*

A: By forming a company, you may not benefit from some of the advantages mentioned above but you may well limit your liability to protect you from exposure to any personal financial risk. The most commonly used vehicle for startup businesses is a private limited company. You can appoint an accountant or solicitor to form your company, or go to the Companies House website to choose an available company name and register your company there. You'll need to adopt articles of association, which is the company's internal 'rule book'. Private limited companies need a least one person appointed as a director, and every director has certain duties imposed on them, which are owed to the company.

A limited company will allow you to keep your own assets and finances separate from the company itself and will be a separate entity from you. People that have invested in your business, even if it is only yourself, will be shareholders and will only be responsible for any company debts up to the amount that they have invested. In order to set up a limited company, there are criteria that have to be satisfied as set out in The Companies Act 2006 as follows:

- The company must be registered with Companies House.
- The company must have at least one director who is at least 16 years of age.

It is usual for an entrepreneur to be the director of their business, but remember that the shareholders are the ones who fund the business and inevitably must benefit from the profits. When setting up a company it may well be that you are the only director and shareholder. It is very important to seek the advice of an accountant when starting a company. The company will be taxed on its profits and may have to charge VAT depending on the predicted turnover.

Q: *What are the benefits of forming a limited company?*

A:

- There is limited liability as investors/shareholders will only be liable for any debt the company gets into according to the levels of their own investment.
- Limited companies are only taxed on their profits and you can benefit from paying yourself dividends on them as often as you like.
- The company is a separate legal entity.
- If you drive and have your own car, you can charge the mileage accrued on business travel to the company, which allows you to benefit from tax-free fuel, and these costs are also tax deductible to the company too.
- You can run the business from your home and claim back the costs of doing so.
- You can choose your own company name provided that someone is not already using it! This will give your business its own identity.

Q: *What are the risks and disadvantages of a limited company?*

A:

- You may have to account to investors or shareholders when making decisions and distributing or re-investing company profits.
- Information about your business, including your accounts, may appear in the public domain.

- You will have to comply with more stringent and onerous accounts rules.
- There are restrictions on raising capital through sales of shares.
- You may not be able to run your business as freely if other people are involved.

When making a decision on whether to run your business as a sole trader or limited company, it is best to take all of the above factors into consideration and work out which option is best for you.

Q: *How do I find the right business premises?*

A: Businesses operate from a wide variety of locations, from homes to large-scale offices. Where you decide to trade from will very much depend on the size, nature and type of your business and the products or service that you sell. Initially, a lot of entrepreneurs opt to start their business from home and, in an ever evolving landscape, others also opt for virtual business addresses or short term licences.

Q: *What are the advantages of trading from home?*

A:

- Costs can be kept down and this will save money on rent or mortgage expenses.
- You can deduct certain expenses from running a business from a room in your home from your tax bill.
- You may be able to maximize your working hours by cutting out travel to and from a workplace.
- You can work more flexible hours.
- You do not have to deal with any issues arising from having additional business premises which means that you can focus on your business.

Q: *What are the disadvantages and risks of trading from home?*

A:

- It may affect your productivity if you are open to distractions.
- You may need to have meetings with customers who you may not necessarily want to invite into your home.
- Your business might outgrow your home.
- You may not be allowed to run certain types of businesses from home.
- You may need to exhibit your goods or services.
- You will not have the opportunity to attract physical passing trade.

If you have decided that it would be unsuitable to run your business from home, then it is important to find yourself the right business premises, and decide whether you want to buy or rent. The first step is to decide what sort of premises you are looking for by drawing up a list of specifications that you might want. For example:

- What type of premises do you need (e.g. retail unit, shop, office etc.)?
- Which area do you want to trade from and why?
- How much space do you need?
- Do you have any other requirements such as parking etc.?

Q: *What are the alternatives?*

A: Whether you want to rent or buy business premises, this will be one of the biggest expenses that you will have to incur. Whilst monthly payments on a mortgage may work out to be cheaper than renting, there will be a considerable outlay in respect of a deposit on a property and a commercial mortgage may be hard to obtain. It is worth speaking to a good mortgage broker or independent financial advisor if you choose to buy your business premises. At the beginning of the life of a business, it is worth remembering that it is important to keep costs down, so this decision will be crucial.

A good starting point are property websites to assist you with finding commercial property to buy or to let. Often, you can input your requirements and the websites will generate leads for you to pursue. You may also wish to visit local estate agents who may be able to help meet your property requirements.

Remember that negotiation is important to get yourself the best deal possible, whether that is on price or, if you are renting, on the terms of the lease. Before making a commitment to any property, it is worth doing some research into it and finding out as much about the local area as possible to decide if the property you have found is the best one to start your business from.

Q: *Is it better to buy or rent a property?*

A: For a business, new or old, buying a freehold property will mean a significant investment which may be better spent on stock, promotion, advertising, or on another area of the business. With property prices on the rise, many businesses will not have the funds or borrowing ability to make buying a property a realistic option, but those who do buy will make it an investment. It is worth remembering that if your business purchases a property, it can later be improved, and may increase in value over time which will lead to the overall net worth of the business increasing too.

Most businesses will opt to lease their business premises as this limits the capital investment required. A short-term lease or licence on serviced offices, if properly negotiated with the aid of a solicitor, will give you flexibility if your needs and circumstances change. However, if you require a longer-term lease this will also have its advantages as you may want your own shopfront, be distinctly separate from other businesses, and may want to exhibit your products or services to the public, attracting walk-in trade. You will need to consider what suits your business best.

If you decide to enter into a commercial lease, you will have to bear in mind that a lease agreement can be lengthy and very detailed. However, it is important to determine the length of the lease, any options to break the lease if required, what the rent and service charge will be, who will be responsible for insuring the property and

how much this will cost, your responsibilities for repair and maintenance, and that the landlord will permit you to use the property for
your intended business.

When deciding whether to rent or to buy, it is important to budget
properly. Whether you are acquiring freehold or leasehold premises,
initial costs will include:

- solicitors and surveyors' costs plus the landlord's fees if this
  has been agreed
- legal disbursements such as stamp duty, land registry fees
  and searches
- the purchase price of the property if you are buying or any
  premium, rent deposit and rent advance if you are renting
- costs of getting the property the way you want including
  repairs, signage, fitting out, furnishing, utilities etc.
- any service charges
- insurance costs
- business rates
- maintenance and repair.

You will need to speak to a solicitor to help you determine the legal
costs and disbursements, and to make sure that you can keep control
of on-going costs.

The advantages of entering into a commercial lease:

1 Requires less investment than buying, which helps cash flow.
2 It avoids the risk of interest rate fluctuation.
3 It avoids the risk of fluctuation in property prices.
4 It is easier to relocate should you need to.
5 You can obtain short-term licences for even
  greater flexibility.

The advantages of buying a property:

1 There will be no risk of losing the property when the lease
  has expired as long as you keep up with your mortgage
  payments.
2 You will have more flexibility on how to use the property.

3 The property itself can be an asset on the business and may even increase in value.
4 The property can be altered, sub-let, repaired, maintained etc., as you see fit.

• •

Once you've done the groundwork, are clear about your destination and feel prepared with your own domain name and business registration, it's time to get your creative juices flowing and consider what will attract customers and enable them to relate to you and respect you. It's time to work on how you want to present yourself and your business to the world via your brand.

2

Build your brand

In business, people buy from people. So, as well as building your company's brand, it is also vital that you build your personal brand too. In this chapter we'll explore how to do both.

It's been scientifically proven that people make decisions about you within the first few seconds of meeting you and, as the saying goes, 'you never get a second chance to make a good first impression.'[9]

As such, when you are trying to persuade a prospect to become a customer or convince an influential person to collaborate with you in a strategic alliance, you need to make sure your appearance, body language, mannerisms, attitude and strengths come across well, and quickly. For it is on these areas that people meeting you for the first time will evaluate and form an opinion about whether or not you are a good fit for them and their own goals and needs.

Not enough people see the power in marketing themselves in the right way by being their best authentic self. How you communicate, your social media, how you dress, how you present yourself: all of that is part of your personal brand.

In business, so much attention is given to building your company's brand identity – from your logo, and your website, to your messaging and your value proposition. And yet, equally as important is how you present yourself to those who might buy from you, invest in you or partner with you. It's not just about showcasing the benefits of your product; you need to spell out the benefits of doing business with you personally, and you need to make a good first impression, otherwise you may face an uphill struggle.

With each new encounter, even before you open your mouth to speak, an evaluation and impression of you is formed, which can be difficult to undo. So set the tone well to show that you are trustworthy and worthy of respect.

According to a 2009 report called, 'Personality Judgments Based on Physical Appearance' in the *Personality and Social Psychology Bulletin*, our first impressions tend to be very accurate.[10] For example, in one experiment, after viewing pictures of people in a self-selected neutral position, observers accurately judged a subject's levels of extraversion, emotional stability, openness, self-esteem and religious beliefs, whilst the combination of physical characteristics, body posture, facial expression and clothing choices enabled observers to form an accurate impression of the subject's personality.

Image-related information is so strong that, in one study in the *Journal of Experimental Social Psychology*, participants struggled to see past physical appearance cues, even when they knew information that contradicted their initial judgements.[11]

So, about that…

Building your personal brand – PACK (Presentation, Approach, Communication, Knowledge)

I've built a business around personal branding because I know how much it matters in business. At The Be Group, my team and I help individuals to identify and define their personal brand and start working towards improving their career trajectory. Essentially, my area of expertise is in helping people to understand how to brand and market themselves.

Guy Kawasaki once said, 'Brands are built on what people are saying about you, not on what you are saying about yourself.'[12] In other words, what do people say about you when you leave the room?

During my time on BBC show *The Apprentice*, I was humbled to have impressed Karren Brady and Nick Hewer with my own personal brand and expertise, so much so that when I left the room, Karren told the cameras: 'Bianca is very professional, very in control of herself. It didn't surprise me in the slightest that she was into personal branding, because she's certainly got her personal brand right.' That obviously made my heart sing, to have impressed someone who I admire so greatly and have so much respect for.

As an HR Advisor for Accenture and now running my own enterprises, coming across as professional is absolutely vital to me and I was delighted that I had done so. It takes a lot to impress Nick and Karren, so this made me feel very pleased and grateful when Nick said, 'Bianca has displayed a professionalism perhaps more than anybody else.'

It would have been pretty embarrassing had Karren and Nick said I came across as scruffy and unprofessional. Thankfully, they said the opposite, which confirmed for me that I am in the right industry and able to put my own expertise to good use in helping others.

Over the next few pages, I will share with you what I know about self-packaging of this nature so that you can market yourself and your expertise accordingly to achieve your business goals. I will explain how the following elements can come together to ensure that people perceive you as you wish to be perceived.

Your personal brand is based on:

- Physical attributes: How you look/what you sound like.
- Rational appeal: Your skills, your education and experience.
- Emotional appeal: How do you make people feel when they're around you? What sort of legacy do you leave them with?

So how do you want to be perceived? What do you want people to think about you and say about you when you've left the room? What's the lasting impression that you want to leave people with?

Write your answers down here.

I want to be perceived as:
_____
_____
_____

When I leave the room, I want people to say:
_____
_____
_____

I like to divide personal branding into four clear key attributes, using the acronym PACK: Presentation, Approach, Communication and Knowledge.

P is for Presentation

Those seven seconds that it takes to make a first impression are largely based on your appearance and presentation – how you look, how you dress, what you say, how you say it and your personal grooming.

So, in terms of how you dress. This needs to tie in with how you want to be perceived. If you want to be perceived as professional in a corporate arena you will need to dress smartly and accessorize appropriately. Neat, well-presented and stylish will be your aim. However, if you are a personal trainer, and want to perceived as fit and healthy and ready to go, a good-quality tracksuit or other fitness attire would be more appropriate. Conversely, if you are an artist or writer, you may want your creativity to come to the fore, in which case your bohemian style may be more appropriate. So consider how you want to be perceived and make your outfit fit. Consider what the appropriate dress is for the meeting you are attending in terms of who you are meeting and why. If you are meeting executives from the music industry, you could get away with a more edgy look, but only if that suits how you wish to be perceived. If a pin stripe suit with cufflinks is likely to give you the perception you are aiming for, then wear that and make sure you are well groomed, with a good haircut, polished shoes, clean and tidy clothes and make-up.

You should aim to come across as the same person in person as you are via other modes of communication, via email, on the phone and on social media. Consistency is vital, so make you're your profile picture reflects your positive presentation and fits with how you wish to be perceived.

Of course, presentation is only one part of your personal branding package. As Alesha Dixon says,

'Looks aren't enough. You have to have substance, you have to have something about you, a talent or skill, to drive your success. Because the exterior is just the exterior. You have to be able to offer so much more.'

Byron and I frequently say this to the business people we advise who spend so much time on how they dress, what they look like and what their website looks like, but not on the actual substance: the credibility, the knowledge. Without the content, you're nothing. Branding is about the whole package – Presentation, Approach, Communication and Knowledge.

A is for Approach

Your approach includes your body language, your story/elevator pitch and how you come across in terms of your personality and your motivation for doing what you do.

Body language, like appearance, speaks louder than words. So your body language should reflect your intended perception. Whilst mirroring the body language of the person you are meeting can be effective to establish rapport, you should focus your attention on your own body language in order to come across as you wish to. Consider whether you are giving them an appropriate level of eye contact. Are you giving them a good firm handshake? Are you standing tall? Is your posture good? Are you smiling?

A warm and confident sincere smile will put both you and the other person at ease and open up the channel of communication in any language. And, when you smile at someone, it shows you as an approachable person who they will feel comfortable talking and opening up to. This body language will help you to project yourself as open and confident.

When it comes to your approach, it's really important that you synch not sink your brand. Here are five tips on how to make a good impression via your approach and ensure consistency.

1 **Be authentic.** People like people who are honest about who they are and what they can offer. Have a professional online

image – people want to see who you are but recognize you as well, so ensure that it looks like you.

2 **Be responsive, otherwise you get a bad reputation.** So if someone emails you or messages you via LinkedIn, make sure you respond within 24 hours, even if it's a holding email saying that you'll get back to them soon; it's really important to respond consistently within a reasonable period of time. It's no good having a professional appearance and then letting yourself down via your approach.

3 **Deliver on your promises.** If you say you're going to do something, deliver on that, so that you become known for being reliable. In fact, where possible under-promise and over-deliver so you exceed people's expectations and really impress them. This also gives you enough time to deliver on schedule should anything come up that you need to react to.

4 **Stay positive in the face of criticism, nerves or mistakes.** By staying upbeat and smiling, even when you have made a mistake or are being provoked into responding in a different way, you will leave the meeting with your head held high.

5 **Be polite and attentive.** Courteous behaviour and good manners go a long way. Showing an interest, asking questions and maintaining eye contact are all critical when it comes to leaving a good lasting impression. So turn off your mobile phone and pay attention. In fact, letting the other person do the talking can be especially effective so ask them to tell you about themselves and then show a genuine interest in what they are saying. Have a few questions ready to ask about their business or interests and nod to show you are listening.

KNOW WHO YOU ARE AND WHAT YOU OFFER

Whilst your knowledge and expertise will come later (under K in the PACK acronym), you should be clear on what you have to offer. Your elevator pitch is essentially a very short summary outlining precisely what you do, who for and why.

A mistake most people make when they go into business is not bothering to create a clear elevator pitch and then, when they bump into a potential investor or someone equally influential, who asks 'so what do you do?', they don't know where to start or, worse, they don't know where to finish.

During the audition process for *The Apprentice*, our first task was to deliver a 30-second elevator pitch. Fortunately, for me, I had been banging on about the importance of the elevator pitch for three years. So, when that moment came I was prepared and did enough to get through to the next round. I felt sorry for one guy who stepped forward and rambled for the full 30 seconds. He said his name, how many kids and dogs he had – all irrelevant to his business – and then the producers said, 'thank you, step back'. He hadn't even got to the point about his business idea.

Fundamentally, to engage people and spark interest you need a powerful and memorable explanation of what you offer that you can recite in around 30–60 seconds, the time it would take to go from one floor in an elevator up to another floor, hence the name. People are busy so you need to convey this information quickly and clearly so that the person listening is inspired enough to ask more or book a meeting or agree to invest/partner/request a call (before the bell dings and they step out of the imaginary elevator).

So keep it simple, succinct and clear. Fill in the gaps:

I am/We are a _____

[insert company type] firm

that works with/helps/teaches _____

[insert target audience]

how to _____

_____

[insert challenges/problems]

so that they can _____

_____

[insert benefits/results]

If you have time you could then add what your goal is/what your reason for existence is. For example:

I want to live in a world where _____

_____

_____

_____

Or, we aim/our mission is to _____

_____

_____

_____

C is for Communication

Once how you look and present yourself is locked down, you need to ensure that your verbal, written and online communications are aligned and effective. It's important to consider exactly how you represent your personal brand online via social media and the internet – everywhere that anyone can come into contact with you.

Face-to-face and in videos, you need to consider three key aspects:

1 Verbal – the content of what you're saying.
2 Vocal – how you sound when you are saying it.
3 Visual – how you look when you're saying it.

The first of these also applies when it comes to online content. And, even when people can't see you, but can hear you (such as on the phone) both the first and second of these elements applies. You should sound clear and confident but also make sure you're smiling on the phone. It makes all the difference.

Wherever you appear online, make sure your profile image is professional (so, if you are going to send potential customers or partners friendship requests on Facebook, make sure there are no photos of you falling out of a club at 3am, as that aspect of you conflicts with your professional image and will alter their perception of who you are). If it's out there, people can look at it, so make sure you're showing them the image you want to project. In fact, you might find it best to focus your business relationships on media such as LinkedIn, Twitter and YouTube, and save Facebook for friends and family.

Or set up a professional page on Facebook which presents a consistent image and invite customers to 'like' that page instead. Encourage people to interact with you by using action verbs, such as 'read my blog' or 'contact me here'.

Remember, conversations are based on verbal give and take. So ensure that you know all you can about your target audience. If you're going to meet a prospective customer, do you know who you will be meeting? If so find an image of them before you meet to make you feel more at ease when you do meet. What do you know about the company? What do you know about the individual and their likes and dislikes? Do you have anything in common that will aid the conversation?

Ask open-ended questions to help you to find out more about that person so that you can communicate clearly and build a strong relationship with them. When you ask good questions and listen, you learn enough to build a good rapport. By doing your homework before and during a meeting, you will gain a better understanding of who your target audience is which will be incredibly beneficial when it comes to writing content that appeals to them and when it comes to conversing with them in future. In this way, what you say and how you say it will be as good as it can be.

Another crucial part of communication is connection. Alesha Dixon has a great piece of advice for people looking to make a good impression,

'Look people in the eye,' she says. 'Show that you're confident and smile. A smile goes a long way! And listen. Doing so makes people feel important. Because people want to be acknowledged, they want to be seen, so you've got to show that you get it.'

K is for Knowledge

When you meet someone in person or are presenting yourself online, you want to give people confidence that you are able to deliver. The final aspect of your personal brand, therefore, is your range of credentials and how those strengths make you worth knowing.

So present yourself as an expert in your field by showcasing your experience so far and the expertise you have gained. Demonstrate how you have used this wealth of knowledge to help others: use testimonials, give examples of successes and list your strengths. This all adds a large dose of credibility to your offering.

Of course, sometimes, when a meeting really matters to you and you feel like you have to come away with a deal or an interview or SOMETHING, this can make your nervous, even if you have all the knowledge in the world. So what should you do in that instance? Alesha advises,

'Fake it 'til you make it. I've shown up for interviews or meetings where I've been so nervous and my heart is pounding out of my chest but [you just have to] fake it 'til you make it. Go in with confidence and if you leave feeling you could have done better, that's the learning curve. You've got to go through those beginners' nerves, because that's essentially how you develop.'

Building your company brand

Marketing is about values.

Steve Jobs, entrepreneur and co-founder of Apple Inc.

The phrase 'people buy from people' applies, not only to the notion of personal branding, but also when it comes to creating a company brand. This is because, in order to sell plenty of what you have to offer, that offer must resonate with a particular group of people – your target audience. And, in order to resonate, your company must share values with the customers it seeks to serve.

The world of business is a crowded place so, in order to stand out and differentiate yourself, you need to dig deeper than just listing all the benefits to the customer when they buy from you. You need to find the core message of your company so that you can communicate to the world what you're about.

That's essentially what your company brand is. It's this intangible thing that will express what your purpose is, and will resonate with the particular group of people who need what you are offering and act as a magnet to draw them to you. So consider these questions:

- What does your company stand for? What are the values and mission of your business? What makes you (and your target audience) tick? Refine it until you get it right.
- Why are you doing this? What is your purpose? Why are you so passionate about achieving your vision? What is your 'why'? (Your 'why' is the purpose, cause, or belief that inspires you to do what you do and get out of bed each morning with a spring in your step.)
- How do your customers feel? What is their experience of your company? How can you improve on the status quo?
- Who in the public eye appears to share those values? For example, Apple's famous 'Think Different' campaign was aligned with famous people who shared their values, from Muhammad Ali to John Lennon and Yoko Ono.[13]

In figuring this out you will see that a brand is more than just a logo and a tagline. Those elements are simply the brand's signature. Your brand's reputation becomes an asset, one which is based on a strong set of values and beliefs which drive the decisions made, products provided and mission strived for. Essentially then, your company needs to stand for something. Not only will it then relate to and draw in customers who feel the same and share those values, but it will also attract staff with whom the brand resonates.

As Simon Sinek says in his book, *Start With Why:* 'There are only two ways to influence human behaviour: you can manipulate it or you can inspire it.'[14] The way to inspire people to buy from you or work for you or to evangelize about what you are doing, is to make sure they get your 'why' and support that. Because, unless you have first mover advantage, which is rare, your customers will (if not now, then soon) be able to buy what you are offering elsewhere. There may be a number of reasons why they might choose your products or services – because they're cheaper, better quality, longer lasting, and so on. But the reason that will drive your business and sustain it over the long term is because customers can see how passionate you are about your 'why' in the way that you present yourself and your brand.

Take Jason Vale, for example: he started out with nothing more than a passion for juicing and a dream to 'juice the world'. Today, 16 years after his first book was published in 2001, he has a multi-million pound business that includes seminars, retreats and juice bars, is the best-selling author of numerous books which have sold millions of copies worldwide, as well as DVDs, apps and CDs on juicing, health, fitness and junk food addiction. Jason is highly regarded as one of the most influential people in the world of juicing and health. His story is a fascinating and inspiring one, and he certainly inspired us when we interviewed him for this book.

Jason's story began when he started juicing to sort out his health problems, which included severe psoriasis. He is now on a mission to encourage as many people as possible to improve their health and fitness naturally. Jason told us:

'I didn't set out to start a business, I just wrote a book in the hope that it would get published and inform people of the advantages of juicing, and then it did. I set out to juice the world, but I had no idea how to monetize it.'

'Your first intention should not be money; number two should be money, number one should be whatever gets you out of bed, whatever drives you, whatever is your passion. If you do it all for the money, if your number one driver is money, nine times out of ten you are going to fall flat on your face.'

Therefore, it's critical to consider: who do you genuinely want to help and why?

'When I started, I just wanted to help somebody else with psoriasis because juicing had cleared mine. I thought, if I can help somebody else with psoriasis it would be amazing.'

Jason's focus on his core intention, on his 'why', has led to him helping millions of people, not only with skin conditions, but also to lose weight and live healthier lifestyles.

Ask any successful self-made person and you'll discover that focusing on their purpose, on their primary driver for creating their business, is what has helped to set them apart from other businesses.

Another example of this attention to purpose is Mark Hobbs, the founder and managing director of New Leaf Distribution Limited, one of the last independent national IFA firms in the UK to remain in private hands. New Leaf is an independent network for financial advisors, mortgage brokers, protection advisors and will writers, and employs 120 regulated advisors who look after professional development for their clients, and help them to build their businesses in a compliant way. Mark also leads a church ministry which has helped over 100 homeless people per month in Manchester, Liverpool, Bath, London and Southend by providing clothes, sleeping bags, emergency packs, coffee, tea and soup.

As well as taking care of his family, Mark also wanted to serve his local community, as his work for his ministry reveals. He additionally wanted to retain independence and focus firmly on the family and small business owner in particular. Mark says:

'The old school financial advisors are not interested in serving those who don't have very much. We are the opposite; we're more interested in serving those families that don't have very much, so that we may help them to have more and gain wealth over the years to come.'

Serving people who need help is Mark's 'why' – that is his purpose in all that he does. 'I'm very excited to be operating in a gap in the market, but I'm very sad there's a gap in terms of the lack of advice for those who need it most, but it does open up a great opportunity for us.'

Alesha Dixon is another example of a super-successful self-made person who is driven by her quest for challenges and her passions.

It was this focus which led her to venture down the less predictable, higher-risk path of the music industry. Alesha explains:

'Looking back at my own life, that was a really scary thing to do, to say, "I'm not going to university, I'm going to be in a girl group". But there was an instinct within me that just drove me, I've always followed that. Sometimes passion prevails, sometimes passion is what makes us who we are and it's an extension of who we are, so it felt more natural to go down that road.'

Trusting that inner instinct to seize opportunities which speak to your heart and your 'why' for doing what you do, takes practice. And we don't always get it right. Every self-made person will have an example or two of times when they've taken on projects which didn't fit with their core purpose or passion. Alesha is no different. She admits:

'I've said yes to a few jobs that in hindsight I wish I hadn't but I'm learning. I love saying no more than I love saying yes because there's a confidence in saying no. You realize, over time that actually you don't have to take every job just because they're offering you lots of money; you've got to think about whether it's creatively the right thing for you. Does it fit? You've got to think about whether it's credible, if it makes sense for my brand, the messaging. Everything that I do now has to have some sort of authenticity to it,' says Alesha. 'I have to believe in it, care about it, and consider who it can help.'

Ultimately then, branding is not so much about what you look like (although it is important that your logo, website and other visual imagery tie in with your brand values to create an integrated brand personality). It's more about who you are as a company and why you do what you do. So, whilst personal branding is about who you are as a person, what you know and how you harness that knowledge to present yourself and deliver, company branding is about your 'why':

who you are as a company. It's about your culture, your mission and encompasses everything, from how you and your team answer the phone to how you make your customers feel after they have purchased something from you.

Purpose and values, like passion, are effectual so they should sit at the heart of all that you do and be woven into everything: your brand identity, your customer service policy, your culture – everything.

In taking this approach, you will be able to build trust in the marketplace and become the 'go to' company for your specific products or services. But first you need to establish a clear definition of who your customer is, what their values and needs are and what you have in common with them. So create a strong customer profile that establishes who they are, what they are seeking, where they go online and offline – all of this you will have done in your preparatory market research (see Chapter 1).

Create a list of keywords which define your brand personality and what you stand for. This isn't a list explaining what you do, but spells out who you are as a business. For example, are you reliable and traditional as a business? Are you fun, friendly and flexible? Approachable and ethical? Honest and kind? Bold and brave? Stylish and professional?

Fine-tune your mission statement and write it here.

Our mission and reason for existence is to _____

_____

_____

_____

so that we can [insert the impact you want to have on the world] _____

_____

_____

Create a brand identity that weaves all of this into it. This is where you package your purpose, your knowledge, your characteristics and personality and articulate it all through your brand name, your logo, slogan, the font you use, your website and the colours you use on it, your packaging, and so on. Sometimes it can help to think of a celebrity who has a similar personality as your brand, or an animal or plant or shape which shares those characteristics. What colour is your brand? Are you an environmentally friendly green or a fast and efficient orange? All of this comes into play when designing a brand identity that expresses who you are and resonates with your audience so that they buy from you time and time again.

A brand for a company is like a reputation for a person.

You earn reputation by trying to do hard things well.

Jeff Bezos, founder of Amazon

3

Small Budget? Getting Your Business Up and Running on a Shoestring

Just do it – taking the plunge

Making the decision to take a risk and start your own business isn't easy, but then nothing rewarding is. When Byron launched his first business, a property services company, there came a time, after he'd done his research, where he just had to get out there and do it. 'I had enough money to last me two months and that was it,' recalls Byron, but taking that risk certainly paid off. 'We started off in a basement office, just myself and someone I had convinced to help me out for a month. Within that time we went from a team of two to a team of four,' adds Byron.

The building they were in reflected the hierarchy of success; the higher up the building, the bigger and more expensive the office space. 'At first we were given the basement but we ended up rising, literally, to the top floor. From there we relocated to new premises and grew to a team of 20 within a few years.'

'We started offering just one service and branched out from there to offer everything from floor plans and photography to gas inspections, to dealing with landlords and estate agents,' explains Byron. 'But, had we not just taken that risk and gone out there and launched, we wouldn't have got the business off the ground during a time when that market was growing. So, whilst overcoming that fear to take the leap is a big challenge, as a self-made entrepreneur, you need to 'feel the fear and do it anyway.' You need to think 'what's the worst that can happen?' And then, know that you will handle it.'

Byron and I work well together because we both have a different approach to risk. I tend to be quite risk-averse in terms of wanting to do a lot of preparation and research before taking those tentative first steps. I need to feel that it is a solid proposition and that there is a promising customer base and likely trajectory and that I will definitely make enough money to survive. Whereas Byron is the opposite. He'll assess the risk and then get on with it anyway.

Byron says, 'If I have a product to sell and need to hire a salesperson who will cost me £18k as an annual salary, I will see that as £1500 per month. If it doesn't work, what will I lose during the initial three-month probation period? £4500 maximum. And, during that time, surely they will sell something, which reduces the risk even further.'

Byron's way of assessing risk makes the leap seem less daunting. So, whilst it is important to do adequate research so you are not leaping into the abyss of the unknown, it is worth taking calculated risks to just get out there and do it. Make sure you have some money behind you, and remember that things often cost more and take longer than you think they will; then get out there and test the market – without spending too much at first.

Byron didn't hire a team of 20 from the outset, he roped in someone else to help him and invested in office space; then he went out and got the customers, brought in the business, learned a wealth of knowledge on the job and grew the company into a success that he was then able to sell.

The good news is, you can do the same without investing much money at all.

Not only that, remember that there is immense value in bringing your existing skills and strengths to the table. Both Byron and I have used our capabilities in our businesses, from mentoring and recruiting to coaching and writing, which reaps rewards beyond the financial. Mark Hobbs used his experience of direct sales and his resilience in facing rejection, selling insurance door-to-door for 13 years, when he set up his New Leaf Distribution firm. Mark says:

'During that time I took 275,000 rejections; I would approach 50 people a day, cold-calling business to business, of which 15 would listen to me and perhaps three would buy, so I would always sell around 15 policies a week.'

That experience of direct sales served him well when it came to increasing his customer base. And it was this realization, that he could use his skills to become self made rather than make a fortune for his employer, that spurred Mark into action to launch his own business, as it does for so many of us.

'I always thought, I don't need to be making millions for an American firm,' smiles Mark.'I need to be doing it for my family and the people I work with, their families. So I started from the basis of no money down, no loans and absolutely no support from anyone, and that was where I wanted to be.'

Evidently, it is possible to start your own business on a shoestring by harnessing the value you can bring to the business.

Minimizing your risk

To start your self-made journey you do not need to be wealthy, even though it can be true that 'you get what you pay for' in terms of quality and 'you've got to spend money to make money'. In fact, it is possible to get started on next to nothing if you know where to look.

And, whilst preparation is vital before you start your business, so that you know where you are headed and how you will get there, once you have sufficiently researched the market and the needs of your target audience and spent some time working out who you are and what your company and personal brand stands for, it's advisable to get yourself out there into that marketplace to test the market.

Until you are operational, you don't know what you don't know. Until you get out there, with a product or service that is ready to test, you can't find out if anything needs tweaking to improve it; if customers who say they will buy, actually will buy. So it's wise to have a test phase and soft-launch your business on a small budget.

The hardest part, when you're starting something new, is making sure you've got a customer base and sufficient finances. The reason that's tough is because you need to prove you have a customer base in order to get the finances, and yet you need the finances to establish your customer base. So this is a challenge in terms of what to do first. That's why it is worthwhile doing a soft launch of your product or service out in the real world so that you can demonstrate demand and, as a result, secure the finances that you need to seed the business in its crucial first year (or, at the very least prove that the business idea is viable before sinking too much of your own cash into it).

The way that both of us have got round this challenge is to find customers ourselves, with just a computer and a phone, to keep costs down and then promote our businesses on a shoestring budget. In general, we have done this through:

- networking to build relationships
- negotiating lower costs
- doing contra-deals to keep costs down
- searching the market to find the best deals
- using referral systems.

Let's explore each of these one by one.

Networking

In Chapter 5 we will talk in depth about networking: why it is important to network, how to network, and what to do before and after an event to make sure your networking pays off. However, to summarize, networking can cost very little. Apart from the cost of some decent clothes and a good haircut, to ensure you are well presented, many networking events are free or low-cost. The only additional cost would be for some business cards which should include a website address. As such, you should ideally have a website or, at least, a holding page, ahead of going networking. But that doesn't need to cost the earth either, as we'll explore later in this chapter.

Negotiating lower costs

Don't be afraid to haggle. Maybe this is an *Apprentice* thing, but many people think the price is the price. It's quite an English mentality to accept the price. But it's always worth asking for a discount. What's the worst that could happen? They say 'no'. Don't be too cheeky and destroy relationships, but if you have a budget and can't go above that, say so: you'll be surprised what you can get.

Sometimes, you have no choice but to negotiate costs down. When I was starting the Bianca Miller London brand, the minimum order quantity on hosiery was 2000 per colour, which had a huge impact on costs. Negotiating that down to a more manageable number really helped to get the brand up and running.

Contra-deals

This is a worthwhile activity to pursue and many small businesses do this. It involves speaking to suppliers, such as logo designers or web developers – anyone who you would ordinarily need to pay for their services – and offering to do something for them in exchange for them doing something for you. For example, you could agree to send some of your customers their way or to give them free services or products in exchange for them designing you a logo for free or for a significant discount.

You could also find another business person who is a similar position to you and agree to share office space as that halves your costs from the outset.

Using deal websites

From using comparison sites such as MoneySupermarket.com and MoneySavingExpert.com to research and source the best business insurance or business banking deals, to buying stationery and equipment, or training courses via the likes of Groupon and Wowcher, there's a lot of money to be saved by seeking out the best deals online. British people spent a massive £16.5bn via deal websites in 2014, so there are clearly many savings to be had.[15]

Although the majority of deal sites focus on consumer products and services, there are two key sites that can save you money by offering discounts on a variety of products and services for businesses. AppSumo is a daily deal site for software which partners with apps to provide exclusive price deals on web apps. Huddlebuy is another useful site which curates the best deals for entrepreneurs. Sole traders can also use the Huddlebuy goldcard to save money on a range of business products and services from leading retailers.

Using referral systems

As well as seeking and providing mutual referrals via networking groups or business breakfast clubs there are specific sites that have been set up to provide you with referrals. You could also try websites which have software for you to add to your website to encourage your customers to mention you to their friends and refer business your way.

Primarily, however, when it comes to referrals, we suggest looking at networking not only as a way to meet with potential customers, but as a method of forming alliances with other businesses with whom you share a target audience, but aren't competing with. For example, if you are a carpenter, you could form a referral network by aligning yourself with a local plumber, a painter and decorator, a tiler, and so on. With homeowners seeking people they know and trust to carry out work on their homes, you can refer business to the other companies in your referral network and, in return, you can expect business to be sent your way too. The customer is more likely to invite you to quote for their business as your introduction has come via a recommendation from someone they already know and have done business with.

Aligning with like-minded business owners, who can refer business to you and vice versa, is a great way to keep your marketing costs down.

Starting up on a shoestring budget

The good news is, you can start a business from as little as £500. All you really need is a mobile phone, a domain name and website, stationery and, if selling a product, samples to show people. There are plenty of people and resources around to enable you to start up on a shoestring. For example, many freelancers do work for lower fees in order to build up a portfolio that enables them to attract more clients. Websites like People Per Hour, Fiverr and Fivesquid provide an out-let for freelancers who will do all kinds of things – from designing a book cover or editing a video to designing a logo and getting traffic to your site for $5 or £5 and up.

Whether you sell services or tangible products, having your own website is a no-brainer, if only because your competitors are likely to have one. Research commissioned by Nominet reveals that 93 per cent of businesses with a website saw business improvements such as more customers and better brand awareness; while 88 per cent said that boosting their online presence helped their business to grow, so it is certainly worth the investment.[16] Yes, these days you can generate custom from social media pages and there are a great many people who are doing just that, either taking orders via a combination of wall postings, personal messages and PayPal links or by setting up a shop on eBay. But we believe having a website is worth pursuing to add to your credibility. Research for Nominet also says that businesses who rely on social media without a website score far lower trust with consumers than businesses who operate both social media and a website. Social media acts like a satellite gathering interest and building a following, but it needs to point somewhere, to a space you own, such as your website. The most trusted businesses have a website and a professional email that contains their business name. A free email (e.g. Hotmail, Gmail) just looks amateur and earns low trust.[17] The good news is, it really needn't cost the earth and you don't need any technical know-how.

There are many free and low-cost resources that you can use to create a top-quality website, and there are plenty of plug-and-play websites where all you need to do is add your words and pictures without any coding knowledge.

That said, you should still ensure that your website looks good. Just because you are spending very little on it, you shouldn't cut corners, because that website is like a shop window. In a retail environment you make sure your shop window looks good; your website is the same. You want customers to see you as credible enough for them to give money to, so whilst you can get a website up cheaply, you don't want it to look cheap.

Having a good, sound website that is aesthetically pleasing but also works in terms of functionality is crucial, because it feeds into your whole plan. That's why, although you can be shrewd and avoid throwing too much money at your website, it's important to know what you are doing and use the best tools around.

So, here's our ULTIMATE GUIDE on how to get your business onto the web on a shoestring budget.

Ten ways to launch a quality website without breaking the bank

1 Register your domain name and investigate DIY website service and email bundle special offers

There are many registrars (or domain name web services resellers); e.g. Go Daddy (uk.godaddy.com), 123reg (www.123reg.co.uk), 1&1 (www.1and1.co.uk) are three of the largest. For a wider list visit the UK Domain site at www.theukdomain.uk where you can also search to see if your ideal domain name is still available. Registrars also provide website development and hosting packages. Or you could investigate good-looking, easy-to-update, one-page sites at Strikingly. com which will let you create and host your website for a minimal monthly fee.

You will have lots of choice here about what type of website domain you wish to purchase (.co.uk, .com, .uk, .me, .wales or .org. uk to name a few). We think it is important to choose a domain name that represents your geographic location; for example, if you are a UK business we would suggest using a UK domain as your primary website. But you may also wish to consider buying the .com for brand protection and pointing it to your UK domain. This prevents anyone from potentially registering your domain and benefiting from your hard work.

The additional benefit of having your own business domain name is that you are able to use a professional email address (e.g. Bianca@ mybusinessname.co.uk). As mentioned above, research shows that businesses with a professional email address are more trusted than those which use free email. Furthermore, why would you want to promote someone else's business every time you send an email?

2 Find somewhere reliable and secure to host your site

There's little point having a brilliant website if your users can't reach it. You want uptime not downtime. 'The site has gone down' are words that no website owner wants to see, even if it is due to popularity (a spike in traffic can often create a server overload). You want to ensure that your site can handle any volume of traffic and make the most of traffic spikes, rather than have a site that is unavailable or incredibly slow during busy periods. Having a site which is fast-loading and reliable is a must. So allocate enough 'web space' to scale up, add new pages and rich media and enough bandwidth to attract more visitors to view more pages. Look at shared server solutions or cloud computing hosting solutions to keep costs down. Ask vital questions, such as what would happen if the site went down at 3 am? Is there round-the-clock tech support? Will they issue a credit or move your site to an alternative server? Can they scale up? How might you be charged if you go over your bandwidth limit? Read reviews to assess quality of service, uptime and potential issues before committing to any provider. Use www.loadimpact.com to simulate and test how much traffic your site can handle.

3 Plan what you want to have on your website

This will inform what kind of solution you should choose or, at least, help you when choosing a theme for your site if you opt for a pre-made one (as you'll be able to find one which matches your required content and functionality). Try www.cacoo.com (a 'wire-frame' tool) to plan your site or simply sketch it out on paper. Look at other websites to see where they position key areas such as product pages, contact forms and so on. A wire frame is essentially a blueprint of your web pages which connects and prioritizes the content and navigational structure with the visual design and functionality of the website. So you sketch out what will be displayed where and how it will be prioritized and structured, plus where your header, footer, logo, content areas, navigation bars, drop down menus, call to action buttons and so on, will be on the page.

4 Brand your website and get your logo designed

Refer to the previous chapter regarding creating a brand identity which relates to who you are as a business and your values. Branding differentiates you from your competitors. It characterizes you and personifies your business. It puts your stamp on your offerings. If you can list up to six words which summarize what makes you different, your core values and characteristics as a business, you are half way there. Also consider a character, celebrity or animal that you might associate your brand with and colours that fit with all of those elements.

Give your brand words to a design student along with your chosen colours (which should evoke those words). If you don't have a graphic design guru friend, or cannot find an enthusiastic graphic design student, take a look at www.graphicleftovers.com and www.graphicriver.net to see if any logos there suit your branding ideas. Alternatively you can get a reasonably priced logo from www.small-businesslogos.co.uk or crowd-source for various people to pitch ideas to you via www.crowdspring.com, www.99designs.com or hire a designer for $5 at www.fiverr.com.

Although this section is all about creating a brand on a budget, remember your logo and brand say a lot about your business. So it may be worth putting some money aside to invest in a professional.

5 Build your website

Choose from an array of low-cost or free website templates, plug-ins, open-source software all designed to help non-web-designers create their own sites. We have listed a few here but for more websites please visit us at www.selfmadebook.uk.

- www.strikingly.com
- www.create.net
- www.wordpress.org
- www.joomla.org
- www.drupal.org
- www.grabaperch.com
- www.wix.com
- www.moonfruit.com

- www.webstore.amazon.co.uk
- http://pages.ebay.com/storefronts/building.html

Most of these provide WYSIWYG editors (What You See Is What You Get) to make it relatively straightforward to create a website with drag-and-drop options and word-processor formatting. These are all of particular use if you are thinking of putting up a site containing static pages with not more than 15 pages or so. Most include robust CMS (Content Management Systems) for bigger sites, particularly Drupal and Joomla. Drupal has a wide range of modules whilst WordPress has a selection of plug-ins to explore to give your site the functionality you want, whether that's to offer membership, sell directly from your site, bolt on paid adverts, a directory, calendar, and so on. These days you can easily incorporate means of enabling your visitors to share your content via social media, and can add photo galleries via Flickr plug-ins. If you know your way round Microsoft Word you will be able to post articles/blogs on a WordPress site or any other site creators with a WYSIWYG editor. WordPress is free, easy to install and update and there are many plug-ins and themes being added constantly.

6 Choose a theme

Different website building options offer different themes. Some come direct via the site, such as Create.net, others are built by a wide array of designers and available for free download or purchase for under £50. Themes/templates are customizable (if you know your stuff; you may need to hire someone to tweak them to suit you). For WordPress, for example, you can find some amazing templates at http://wordpress.org/extend/themes, http://themeforest.net, or http://www.templatemonster.com/wordpress-themes.php.

7 Outsource at low cost

Most of the aforementioned website builders are very user friendly and, if you read the documentation and follow the guidelines, you should be able to install, set up and play around with the set-up of your website yourself. However, if you need anything bespoke, or help with installing or setting up plug-ins, editing or customizing themes, we would recommend using freelancer websites like Odesk, Fivesquid, Elance or People Per Hour to source a website developer. Search for WordPress expert, for example, and you will find hundreds of professional experts who charge a range of fees. Ideally your candidates will have coding skills in PHP/CSS, your chosen web software (such as WordPress) and have feedback to back up their expertise. Always ask to see websites they have created previously and look for their logo at the bottom of the site to check authenticity. Remember your website is your 'shop window' online so you want to ensure it is inviting and professional. Alternatively we have our preferred web designers listed on our website who are tried and tested. Or if you like the look of a website why not ask them for their designer's contact details?

If you do go for WordPress, as well as searching for experts on freelancer websites, you could try www.designcrowd.co.uk – a hub for a specialist group of WordPress designers from around the world.

Be clear when writing your brief/specification. Clear communication is vital when hiring someone to design and/or develop your website. You need to specify exactly what you want in terms of functionality (what you want your users to be able to do on your site, such as sign-up to a newsletter, share some content or click to buy), plus the colour scheme/design and the image you are aiming for, navigation/positioning of content and the type of content you'll be using. Provide clear guidelines, get clear action steps back and agree them then, provide detailed feedback. It is also essential to ensure that the website has a user-friendly 'back end' which you can update yourself. Hiring someone to make small changes as the business develops can be expensive and unnecessary.

8 Make use of Google's free tools

Try using Google Webmaster Tools (www.google.com/webmasters/tools/home) and Google Analytics (www.google.com/analytics/) to gain insight into what is working and what needs attention, once your site is live. For example, these tools will show you which keywords and search terms are driving visitors to your site, as well as the websites that are referring traffic your way. You can also gain free analysis online which analyses your web page content, structure and headers. And make sure you stay on top of dead links in order to get rid of them as they can hamper your SEO.

9 Employ students/interns

If your website is successful and your business starts to thrive, you may need help fulfilling orders, answering phones, creating or sourcing more products and so on. Hiring talent can be a minefield but, as well as outsourcing tasks via the freelance marketplaces mentioned earlier, you can also use sites to find free or low-cost talent, such as Internwise and http://graduatetalentpool.direct.gov.uk and https://Enternships.com. This can be win-win, as they require the experience and you require the talent, but you must ensure you are willing to allocate time for training.

10 Make sure your website is fully functional

As well as ensuring that your website is aesthetically pleasing, it must function well so you need to consider your customer's journey and ensure that their experience in using your site is a positive one.

Your customers should be able to go online, choose the product, get it in the basket, make the payment and get an email saying thank you for your order. That customer journey must be effective and a phone number is also essential in case they want to speak to you or ask a question (Where are you? Are you open? What time do you close? Do you have my size in stock? etc.). Online, your competitors are only a click away.

What's more, the customer journey doesn't stop when they buy the product or service you are offering. As well as getting the product to them in the right amount of time, it's equally important to make sure that the customer is happy and feeling like they have that connection with you.

All of this can be done on a shoestring. You really need not spend much on setting up your business. Now all you need to do is shout about it from the rooftops. So, about that...

Part 2: The Action

In Part 2 we will guide you through the next steps after launching your startup. It's all about consolidating your position: finding sources of funding, promoting your business and getting your message out there. We'll explain different marketing methods and look at how networking can work for you. We'll explore social media marketing and show you how to make the most of Facebook, Twitter and LinkedIn, among others. We'll also discuss sales techniques, including how to attract customers and keep them coming back. Expert advice comes from Nominet (who operate the UK domain registry), social media influencer Jay Shetty and Gordon Merrylees, Head of Entrepreneurship for the Royal Bank of Scotland, NatWest and Ulster Bank.

4

Advertising and Marketing Your Business

Before you launch your business, you need to create a marketing plan. In your plan, you need to consider:

- Who do you want to be aware of your launch? How are they going to find out?
- How will they know where to find you?
- What is the key message about your brand?
- How might you spark curiosity and capture audience details prior to launch?
- How might you connect and engage with your audience so that they feel involved?
- What will you do during the launch and post-launch? There's no point launching and then doing nothing; you need to keep the momentum going. So what's your action plan for that?

In Chapter 3 we looked at the impact of networking on building relationships with other businesses, but it is essential to do this with your existing and target customers too. So, consider how you might connect with them. For example, as part of our campaign for Bianca Miller London, we encouraged our customers to send us a photograph of themselves wearing their hosiery, and hashtag the colour that they chose using social media, because we wanted them to feel part of the launch. Bringing people in and making them feel involved is really key.

We used Twitter, Instagram, Facebook and LinkedIn to promote the launch of Bianca Miller London, as well as having a database of people who had signed up for more information.

It's a good idea to have a database of email addresses ready before you launch. You can buy one or set up a simple 'sign up' page which explains what is coming and encourages people to opt-in to receive information from you. As an added incentive you could also offer a benefit, such as a discount on their first purchase or a free report on a topic of interest on them.

With Bianca Miller London, we had a running start because we already had a database of a few thousand people, all of whom had signed up on the website. Alternatively you could add a video to your site that entices people to want to know more.

But remember, if you're going to tell everyone your website is going to launch at a set time, it needs to launch at that time and it needs to look good when it does. If you're going to build anticipation, you need to deliver that excitement when you launch, and then hold your audience's attention.

After you've launched and taken orders you need to keep the customer engagement and interaction going. So, once you've sent the item, check that they're happy. If they aren't happy, make sure you demonstrate your commitment to excellent customer service by resolving the problem quickly and to their satisfaction. A large part of business is retention, which means repeat business from customers who have already bought from you. Many businesses focus on attracting new customers, rather than retaining existing ones, despite the latter costing a good deal less. So, always consider this in your marketing plan – how will you communicate with customers AFTER they have bought from you?

Marketing strategies and objectives

You have to be clear on what you're using to get the message out there. All of the homework that you have done so far will help you to know your customers and, consequently, know which marketing medium and message will suit them best. This is going to be helpful because there are A LOT of marketing channels to choose from. There's traditional advertising and editorial in magazines, driving traffic to your website via good SEO (Search Engine Optimization) and Pay-Per-Click (PPC). You might choose to partner with others to do collaborative marketing, set up a blog on your own website and write guest blog posts on others, or you might opt to exhibit at events. Another key method of getting your messages in front of your audience is via social media marketing, which we shall cover in Chapter 6.

Indeed, social media is a great tool because you can attract followers and build interest, although it doesn't work for everyone. So, effective marketing is about understanding your customers: what do they want? How do they want to engage with you? And how do you get them from engaging with you to buying? A lot of the time people use social media as a method of having an online presence, but then fail to capitalize on it. Marketing is not just about putting your message out there, it's about what you DO with the information you gain from customers and from the interactions you have with them.

Whatever marketing strategy you adopt, your aim will be to get the right message in front of the right person at the right time. You could have the best product and website in your market, but if people don't know about them, you won't get any sales. Therefore, you need to dedicate sufficient time and money to telling people about your offering and driving them to your website. And you don't just need to tell people once, you need to tell them and then tell them again and again. Repetition is key. That's why building a good quality email list is so worthwhile, because you can contact the people on your list at regular intervals, reminding them what you have to offer, how it will benefit them and, just as crucial, demonstrating your expertise in your specialist area.

Pulling traffic in to your website is known as inbound marketing, whilst push-marketing (including email marketing, advertising and PR) is known as outbound marketing. It is often worth devoting a portion of your marketing budget across a variety of marketing channels and tracking which is working the best, either by asking for or including a tracking reference number when a customer places an order or by asking them where they heard of you. Once you know which marketing method is generating the best ROI (return on investment), that's what you roll out with and invest your marketing spend on.

Where does your target market tend to go – online and offline? For example, which websites do they frequent and which magazines do they tend to read?

As well as finding out which marketing channels are most appropriate for your target audience, you should also consider what your objectives are, as they too will determine your choice of messaging and media.

For example, initially, you will want to shout from the rooftops about your soon-to-launch business, so your objective will be to source and attract potential customers, and persuade them to visit your website. After that you will want to encourage them to take some kind of action, so you can gather as many leads/sign-ups as possible. Your objective then is to encourage people to sign up, book a meeting and so on. To do this you will need to focus on building credibility and gaining trust. The next part of the marketing cycle is selling – securing the sale by closing the deal. So you will need to convince your would-be customers to place an order with you. Once you have delivered your product or service to them, your objective will be to secure repeat business or, at least, the likelihood of repeat business. So you need to follow up the sale, ask customers to provide you with a testimonial and/or referral (if they are happy with your product/service), and continue to keep them updated on what you are offering. And then the cycle begins again – attracting, persuading, selling and following up… and repeat.

Which objective you are focused on at any given time will affect what activities you focus on in your marketing plan. So, if building credibility and trust is your aim, starting a blog and creating a strategy for guest blogging (inviting guests to blog on your website, as well as blogging on theirs) might be the best use of your time, along with securing interviews on local radio stations. Meanwhile, if you are focused on attracting fresh prospects, an enticing video that you post all over social media might be a priority, along with a press release announcing your newness to all relevant publications, plus a bit of telemarketing or direct mail. You might also choose to offer a heavily discounted deal on a daily deal website, like Groupon, or offer giveaways to publications in order to secure editorial coverage.

There are a lot of marketing methods to choose from, so let's delve into these a bit further.

Marketing methods explained

Email and text marketing

Email and text messaging have overtaken direct mail as the best way to deliver messages to customers. Text messaging CTR (Click Through Rates) do tend to be higher than those for emails because our inboxes are so cluttered these days.

Both options are cheap and fast but you need to make your messages engaging enough to be opened, read and, importantly, acted upon. You can send people who sign up to your list details of special subscriber deals and discounts and, if you use online email marketing software, you can even see how many people opened your emails and which links they clicked on.

However, it's important to ensure that you only send solicited emails to people who have opted in to receive your messages and always include the means to opt-out within every message, so that people can unsubscribe if the content is no longer relevant to them (in which case, you don't really want them on your list). This brings us on to the next rule of email marketing which is to ensure that everything you send is RELEVANT to those on your list and, ideally USEFUL too. And keep it short. Finally, write subject lines that entice the reader to open the message, include calls to action and time-sensitive offers, and don't send messages too often.

You can send professional newsletters for free or next to nothing if you use automation and have a longer list. Email marketing websites like Mailchimp can be used to distribute your e-newsletters (free for up to 2000 subscribers and 12,000 mails per month). You may also wish to consider using a virtual phone-answering service to pick up any calls or enquiries that come in from your website in your absence.

Content marketing

As well as building your credibility and positioning you as an expert in your field, your web content can drive traffic to your site and improve your page ranking with search engines, such as Google.

Blog posts, for example containing 'Seven ways to... [do something your target audience is keen to do]', podcasts, webinars, white papers, videos and checklists are worth spending time on and can be repackaged. So a podcast can become a Top Tips feature and transcripts of videos can be published as features. The key, as well as posting good quality engaging content on your own website, is to create content for use on other websites and drive traffic from those sites to your own. If you can't write your own content, you could hire a freelancer to do it for you. Once you have published your content you can get it listed in directories such as Yell, Review Centre and Trust Pilot, and list your podcast on iTunes and other podcast directories. You can also promote links to your own site content using social media.

Editorial in targeted magazines

Publications need content and if you can supply them with an interesting story about a new product or service, you could get free publicity that may be read by thousands of potential customers. All it costs you is the time it takes to write and distribute, and to follow up what you've submitted.

So, seek out stories in the news that feature current topics relating to your product or service. If the economy is in dire straits, any story helping people to save money will be useful. Similarly, if sugar is getting a hard time in the media, your healthy new smoothie machine could make interesting news.

Essentially, editorial in magazines is not only free, it is worth a lot of money. Think of the cost of advertising in those magazines: it is worth that much or more to gain editorial coverage, because people buy magazines to read them rather than to look at the adverts. So, if you can send a press release in to a health and fitness magazine and tie it in with National Smoothie Week, there is a good chance you'll get featured. Timely, interesting angles will get the editor's attention. Furthermore, if you can promote yourself as an expert in your field and get on the radar of editors and writers, you may become their 'go to' person when they need an expert quote on a specific topic.

You can find a list of publications at media directories such as media.info or gorkana.co.uk and use submission services such as prweb.com and sourcewire.com to submit to them. You can even receive feature lists and press requests to give you an even greater chance of getting your story published: try journorequests.com.

Daily deal websites

Daily deal websites such as Groupon, Living Social, Google Offers, and so on provide customers with discounts. They promote offers to a large list of people and so, if you are keen to generate brand awareness, or have sufficient products to upsell to those who take up your offers, this could be a worthwhile marketing avenue to go down.

That said, many people who take up the offers are only interested because of the low price, so it can work more as a loss leader in some instances. However, if you have something which doesn't take a lot of time or money to provide and could generate passive income, such as a range of online courses, these deal sites could work really well for you.

It is important to think about how this aligns with your overall marketing strategy for the business. For example, if you are creating a luxury product or service you might want to consider how being aligned with a deals site could reflect on your brand as a whole.

It is also worth looking at what percentage the deal site wants to retain from the product sale (after discount) and see if it is commercially viable to provide the offer to a potentially disloyal customer base.

Search engine marketing

There are two types of search engine marketing. Paid listings are when you bid on keywords to effectively sponsor a search listing which is triggered when web users search using the keywords that you have bid on. However, before you invest any money in this area, it is worth spending some time getting to know how to generate a good flow of traffic to your website from free search engine listings. The name of the search engine game is to get your site ranked as close to the top of the first page of search results as you can but, with search engine algorithms and ranking criteria changing frequently, it can be difficult to stay on top of the latest strategies. However, given that Google is the primary search engine, there are certain rules that have always stayed the same.

SEARCH ENGINE OPTIMIZATION (SEO)

The bottom line is that Google wants to satisfy its customers, so it wants to ensure that the search results it displays are top quality and relevant. As such it makes hundreds of changes to its ranking algorithms annually, but, as long as you ensure that your site copy (text) including your headlines, page titles and descriptions are relevant and credible without duplication, you stand a good chance of coming high up in results.

Here are the must-haves to optimize your site in order to make it as likely as possible to rank well in search engines.

- **It must be technically sound.** Search engines must be able to crawl your web pages so they need to be functioning correctly when you submit your site to Google. Make sure your website is compatible with multiple browsers and mobile devices, loads quickly, and that all links work. You can check for further technical specifications on Google's Webmaster pages and use tools there to identify any broken links.
- **Keyword selection.** Although the ratio of keywords that appear on your site in relation to other words is less of a ranking point than it used to be, it is still worth considering what your target audience might type into a search engine to find sites such as yours, and to ensure that you use those words in your web copy and in your 'behind the scenes' page descriptions and titles. But don't pad out your title with keywords as you will be penalized for this. Rather, make sure your title uses keywords but remains descriptive, relevant and accurate.
- **Good content: authority and quality.** Reputation is imperative to Google, both its own and that of websites it directs its users too. So, in order to build a good reputation, you need to show that your content is of good quality. Google signals the authority of your content via the Page

78

Rank it has assigned to your web pages and via social media authority (i.e. how often your content has been shared). So, you can gain a positive authority ranking by making sure that all content you publish on your site is unique (not duplicated) and fresh and, ideally, has lots of inbound links linking to it from other equally reputable websites.

Maximize dwell-time and minimize bounce rates (single page visits) by ensuring that your content delivers what it says it will deliver in its title and description. Also, the more you can engage readers and enable them to post comments, reviews and share your content, the better.

Ultimately good-quality, helpful and engaging content not only impresses Google but also impresses your web visitors, who are then more likely to revisit. All of this bolsters your perceived authority and ranking in the eyes both of Google and of your web visitors.

- **Inbound links and online directory submissions.** Another benefit of creating great content is that you are more likely to attract other webmasters to link to that content and, the more websites out there pointing towards yours, the better your ranking will be. After all, a high number of inbound links shows Google that your site is relevant and authoritative. So, as well as writing super-relevant content, you should make sure that your 'share' buttons are clear and functioning, that you register your site on relevant targeted directories and request 'guest blog' spots on other high-traffic sites to build credibility and link back to your site.

You can also post comments on relevant forums with a signature file at the end which links back to your website and create content on social sites such as Reddit and Digg, among others. Finally, spend some time trawling the web to find online directories that list sites such as yours. Some will be fairly generic but others will be more specific. For example, Byron runs an online wedding directory (www.happybrideguide.co.uk) which provides brides and grooms with a complete solution and a 'one-stop-shop', but which also gives anyone in the wedding industry, from wedding dress boutiques to luxury car drivers, an opportunity to get their website in front of the right audience. There are lots of online directories operating within all kinds of markets, so seek them out and get listed. Not only will you benefit from the traffic and sales you generate from your listing, it will also help with your search engine page ranking in terms of the in-bound link and credibility algorithm. Remember, the more sites that link to you, the higher Google will rate your authenticity and credibility.

Paid search: PPC (Pay Per Click)

Organic free search engine results can take a few weeks to show up; however, paid listings enable your website to show up instantly. PPC allows you to test which keywords and search phrases result in the most traffic, giving you useful knowledge with which to tweak your site content and gain a better organic search ranking too.

The way PPC works is that you set a minimum daily spend for your bids on relevant keywords, and then you write clickable ads that will show up on the search page based on the amount you bid on relevant keywords and a quality score. The quality score is determined by how many times an ad is viewed and clicked rather than not clicked. So your ads need to be compelling as well as relevant.

When your ads are clicked you can analyse the results to see what is working best and tweak your campaigns accordingly. You can even choose negative keywords that won't trigger your ad. For example, if you are selling second-hand items, you could select 'new' as a negative keyword.

For some businesses, PPC can work phenomenally well. For example, with his property services company, Byron has invested £2000 pcm into PPC and got a significant return on investment. However, when I presumed that I too would generate a similar return on my investment, it didn't happen. Why is that?

The key here is to understand the motivations of the customer. With Byron's property business the need is immediate; for example, if the customer has a problem which requires a prompt solution, such as an emergency repair. Moreover, the products available are already familiar to the customer. This means the customer's decision comes down to a few factors: price, website and customer service. They need the service, they need it in their area and they want the best price.

Whereas the services offered by the styling section of my personal branding company are very niche; they appeal to a smaller market and there is far less urgency. In addition there is no set industry standard, and the service is tailored to each person's needs – there is no 'one size fits all price', and no call-to-action at that level. The need differs in that it is a luxury not a necessity.

Top tips for maximizing your PPC success:

- Write engaging copy that asks a targeted benefit-rich question, such as 'Need a nail varnish remover that doesn't smell?' or 'Want hosiery that matches the actual colour of your skin?' Be precise; for example 'brown leather boots' rather than 'boots'.
- Use compelling calls to action. Reveal value to your potential clickers by spelling out precisely what they'll get, then include a call to action, such as 'Learn More' or 'Free Download Here'.
- Visit Google Adwords to learn more about how to get the best from your PPC campaigns.

Advertising and sponsorship

Advertising on billboards and in magazines, or sponsoring roundabouts and charitable events, can be effective ways to build brand awareness but tend to be expensive. Display adverts (online text-based or graphical ads placed on targeted websites) can be a worthwhile alternative. You are charged based on CPM (Cost Per Thousand Page Impressions) rather than CPC (Cost Per Click).

Google AdWords enables you to get your text ads to appear across a network of well-targeted websites that have opted in to display ads. Furthermore, Google Content Network allows you to target users who have already visited your website before (re-targeting) and choose specific sites based on keywords or location.

You can also advertise on social networks such as Facebook, where the targeting is unrivalled. With users giving away so much information, from marital status to interests and 'likes', you can target your ads very precisely. For example, if you are a wedding photographer, you could choose to show your ads only to women of a specific age who live in a certain area and have updated their marital status to 'engaged'.

When it comes to sponsorship, you can approach those with large mailing lists or high-traffic websites which target your audience and see if they'd accept a sponsorship deal, whereby you pay to sponsor their email newsletter or a section of their website, and get your brand in front of their readers.

Collaborative marketing

We've already talked about referral systems and establishing partnerships so that you send business to a business which sends business to you. It's worth exploring this kind of collaborative marketing when you write your plan. List all the good quality websites you can find that are not competing with you but which target the same audience. Consider what kind of partnership or collaborative marketing campaign you could run. As well as simply recommending each other to your customers, you could run an email campaign offering discounts to both mailing lists using a specific discount code within a certain timeframe. The possibilities are endless.

Blogging

The best kind of website visitors are those who know, like and trust you and, in general, such visitors come from reading your blog posts, from social media and from search engines (whether via paid or free listings).

Blogging keeps your website fresh with new relevant and engaging content. Each time you write a blog post, you add a new indexable page to your site. In so doing you are giving search engines a fresh opportunity to drive traffic to you. You're also providing people on social networks with a new piece of content to share which bolsters your social media reach.

Not only does blogging help drive traffic to your site, it also helps convert that traffic into leads, but only if you add a call to action to each blog post. For example, you might offer a free checklist, factsheet, product/service trial or ebook: something that the reader would readily share their email address in order to gain – something of value.

Your blog will also help you to position yourself as an expert in your field and may answer certain questions that customers might have. If a customer asks you how your product or service could benefit them and you can send them to a blog post which not only answers their question but also provides additional information, they will be impressed.

What's more, there's longevity in blogs because, even after the main hype around your new post fades, once it is ranked in search engines it is there forever, so will drive traffic to your website for many months and years to come.

The key to inspiring people to read and engage with (and, ideally, share) your blog posts is to make sure they are relevant and speak directly to their audience. How do your blog posts help readers to solve their problems, rise to their challenges and move forward? It's also important to invite people to comment and share. Ask people, 'Did you find this post helpful? If so please consider sharing it.'

In fact, whichever channels you choose to use, much of marketing comes back to relevance. Relevant content, audience, keywords and so on. So, the more you know about your audience, the better your marketing results are likely to be.

The power of expertise

Equally, the more you know about your topic, the more you'll be able to secure coverage across a multitude of media. Why else do you think Jason Vale proclaimed himself the 'Juice Master' from the outset? He was able to establish himself as a leading expert at a time when nobody was juicing in the UK. Consequently, he went on to appear on TV shows, such as *This Morning*, and got his first big break in radio.

If you create something from the heart which showcases your expertise, you are more likely to find people who will evangelize about it. This was certainly true for Jason who, full of optimism after his first book was published, asked his publisher when they'd like him to start work on his next book. They told him that the book wasn't doing very well and had only sold a couple of hundred copies. Jason responded:

'I told them, with all due respect, I hadn't been anywhere, so who would know about the book? My mates in Peckham had been the only ones who knew about it and supported me by buying it.'

But, as Jason found out, all you need is one influential person to discover what you are doing and rave about it to act as the catalyst for success. As he explains:

'Gareth O'Callaghan, an Irish radio DJ said he wanted an interview. He was one of the 200 people who had read the book. So there I was in the London studio with a live link to Ireland and I hardly spoke. Gareth was telling his listeners, "If you never do anything else today, you've got to buy this man's freaking book, it's sensational!" He told me he never promotes books but he couldn't help himself. He said, "You will never read anything like it." And it went straight to Number 2 in Ireland.'

By putting his passion and expertise into his product, the product sold itself once it was in the right hands (of an influential radio DJ).

As explored in Chapter 2, if you can become the 'go to' person on a certain topic, you can reap the fruits of your labour. I have become known as a personal branding expert/women's fashion guru, and Byron is known for his expertise in providing consultancy and innovative strategy for businesses. Therefore, we tailor our marketing to those areas in order to sustain our position as experts in our field, just as Jason has done with juicing.

Summary

- Plan your launch and what you intend to do to follow up. Use findings from your market research to decide where to place your marketing messages and what to say to generate the best response.
- Figure out your objective and base your marketing activities, messages and channels on which stage of the marketing cycle you are in.

- Measure your results. Marketing is as much about metrics as it is about messages, so it's important to analyse your marketing results to see where customers have come from. Which marketing methods and messages, headlines and adverts, website links and search engines are producing the best results? Which audience segments are clicking and buying from you? Once you have this data you can focus on those audience segments, messages and media to generate the best return on your marketing spend.
- Aim to do three things per day to promote your company, whether that is to send a message to your mailing list, write a blog post and/or submit a giveaway via a press release.

. . . .

Expert insight

Q&A with Nominet

We caught up with Nominet, the people behind The UK Domain to find out a little more about the importance of securing the right domain name, and to get some tips about why every business today needs to have a website and use a professional email address, and how to go about it.

Q: *Who are Nominet, The UK Domain and what do you do?*

A: Nominet is an internet company and trusted guardian of the UK namespace – one of the world's largest country code registries. In the UK, Nominet exclusively operates the .uk country code registry, as well as the Welsh domains .cymru, .wales and 35 other branded and generic top level domains, including .bbc and .london. Nominet has offices in Oxford and London.

In addition to operating the registry database, which lists who has which domain name, Nominet also provides the technical infrastructure which allows a computer on the internet to link to the correct website when a URL is typed into a browser, or which directs an email to the correct recipient.

We are also a company committed to delivering public benefit and tackling social challenges. Since 2008 we have donated over £44m to the Nominet Trust, an independent charitable foundation. The Trust is the UK's leading funder for 'social tech' projects and to date has benefited over 10 million people.

Nominet has operated the UK domain for over 20 years.

The UK Domain inspires and provides advice and guides for businesses and individuals to help them get online with a professional website and email address. Today over 3 million UK businesses and millions more consumers use a domain name ending in .uk and rely on our registry services. The UK domain family, including .co.uk, .uk, .org.uk and .me.uk is managed and operated by Nominet.

Q: *So, how has The UK Domain been working with startups and small businesses?*

A: We recognize that starting a new business is a stressful time, as there's limited time and funds, and much to do, often involving long hours and financial risk. With more and more consumers researching online prior to purchase, securing your company website domain name is as important as choosing your company name.

Remember: Choose your domain name at the same time as you decide on your company name to ensure that it matches. This avoids you choosing a domain name that has already been registered by someone else.

Regularly reviewing the official government stats on numbers of businesses online and monitoring trends, we also carry out our own research. Two headline stats to keep in mind are that over 90 per cent of consumers now check out local businesses on the internet conducting online research prior to making a purchase; and 70 per cent of

UK internet users first learn about a product they purchase by going online. The case for every business to run a website is irrefutable.

At The UK Domain, we also conduct annual research into domain name trust and awareness and have found that 73 per cent of people in the UK would prefer to click first on a website ending in .uk when searching online to buy products and services.

Managing the .co.uk and .uk domain names in close partnership with our reseller channel of 2500 registrars has given us an insight into new business startsups, website creation and success factors in driving traffic and raising awareness, making you 'findable' online, building an online following and growing a brand.

We wanted to share this knowledge widely with startups and mature businesses waking up to the need for a website, students seeking to create an online CV website to boost employment prospects by standing out from the crowd, and families wishing to secure a vibrant digital future online.

So we've created several free guides and advice booklets with tips and best practice advice for when you're setting out on your digital journey. Anyone can download these at no charge from the UK Domain website: http://www.theukdomain.uk/advice/guides/. We'll add more as they get authored and published.

We have also been working with organizations like Do It Digital, The Federation of Small Businesses and a number of regional Local Enterprise Partnerships to help advise and support early stage businesses.

Q: *How do I choose a great domain name for my website?*

A: Besides all the great free advice and tips on growing your business online at The UK Domain website there is also a handy domain name search facility where you can type in any domain name you are considering registering. If it's already taken (registered) it instantly tells you and suggests alternatives that are available. And you can search again until you find one you love that is available. A .uk domain name only costs a few pounds per annum so it's great value.

When you see one you like, you just select it and The UK Domain presents a selection of registrars (domain name and web services resellers) that you can click through to, who will help you register it for your exclusive use, and even help you set up your email on that domain, and create a website, provide hosting and a range of internet services to get you online – it is fast and affordable.

> **Tip:** Common reasons why some businesses do not set up a website are: not being sure where to start; a fear of cost; and worrying about how time consuming it may be. Our goal is to take away the pain, make it simple and straightforward and help you get your business online presence set up in minutes. We are here to help.

Q: *What domains would you recommend for a business owner to purchase and why?*

There are two parts to a domain name. The part before (to the left of) the dot(s), and the part after (to the right of) the dot. The part to the left (your domain name) should either be your name or your business name, ideally without hyphen or symbols, as you will need to say it and spell it over the phone many times. So keep it simple. It should be short, memorable and professional. You have to live with it for a long time, so get a good one. The part to the right of the dot needs to inspire trust and credibility and should be well recognized to encourage click without risk. Research shows that around three quarters of UK consumers prefer to click first on a website ending in .uk (.co.uk, .uk, .org.uk) as it shows where you live and operate, and shows you are a UK enterprise, targeting UK consumers and, as domains ending in .uk have been around for over 20 years, they are well recognized and trusted.

> **Tip:** Research has also shown that businesses who only operate on social media (e.g.: only have a Facebook page) are far less trusted than a business that uses social media with their own website. Consumers expect your business to have a website. Don't disappoint them.

A .co.uk address is one of the most established and popular domain names in the world. It's the gold standard for UK businesses. The shorter .uk builds on that trust and recognition, but being shorter makes it a whole lot easier to say and remember. The well-known and respected .org.uk is the ideal choice for charities and good causes; there is even a .me.uk for a personal website, where it's all about you, your journey, your experience or personal project. But of course, it's your choice.

A .uk domain name is easy to register for a very small annual fee of around only a few pounds. Our registrars (domain name and web services resellers) can help build your website for you or offer some speedy drag-and-drop templates, and set you up with a professional email. So what are you waiting for?

Q: *What is your insight into personal and business branding and the benefits brought to startups?*

A: OK, a few quick tips: don't neglect your email address. A gmail or hotmail says nothing about you other than you didn't bother to upgrade your free email service when you started a business. It also makes you look like 'a one-man-band'. A more professional approach is to make sure your company name is present and correct in your business email. Build your brand at every opportunity.

Keep your website simple. Start simple. A basic website often just needs opening hours, contact details, a map, examples of past work, quotes from happy customers and some background on who you are, what you do, what you offer and how to get in touch. You can easily develop it and expand as your business and needs grow. There is plenty of help to be found, so don't hesitate to ask an expert. To find a Nominet approved registrar to speak to please visit: https://www. theukdomain.uk/advice/choosing-a-registrar.

For more quick tips visit our blog: https://www.theukdomain. uk/blog/.

Q: *Do you have any key messages for tomorrow's entrepreneurs?*

A: Your road is well trodden and many lessons have been learned. Don't fail to seek help from industry experts and online. There is plenty of expert help and advice, not to mention special promotional offers to point you in the right direction and help your limited budget go further. The UK startup market is running at about 50,000 new company startups every month, so remember you are not alone!

5

Networking Your Business to Success

> Your network is your net worth.
>
> *Napoleon Hill, author of* Think and Grow Rich

A core business truth that has existed ever since the very first business transaction took place is that 'people buy from people'.

So, whilst the features and benefits of what you are selling may be important, so too are the relationships that you build with others and the people that you communicate with. This is true more than ever before, because today enterprise is ALL about connection and community. It's about conversation and collaboration.

Customers have high expectations of businesses, largely due to the sheer volume of choice, and people recommend businesses to others. This is why it is critical to go where the conversations are – both online and offline – to actively participate in dialogue that is relevant; to help connect people and be the link in the chain from one person to another; to become the 'go to' person for whatever it is you offer; and to engage in conversation with potential customers. By going where the conversations are, as well as spreading the word about what you do, you can tap into the 'people power' that is prevalent in enterprise today and enable other people to generate a buzz alongside you.

In addition to getting you out where the action is – where the conversations are – networking (both in person and via social networks) enables you to find and build strong relationships with potential supporters, advocates, partners and evangelists. As you grow your network and give your time to them, you will earn respect and equip people with all they need in order to recommend you and/or collaborate with you.

As CEO of LinkedIn, Reid Hoffman says, 'Success in the modern world depends on the real connections you have.'[18] So, connecting with the right people at the right time is a vital ingredient. Surrounding yourself with the right people is as important to your flourishing in business, as it is in life. This is why networking can serve as one of the most powerful and cost-effective tools in your arsenal.

The late Jim Rohn – entrepreneur, author and motivational speaker – said, 'You are the average of the five people you spend the most time with.'[19]

As his business has grown, Jason Vale has focused on building strong relationships. This has resulted in a whole host of celebrity clients and good relationships with people in the public eye who are often successful, in part, because of how well they treat other people.

'It's important to add value to relationships,' says Jason. 'For example, when I asked Alesha Dixon to be on our magazine cover, I made sure there was a win for her too. I invited her to promote whatever she wanted to and be able to use good photographs. I wanted to add some value. So, when the magazine went to number one, I was so pleased, because I realized there would be a good upside for Alesha, who'd think it had been worth doing.'

Often, this can work well in your favour.

'Last time Gary Barlow visited my juice retreat, he asked me what he could do for me,' recalls Jason. 'I told him nothing, but he said, "You've got a new place opening. I want to play at the opening." I told him I couldn't afford him, but he offered to do it for free. I told him it would be ok if he changed his mind, but he was adamant and said, "No, I promised you". So that is turning into a bit of a JuiceFest.'

None of this would have happened if Jason didn't treat his guests and contacts with the utmost respect, and go the extra mile to make them feel at home. You definitely reap what you sow in business.

Indeed, to succeed in business, developing relationships with those who can help you to do so is vital, so choose wisely. If, for instance, you are the smartest person in the room, the chances are you are probably in the wrong room! So take a closer look at your own network and consider who you respect, admire and feel proud to know; who you look up to and aspire to be like; who is achieving great things in relevant industries – and do what you can to develop stronger ties with these people. Then, consider who is missing from that network or who doesn't fit quite so well?

What is networking?

Networking is not called networking by accident. It takes a lot of work and effort to build a valuable network in business. But it is worth doing so. In a nutshell, networking is the 'art' of establishing mutually beneficial relationships. It should never be viewed as one-sided, as a way for you to find people who can help you to sell more. No. Networking is all about finding the win–win in relationships. It is about reciprocity – give and take.

And it's not difficult to find places to network. Indeed, such is the power of networking in business today, there are probably as many networks out there as there are grains of sand on a beach! Popular networks include weight loss groups, such as Weight Watchers, and parenting groups, such as Mumsnet. The number of networks available worldwide has increased exponentially thanks to the internet; members of each united by a common cause or interest.

However, networking should not be regarded as a part-time activity which only takes place when you visit your local Chamber of Commerce networking event or business breakfast. In reality, networking is a process you should engage in '24/7' – at the petrol station, on holiday, even as you ride in the lift to the top floor for a business meeting (delivering your well-honed 'elevator pitch').

Why should you network?

Networking should be at the very core of your business development and recruitment processes because the benefits are so plentiful. By increasing your quality contacts you can seriously advance your business.

Ten reasons why you should attend networking events

1 **Increase your visibility.** Networking gets your face – and your brand, product or service offering – in front of the right people, at the right time, in the right forum on an ongoing basis. Some business gurus call this 'top of mind awareness', which is key to any marketing initiative. Essentially it means that, when the people you meet think of what you offer, they think of you first. It puts you at the top of their mind as the 'go to' person for that type of work or product.

2 **Create opportunities.** By constantly developing relationships with business potential, you increase the chances of starting a relationship that will result in strategic alliances, joint ventures and referrals – each of which can be incredibly valuable.

3 **Stay 'on trend' in your industry (and in your target market).** Networking events laid on by your professional association – or an association affiliated with your target market – provide you with an opportunity to absorb vast amounts of information about current and future trends, potentially giving you a competitive advantage.

4 **Get connected with 'movers and shakers' in your industry (and target market).** Getting in front of influential people can serve you well, so do your homework. Research who might be at the networking events you are thinking of attending. Be clear which events attract the type of people you want to meet to yield the biggest return on your investment of time. Be selective.

5 **Learn from (and be motivated by) influential speakers.** Some powerful and prolific speakers appear at networking events. Attending such events gives you the chance to learn from respected experts in their fields. Gifted speakers have

the potential to ignite a flame in you that starts the fire for business success.

6 **Source suppliers and solutions.** Networking events can provide an excellent directory of accountants, printers and sales personnel for you and any clients you may have.

7 **Fine-tune your brand message.** Practice really does make perfect. You can use your networking events to practise and hone your 'elevator pitch'. Be certain that it conveys – in 30–60 seconds – which solutions you provide, for whom you provide them and the benefits of working or doing business with you. Practise your elevator pitch until it becomes second-nature to you – like riding a bike.

8 **Socialize and avoid cabin fever.** Human beings are social creatures in need of certain types of stimulation that can only come about through face-to-face interaction with others. As remote working has become more widespread, more people than ever before work out of their bedrooms, basements and attics. Consequently, the need to socialize, re-charge your batteries (and, some might say, preserve your sanity) assumes all the more importance.

9 **Spot (and recruit) talent.** Networking events are typically fertile grounds for potential employees. If you are in the business of growing your team, the right candidate for one of your vacancies may be only one conversation away.

10 **Uncover the 'hot buttons' of your target market.** Take advantage of conversations you have at networking events to reveal what makes prospective clients tick (and what ticks them off). Then, make it your business to create products or services that provide the solutions that they seek, making you a hero (or heroine) in their eyes.

Evidently, there are many reasons why networking should become a core part of your business development toolkit. For some, networking comes easily. But, for the majority of people, walking into a room full of strangers can be a daunting process.

However, before we explore how to network effectively to generate the best results, let's look into the preparation required *before* attending.

Preparation: before the networking event

Finding events

First you need to find a networking event to suit you. Apart from relying on good old-fashioned word-of-mouth and asking those you know to recommend networking events, social media platforms can provide useful information – particularly LinkedIn and Facebook, which advertise networking events through your connections, 'friends' and (special interest) groups.

Other websites with excellent networking potential include:

- www.eventbrite.co.uk
- www.findnetworkingevents.com
- www.meetup.com
- www.selfmadebook.uk where we will list some of the events we have found.

Private members' clubs may also yield good networking opportunities, although their membership fees can sometimes be prohibitive.

If you cannot find a networking event that suits your needs, we encourage you to take a leap of faith by creating your own. Indeed, in 2017, we launched our own invitation-only networking platform, 'Networks of Power' (NOP) to provide a private networking opportunity for clients and associates in our network.

What do you wish to achieve?

Your preparation for a networking event is almost as important as the event itself. The primary focus of your preparations should be on goal-setting.

Rather than concentrating solely on your 'big picture' goals, it is important to set smaller, achievable goals that quantify the success of each element of your offering – all of which feed into your overall objectives.

People sometimes confuse general goals with networking goals. 'I will secure two new clients this month' is not a networking goal. Even if this is your objective, you need to set benchmarks directly connected to your networking efforts, such as 'I will set-up two coffee dates with new contacts for next week'.

These mini-goals fuel your sense of continual achievement and quickly add up to fulfilling your overarching objectives.

With your networking plan now firmly in place, it is time for you to get dressed...

What should you wear to a networking event?

Researchers have found that perfect strangers start to assess each other the moment they enter a room. The late fashion designer, Coco Chanel, famously said 'Dress shabbily and they remember the dress; dress impeccably and they remember the woman.' Presumably, the same is true for men.

So, before you step outside the front door in search of the next big opportunity, please take a moment or two to review our top three tips on how to dress appropriately for a networking event:

1 **Wear a 'conversation opener'.** People from all walks of life attend networking events. The very first thing they will notice is your physical appearance. Your aim is to project a polished, professional image. A superficial item, such as an attractive watch or handbag, or a pair of polished shoes, could very well open the door to a more meaningful conversation. You do not need to break the bank, just show your personal brand.

2 **Stand out!** You can transform an otherwise conventional look by adding an unconventional tie, scarf or necklace to your outfit – nothing too outlandish, just unique. Equally you should not wear an untested outfit; fidgeting because what you are wearing is uncomfortable is not ideal, as you should be concentrating on the networking opportunity rather than adjusting your garments.

3 **Dress for success.** Dress in the manner in which you wish to be addressed. If you dress like you are the CEO of your own company, you will more than likely be addressed as such. What you give out is what you get back. To be clear, dressing like a

CEO will vary depending on the type of company you are representing. For example, a tech brand CEO is quite widely accepted in casual clothes – a financial advisor may not be.

Once you've done your homework to find suitable networking events to attend, set your goals and planned your wardrobe, you are ready to get out there and start networking.

How to network: during the networking event

The problem is, much like public speaking, networking is deemed as an intimidating activity for most people, but it needn't be. The reason many people are averse to networking is because they feel nervous introducing themselves to people they don't know. Furthermore, for many people, even entrepreneurs, walking into a room and selling themselves and what they do, just doesn't feel like a natural way to behave. However, if you view things differently, you can get over that perception of networking as intimidating and start to enjoy it.

Here's how:

- **Focus on the giving part of networking rather than the taking.** Successful networking is not just about what you are going to get from a relationship, it is also about what you are going to give to it. By seeing networking as providing others with help, be it via introducing them to someone who can help them or finding out their business objectives to see how you might be of service in some way, you take the selling part out of the equation.

- **Focus on listening rather than talking.** It is far less daunting to walk up to a stranger in a room and ask them what they do and why they do it, than it is to start talking about yourself. If you show an interest in others, you can take the onus (and spotlight) off you, engage in conversation and figure out what you might be able to give and how you could potentially help them. And, if you can't help, you can tell people that you're glad you've met them as you now know where to come should any of your customers need services such as theirs. Importantly, although you'll have arrived at the event with a strategy in mind, don't start looking for the next person to talk to whilst engaged in conversation with someone else and don't be planning what you want to say whilst they talk. Rather, stay 'in the moment' by showing your interest and listening carefully. Always make a point of being attentive by listening more than you talk, be considerate in your interactions and gracious with your time.

- **Ask questions.** Everyone likes talking about their business, themselves and to give advice (even when you don't ask for it) so engage people in conversation by asking questions.

12 tips to make your networking work

1 **Find the host.** Make a beeline for the organizer and you'll be heading in the right direction. The organizer may then introduce you to other attendees, easing some of your pre-event nerves.

2 **Be yourself.** Networking events are supposed to be springboards for relationship-building. If you cannot be yourself at the event, you will inevitably start these new relationships with a fake persona, which is no foundation for any relationship – let alone a professional one. Do not try to be the person you think other people want to meet. Just be yourself. The connections you make when you are being your 'authentic self' are the ones you will want to maintain.

3 **Be confident in your knowledge.** Realize that you know your business or industry well enough to let the conversation develop organically. You will almost always have a more enjoyable experience and make a more positive, longer-lasting impression if you do.

4 **Engage.** Maintain eye contact with the person you are talking to. Nod your head and incline yourself towards them when you are speaking. A little body language, or 'non-verbal communication', can go a long way in making your conversation

partner feel comfortable. This helps to build rapport though trust – the foundation on which you may later do business.

5 **Mind your manners.** It is true to say that networking has its own set of informal 'rules', but it is not exempt from society's norms and values, such as having good manners. Contrary to the mantra of cut-throat business, which places a premium on rudeness and aggression, traditional wisdom says good manners go a long way in most of life's endeavours.

6 **Rise to the top (using your 'elevator pitch').** There will always be an opportunity for you to 'sell' who you are or what you do in a very short space of time. There is a skill to delivering an 'elevator pitch'. It must be casual yet efficient, which is a difficult balance to strike. Most importantly though, it must be clear and concise. If your elevator pitch is such that you've just told them your whole life story, there's nothing more to say.

7 **Do not give to receive.** Networking is a potent marketing tool, but only when it is a 'win–win' for all the parties involved. If you are genuinely willing to share your contacts and resources, others will be more likely to follow suit by returning the favour. What goes around, comes around! If it is not already an innate feature of your personality, then develop a sincerity in your giving that has no expectation of something in return. Try it and see. Karma really is in force when it comes to networking.

8 **Pay attention!** If you are in the mould of asking intuitive questions and considering how you may be able to help others, you will start to 'connect the dots' between who you are interacting with and other people in your network. Now is your chance to make these connections and become the link in the chain. Any feedback received from both parties will help you to make a proper assessment of your match-making skills.

9 **Take note.** When someone gives you their business card after having a conversation with you, feel at liberty to take notes on it. This will enable you to be more specific in your follow-up communication.

10 **Avoid spamming.** Perhaps with the exception of the pork variety, nobody likes spam. Do not hand out your business

card to all and sundry. If you have not achieved your objective of building up sufficient rapport with someone to encourage them to ask for your card, then do not offer one.

11 **Think quality over quantity.** Networking is a numbers game; however, it is not about meeting a lot of people, it is about meeting the right people. Focus on the quality of your contacts over their quantity. It is better to shoot for a few quality contacts that result in numerous opportunities over many contacts that result in nothing. In any case, people can often sense when you are talking to them purely to collect their (or dish out your) business card. There is a difference between 'working the room' and having conversations of value, and simply bouncing aimlessly from person to person. When you recognize that a person cannot do anything for you directly, it is not about moving on swiftly from them, rather you can make a valued connection by introducing them to someone else. People who quickly dismiss those they deem 'not of interest' are remembered and soon get a reputation for this activity.

12 **Join the party and ask questions!** In networking circles, it is perfectly acceptable to join a conversation that is already in progress – a great way to get involved in the discussion is to wait for a natural pause in the conversation and then ask questions, or introduce yourself and offer your opinion.

Making it count: after the networking event

So, you hatched a plan of action and executed it to perfection at the networking event. All done, right? Wrong! You have not yet 'closed' the deal. In other words, you have not taken all the steps necessary to develop a mutually beneficial relationship.

Here is our three-point checklist to ensure that you do:

1 **Follow-up (and follow through).** You should always follow-up with an email, text message, handwritten note or phone call.

Here's a follow-up email template to get you started:

Dear _____ [insert first name or title followed by surname, depending on the nature of your conversation. If: if in doubt, remain formal]

It was a pleasure to meet you at _____
_____[insert name of event and date].

As promised, here is an introduction to my business and what my role is.

Can you tell me a bit more about your business and your typical customer to enable me to provide you with any referrals when possible?

We are looking for _____
_____ [insert search term], do you know anyone who can assist me in this area?

I have sent you a LinkedIn request and would be delighted to connect with you on this platform.

I look forward to hearing from you and working with you in the near future.

Kind regards
[insert your name]

Follow-up SMS text message template:

Hello _____ [insert first name or title followed by surname, depending on the nature of your conversation. If: if in doubt, remain formal. Great to meet you today. This is my mobile number and direct line. Please do save my contact details. When you have a spare moment, here are my LinkedIn contact details. [LinkedIn handle]

Feel free to have a look at what I do and the services I offer. I look forward to hearing from you and working with you in the future. Kind regards [insert your name]

2 **Let it go!** Rather than stockpiling business cards, discard them. As soon as you leave a networking event – or on return to the office – enter the business card information into your mobile or, at the office, add to your spreadsheet of contacts. We would also suggest adding a note (to your mobile or spreadsheet) of where you met and what was discussed, for future reference.

3 **Tap into tools to help you.** There are some people who, despite their best intentions to follow-up with people they meet, always miss the window of opportunity to do so. If this sounds like you, factor this weakness into your daily routine. There are scores of mobile apps and online tools available that can assist your networking efforts by reminding you to follow-up with new contacts. For example, you can set an alarm to go off the week after you first enter the contact details of the person of interest into your mobile.

Networking – an important tool in your toolbox

Connecting with people: developing rapport and relationships – this is what makes the world of business go round. And networking is a wonderful way to build your list of people who can provide you with potential customers, staff, knowledge and so much more, whether immediately or at some point in the future. That's the beauty of net-working: you never know when your meeting someone will turn into a prime opportunity.

We have found this to be true for each of our businesses.

Bianca: Making a good impression pays dividends

For example, when I was employed by Accenture, I delivered the training for their graduate scheme. During that time, I met the team who facilitated the company experience. I scored one of the highest scores for training delivery whilst I was there so had made a good impression. When I decided to start my own business, I went back to them and asked if they remembered me.

They did and were able to introduce me to my first two training facilitation clients, The London School of Economics and a global bank. Having that connection and rapport with someone I'd met and built a relationship with – not by having an agenda but just by being me – essentially kickstarted my business. In other words, I was able to start my business on the back of something that, at the time, felt quite inconsequential.

That has proved to me how important networking is and how important it is to make a good first and lasting impression, because you don't know where a referral is going to come from or if you might need that person's help in the future.

Byron too has found that, by positioning himself as a 'go to' person within certain niches, he has built a strong pipeline and reaped significant rewards from networking many months after the initial connection was made.

Byron: Building a pipeline

Having niche businesses I found that most of the networking I did wasn't converting immediately into sales and yet, three, six or nine months later, my efforts would come to fruition because someone would remember me and get in touch. I found that the networking I did became a sales pipeline. These days I have a wedding directory and a luxury chauffeuring company which have a more mass market appeal. So, as a result of networking we're actually converting business on the same day or soon afterwards.

Either way, it's critical to evaluate your objectives. Nobody should go networking for networking's sake. By shifting the way I networked at first, from pitching for business to taking an interest in what others do, I was able to establish a rapport with people and build a pipeline of those who, a few months down the line, might get in touch.

Networking is a vital tool in any self-made person's toolbox because it is all about developing reciprocal relationships. Ultimately, people buy from people, so the way in which you present yourself, focus on giving rather than receiving and follow up after you've connected, helps you to stand out and be remembered. Rather than going into networking expecting to gain instant results, you should view it as a long-term activity into which to invest significant effort. The more frequently you network, the more regularly you are going to earn an income from it. This is because you are constantly building that all-important pipeline which will feed your revenue over the long term – be it via referred business, direct sales from a networking contact, an introduction made to an investor, or through a joint venture or any of the other revenue-generating activities that come from connecting with people. So get out there, connect, engage and listen.

6

Social Media Marketing

Recommendations from friends and other respected influencers are way more powerful than any advert. That's why it is important to connect with those influencers if you are running your own business and want to drive people towards it.

After all, business nowadays is all about connection and conversation; community and collaboration. Being found on Google is no longer enough so you need to go where the conversations are happening – in social networks via social media. You also need to be an active participant in relevant dialogue so that you engage with the right people at the right time and also enable other people to generate a buzz on your behalf. However, with more businesses competing for people's attention, you really need to get your social media strategies right and maximize the time you spend on social networking.

Each social media platform gives you some method of presenting information and communicating with targeted groups of people so that you can gain visibility, credibility (via posting useful content/ linking to recent blog posts) and engage in conversation to create, build and sustain relationships in real-time online.

The fruits of your efforts should then result in social media collaborations, recommendations and transactions; not just in terms of custom, but also in terms of gaining crucial knowledge and finding supportive partners.

Byron and I have devoted many an hour optimizing our profiles and Byron has become somewhat of a professional LinkedIn user, with in excess of 14,000 connections, in the top 1 per cent profiles. For me, years of active networking, public speaking and active profile building have resulted in over 18,000 connections on LinkedIn (and being listed as a Power Profile and one of the 'Most Viewed Leaders on LinkedIn in the UK for 2015' alongside Sir Richard

Branson, David Cameron, James Caan and Julie Meyer). I also have over 18,000 Twitter followers and thousands across Facebook and Instagram. We are telling you this to illustrate that we devote time to social networking each week because we know how important it is to go where the conversations are and engage with people.

So, in this chapter we shall explore the following social media platforms and how to use them to your advantage in growing your connections, prospects and generating business as a result.

- LinkedIn
- Twitter
- Facebook
- Instagram
- YouTube

LinkedIn

LinkedIn – the social network for business – has over 500 million members worldwide, which is more than three times the number it had in 2012.[20]

So, if your target audience includes other businesses, or even if you target individual consumers but wish to partner with like-minded businesses, if you are seeking career opportunities or wish to hire talent, LinkedIn is worth adding to your list of social media networks in which to participate. It provides a useful platform to stay in touch with news and with those you know in your industry, and is a great way to build links with potential new customers, partners and staff.

According to HubSpot research in January 2012, LinkedIn is almost three times more effective than other online platforms in converting visitors into actual leads (277 per cent more effective than Facebook and Twitter).[21]

Certainly there is a global reach that is more apparent on LinkedIn than other networks. If you need to find a distributor in the USA or are looking to be commissioned to create stuff for clients overseas, it's a vital tool.

According to James Potter ('The Linked In Man', LinkedIn expert), in order to really make LinkedIn work for you as an effective tool in your social media armoury, you need to 'gain some under-standing of how the platform works' (handy that you are reading this chapter then), 'take the right approach and have a well-constructed profile, in equal measure. One piece in isolation won't do it. Your profile should be not just good, but great, as 60–80 per cent of people allegedly look you up online before they decide if they should meet you, plus you should have a connection strategy,' says James.

So let's explore how to do just that.

Complete your profile

I have helped many of my clients to create a polished and complete profile for LinkedIn; for those who wish to create their own it is essential to follow these steps:

1 Add a professional-looking photo rather than a Facebook profile pic. Remember LinkedIn is for professional business networking so your photo ought to reflect this. This is not a platform for selfies and family photos.
2 Make your headline descriptive and stand out, as it is this that is shown in search engines before anyone clicks through to your profile. Rather than say 'MD/Founder of ABC, define what you do/offer.
3 Describe what you actually do/have done rather than just listing job titles.
4 Include SEO keywords in your summary. What search results do you want your profile to come up for?
5 Quantify your accomplishments by using statistics where possible, e.g. 'I have helped increase revenue by 25 per cent'.
6 Drag-and-drop prioritized sections of your profile to reorder them based on which bits you'd most like to highlight.
7 Use available apps to add depth and personality to your profile, such as SlideShare to include presentations or the Amazon Reading List app if you read lots of industry-relevant books.

8   Add a video to your profile to really stand out from the crowd by signing up with a SlideShare account, creating a PowerPoint or Prezi presentation which outlines your areas of expertise and filming a welcome video featuring customer testimonials or you explaining to the camera in a few sentences what you do, why and who for.

9   Add recommendations from happy customers and people you've worked with to boost trust and provide 'social proof' to convince people you are worthy of their custom. You'll need to request them and then remember to add them. Again it can be a good idea to recommend others as they will get a notification of your recommendation which will ask them if they'd like to recommend you. You can request recommendations directly from connections or ask people you've done some work for to recommend you when you send your invoice.

10 Link to your other social media profiles on (e.g. Facebook, Twitter, Pinterest) and include a link to your website.

11 Ensure that your profile is public.

12 Include skills to show on your profile and enable receipt of skill endorsements from other LinkedIn users. You can list skills under the More tab or in Edit Profile mode, or click on Skills. You'll be given a choice of those already listed for you to pick from, or you can add skills that are not currently listed. Endorsements boost your credibility for having a certain skillset, as well as showing you how others perceive your skills. As you may be compared to others with the same skills, you want to try and get as many endorsements as possible. It's worth endorsing the skills of your contacts too, as they will often return the favour; this is also a great networking opportunity as it reminds your contacts about you. Also, as you endorse someone or vice versa, this will show up in your LinkedIn newsfeed generating more exposure for you.

Complete your company page

As well as having a personal profile, you can add a company page to LinkedIn. Whereas on Facebook, the company/business page is the one you should prioritize, on LinkedIn it's important to focus first on building your personal profile, as people buy from people and it is primarily a business network rather than a social one. That said, the company profile has great functionality and enables people to go beyond one-to-one connections to follow company pages too.

You can use your company page to share information about your products and services, demonstrate your connections and display recommendations. To make the most of your company page:

1 Add a banner photo (similar to the Facebook cover photo but smaller). This is a fantastic branding opportunity to visually showcase what you do/what you're about.

2 Update your company status with news, events, milestones. Company page visitors/followers can like/share and comment on your updates.

3 Use targeted updates. You can target who you want to reach by choosing to share with everyone following you or with specific locations or industries. You also get stats from LinkedIn for this service.

4 Gain followers by posting a link to your company page in your email signature file, plus adding a 'Follow XYZ Company on LinkedIn' button on your website, blog, and so on. Get the code for your own company Follow button here: https://developer.linkedin.com/plugins/follow-company (to drive engagement, LinkedIn suggests you need a minimum of 100–200 followers of your page).

5 Add products including free guides/ebooks/downloads or a free assessment or event.

6 Ask people for product/service recommendations.

7 Get a Share button to put on your website so that people can share your site or blog on LinkedIn. Go here: https://developer.linkedin.com/plugins/share-plugin-generator.

What to do on LinkedIn: your activity

'LinkedIn is just like a big room, full of business people. Having a profile and being present is not enough. You need to comment, engage with others and be part of the conversation and community to get that engagement,' says James Potter.

He adds, 'Setting up a profile on LinkedIn and then doing nothing means you are unintentionally doing the equivalent of walking into a room of over 150 million business professionals and standing at the edge, smiling sweetly and waiting for someone to come and talk to you.'

So, once you've got your personal profile and company page up and running, what next?

- Update your status (both for your personal profile and company page) regularly to keep your profiles/pages active, fresh and up-to-date. Post new business milestones, product or industry news, awards and so on. Curate content to position yourself as an expert in your field. Remember this is a professional business network so make sure your updates are relevant and business-focused rather than personal. There is no need for hashtags. Just consider what you've been doing and which type of market you've been serving.
- Drag the LinkedIn Share Bookmarklet into your Browser Bar so that you can curate and share content on LinkedIn as you browse the web.
- Join relevant industry groups; interact and participate – ask and answer questions. Set up alerts to notify you when someone responds. Ideally aim to focus participation within three core groups to which you are able to regularly contribute. Use them, not just to learn about the industry within which you are active, but also to see where there are unmet needs and frustrations around the kinds of solutions that you provide. Then get in touch with people who need what you offer.
- Follow influencers. There are a number of people you can follow from Richard Branson and Guy Kawasaki to Barack Obama.

- Ask for recommendations. You may have some from a while ago or relating to skills/services that you are no longer focusing your time on, so ask recent clients/ colleagues to write a few words of recommendation for more relevant/recent skills and services.
- Use LinkedIn Answers (http://www.linkedin.com/answers) to position yourself as an expert in your field. This is a place where people ask questions (some of which you will be well-positioned to answer) and you can answer them and add links to relevant content on your site/blog, etc. Leads from the Answers forums can be generated up to a year or so after you've posted an answer, so it's a forum with longevity.
- Search for Events from the More menu in the navigation bar. You can browse by location or industry type.
- Use LinkedIn Today to customize your newsfeed. You can tailor it to suit your business interests and industry. Simply click on News, select LinkedIn Today and customize the news using the cog icon at the top-right of the page. Choose to follow specific sources or industries.
- Use LinkedIn Signal (in the News drop-down menu) to track what people are talking about on LinkedIn. You can search for your name, your brand name, products, competitors or topics of interest. It will include second- or third-degree connections as well as first-degree connections. So if anyone mentions you or your company at all, you can respond and start up a conversation.

Grow your network

As a first step, connect with your old school friends, colleagues, clients and other business contacts. The size of your network directly impacts your search ranking on LinkedIn. So, if you have 500+ contacts you will rank higher than someone with the same skills who has 100.

As with any social network, you want to go for a good number of quality connections and grow your network on LinkedIn. However, with LinkedIn, you cannot request a connection from someone unless you can say that you have interacted with them in some way – either as an ex-colleague, a friend or someone you know through some other means. That said, there are other ways to connect. Connections breed connections so it's worthwhile actively seeking out connections as you'll find 'so and so is now connected with so and so' will lead people to connect with you.

- Connect with people who are in the same group as you. So, if you find someone on LinkedIn who you'd like to connect with, you can view their profile to see which groups they belong to, and join any which are of interest, then invite them to connect.
- After connecting with someone, always spend time browsing through the lists of people that LinkedIn says 'you may know' as they could be potential clients, referrers or partners.
- Look at who has been viewing your profile. You can see a few of these in the right-hand side of your profile and also by viewing Notifications (the flag at the top of your profile). If you have a paid account you get the whole list of people who've viewed your profile; the free account limits this list but it's still worth reaching out and connecting with those who have.
- Use Advanced Search to find people by title, company, location or keyword to connect with. Then look at people's profiles. Remember a good number of them are likely to look at yours in response. So if you want someone to look at your profile, go and look at theirs.
- Use tactics to view the full names of third-degree connections who are out of your network (something that LinkedIn prevents you from viewing if you have a free account). Look at the activity sessions in their profile to see their full name. If they rarely update their status see if anyone has recommended them, or look at the 'Viewers of this profile also viewed' function to see if you can find the name of the person you are trying to connect with.

- Whenever you meet someone new, whether that's online or offline, follow up with a LinkedIn connection request while your conversation/meeting is still fresh in their mind.
- Use LinkedIn to generate leads by sparking conversations. Do some detective work to find a map of the kind of people you should be talking to, examine their recommendations and see what they've done before and are doing now. When you call, invite to connect or email them you can tell them you've looked at their LinkedIn profile and mention something you have in common or agree with something they've recently posted, and so on.
- Follow companies you are keen to do business with, partner with or sell to. Keep an eye on changing roles as this creates opportunity. As someone joins or leaves a company for pastures new, this can provide ample reason to get in touch.
- Share your profile on your other social media networks. If you update your profile in any way, LinkedIn will provide you with the means to tweet or share on Facebook.

Twitter

Why tweet?

In a nutshell, Twitter enables you to interact directly and quickly with specific groups of people (your followers) by posting a short 140-character message. The micro-blogging 140-character limit was established to make Twitter mobile phone friendly, but now it is simply a great way to enable Twitter users to send and receive concise and rapid-fire information.

As well as interacting with your customers and keeping them up-to-date, Twitter also enables you to:

- create a buzz about events (both in advance and during them, thanks to the real-time updates), products and services
- track what people are saying about your brand and your competitors' brands via http://search.twitter.com

- generate leads by tweeting links to your website, blog, sign-up page
- offer real-time customer service and support
- expand your network of contacts
- generate media coverage for your business.

In fact one of its most significant benefits is that it enables you to develop direct relationships with influential taste-makers (i.e. journalists and bloggers) who may feature you in the media they are connected with.

Where to start

- Sign up and create a username, otherwise known as a Twitter handle. Your Twitter handle could just be your name. However, people searching for you will still find you even if you don't use your name as your 'username', so it may be better to create a username that relates to your area of expertise, or includes your brand/company name. Avoid using numbers, underscores or random irrelevant names. Search engines don't take kindly to numbers as Twitter handles (they can be seen as fake accounts) and you are missing an opportunity to promote your brand if you choose something that has no relevance to your brand or what you do. NOTE: When setting up your profile, do not tick the 'protect my tweets' box as nobody will be able to see your tweets – which kind of defeats the object.
- Create an attention-grabbing profile/biography which reveals your value and provides a snapshot of who you are and what you do. Don't hide your individual value behind your job title. As mentioned above, don't simply say 'MD of ABC', make it clear what you do and what ABC does, e.g, 'Founder of ABC. Saving people time when decorating their homes in the south-west, DIY-lover, blogger, swimmer.' This is true across all social media accounts you set up. It's vital to make it clear who you are, what you do and where you are based. Include your company and your role within it,

area of expertise, hobbies and interests in no more than 160 words. And remember, search engines tend to display your Twitter biography as their description of your link on their results pages. Make it compelling enough to click.

TIPS ON WHAT TO DO NEXT

- Personalize your profile. You can add some personality and branding to your Twitter profile by using the Design tab. This enables you to either select a ready-made background, or upload your own customized background and header.
- Ask your logo designer to give you the hexidecimal colour code for each colour used in your logo. Keep that information as a text file on your computer. You can then use one of those colours as a main background colour when customizing your Twitter background. Solid blocks of colour are easier on the eye. Design a background image to match.
- Start tweeting. Although you are shown a bunch of people you might wish to follow when you first set up your account (usually celebrities and popular people with plenty of followers, and it's fine to follow a few of these before you start tweeting), it is wise to hold off on following until you have at least tweeted something. This is because those you follow may click to your profile to follow you back. They will be less likely to reciprocate the follow if there's not much to follow. So get tweeting first, then start finding people to follow.

How to tweet?

Click on the Home link in the top bar and tweets of those you follow will appear in your Twitter timeline. On the left-hand side you will see a box which is where you write your own tweets. As you type it shows you how many characters you have left (out of 140).

Click the camera icon to add a picture and the location icon to add where in the world you are tweeting from.

All tweets must be a maximum of 140 characters, but to have a better chance of being retweeted, you should allow space for an '@' symbol, your username, the letters 'RT', and two spaces (one after RT and one after your username).

How often to tweet?

In terms of frequency, data from HubSpot software reveals that '15–25 tweets per day is the sweet spot for increasing following'.[22] More can be too much, while tweeting once a day may not impact. Other sources suggest four times per day is the perfect number of tweets. See what works for you. Use tools to schedule and plan your tweets to minimize the time you have to spend actually tweeting.

What to tweet?

You might tweet:

- Event photos, office photos and product shots.
- Offers, such as to download an e-book and then sign up to your mailing list, or to get a free sample by signing up. Twitter can be a terrific lead generator if used wisely. Include links to a landing/sign-up page to capture details and generate leads.
- Words of wisdom from others/yourself.
- Links to your own blog posts or useful resources on your website – drive traffic there. (Use Twitterfeed.com to automatically feed your blog to Twitter.)
- What you are reading or watching: interesting articles, websites, blogs, videos and other content.
- Questions to encourage interaction from your followers.
- Observations about topical news stories, especially trending topics.
- Direct messages to other Twitter users using the @ sign.
- Retweets (RTs) to tweet something someone else has tweeted to your own followers.
- SEO keywords relating to your business.

Avoid tweeting:

- anything too personal
- too many retweets and not enough tweets.

Remember: you are what you tweet and deleted tweets may still be archived, so think carefully before you tweet and avoid saying anything you wouldn't say to a stranger at a networking event.

Tweeting top tips

- **Use hashtags.** Include hashtags when you have the space to as part of a marketing campaign. So, if you are promoting an event, include a # before the event title e.g. #socialseminar. You will be able to see how often that hashtag was mentioned when searching for it later, when you will be able to aggregate a list of tweets containing the event hashtag. Also include relevant trending topic hashtags in your tweets, so that you can piggyback onto trending topics if related to your business. Include hashtags that users you want to connect with are using in retweets, so that you reach those looking at tweets with that specific hashtag. Use wthashtag.com to evaluate what is trending.
- **Tweet shorter.** Give your tweets 10+ characters worth of 'legroom' to enable retweets that include your username and don't leave out important keywords that you have included. This means you should practise tweeting to 120–130 characters – a worthwhile habit to get into as there is data to support the fact that tweets of this length having the highest Click Through Rates (CTR).
- **Be remarkable.** Make your tweets remarkable to encourage influencers to retweet you. Not only to gain visibility, credibility and generate a larger number of followers by spreading your tweets far and wide, but also to gain more authority value from search engines which essentially grade the value of links posted to rank your authority. They do this by examining how many followers

those who retweet your content have, and by using signals such as the number of social media shares your links gain to determine ranking for certain keywords (social search), so it's vital to tweet remarkable and relevant stuff that appeals to the most influential people within your Twitter network.

- **Compel people to click your links.** Tweet calls to action. Write a list of tweets that promote something you are offering, whether that's a free guide, prize draw, interesting case study, and so on.
- **Retweet.** When you see a tweet that you think your followers will appreciate (because it is useful, informative, interesting or entertaining) retweet it. Seek out blog postings, photos and tweets that already contain messages you wish to deliver, then retweet them or link to them. In doing so, not only will you save the time you would have spent writing your own content, you will also create external validation and a network connection with the content's author. This is important for two reasons:
  - It's a great way to boost your own credibility as someone tweeting useful and engaging content within your area of expertise.
  - It supports other people.

When to tweet?

OK, so you want to tweet when your tweets are going to be most visible to the most amount of people. Due to the real-time nature of Twitter and the volume of tweets (55 million per day) there is little point tweeting when people are not on Twitter. Far better to tweet when your target audience is online to get the most TWITTER TRACTION.

So when is the best time to tweet? There are two sources of data which contradict each other somewhat. Bitly suggests Monday–Thursday between 1pm and 3pm EST (so between 6pm and 8pm GMT), whereas Dan Zarrella, social media scientist at HubSpot suggests midweek and weekends between noon and 6pm EST (5pm and 11pm GMT). So while the optimum timings do overlap, one says not at weekends and one says at weekends. You could compromise and aim for between 1pm and 3pm EST (6pm and 8pm GMT) on a Wednesday as the best time (which fits with both pieces of research).

However, the best way to maximize the effectiveness and timings of your tweets is to use a range of tools to determine the best time for YOU to tweet. Forget the rest of the world, these tools analyse your own activity and that of your followers, and tell you when your followers are most active on Twitter.

Try using one of the following tools to gain MAXIMUM EXPOSURE:

- **Audiense** (formerly Socialbro) provides reports that tell you when your followers are online, by the hour and by the day of the week, plus the potential exposure you'll get by the hour/day. It tells you when you tend to get the most RTs and replies, and outlines your reach by the hour/day.
- **TweetWhen** by HubSpot reveals the best days and times of day to get the most RTs per tweet.
- **Tweriod** examines your Twitter activity and suggests the best times to tweet based on analysis of your followers' and your own tweets. The Tweriod tool can be integrated with the Buffer app (more on that later) because you can use the information regarding your best time to tweet gained from Tweriod and connect that information into your Buffer account so that scheduling of tweets is set to the optimum times.
- **Timely** analyses your last 199 tweets and suggests four different hours that may be best for you. It then automatically schedules your tweets based on those hours.

You may find that these tools, due to their varying algorithms and measuring methods, may bring up very different optimum times to tweet. It's therefore worth experimenting with these tools to see which works best for you.

However, while timing your tweets to gain the maximum visibility is a critical part of mastering Twitter, so too is building relationships and engaging with your audience. There is little point being highly visible if there is little actual connection.

Find and follow

With Twitter, you follow (i.e. 'subscribe to') anyone whose updates you are interested in reading. You can search by name and Twitter gives you a list of recommended people, based on who you currently follow (i.e. if you followed him/her, you may like to follow him/her)... plus random popular people. (NB Well-known people/celebrities have a white tick in a blue box next to their name if their Twitter account has been verified, which means it is the real them, not someone posing as them – there are many imposters on Twitter). Use the Who To Follow box to view suggestions and Browse Categories to find relevant people.

Devote some time to finding people to follow and building your Twitter network. Get to know people you follow by regularly looking at your Twitter stream (where all tweets from those you follow will appear).

Invite current and former colleagues to connect and habitually add relevant people you meet professionally within days of meeting them.

Do your homework on your potential connections before initiating communication. By building a detailed profile of valued connections, you will be better placed to add value, discuss topics of interest, create a more targeted message and introduce them to other well-matched connections.

WHO TO FOLLOW?

Here's a list of the types of people you should follow. Many people forget to follow their own customers: brand-loyalists who are best-equipped to get evangelical and spread the word about your business. Your customers may not have thousands of followers (so may not qualify as influential) but they can have an impact on their own smaller networks.

- **Leaders and experts** within your business sector/industry to learn from (and RT) their insights
- **Competitors** to keep track of their activities and messages

- **Customers** to enable better interaction and provide them with messages to spread the word to their own followers (who could also become customers).
- **Editors of magazines** you'd like to feature in and other taste-makers/influencers
- **Journalists and bloggers** who specialize in writing about topics that you're an expert in.
- **Content-seeking companies** who need online experts or partners.

Find people to follow by using:

- Twitter's Who To Follow feature. Click this and then use relevant keywords to source relevant people.
- Search.Twitter.com. This enables you to find people who are tweeting about specific topics of interest. For example, you might want to find people who have tweeted about social media, parental support or raising finance. You can then follow people who have tweeted about those topics.
- Tweet.Grader.com. This reveals the Twitter Elite within specific locations or who fit specific keywords. Audiense. com also enables you to track people who are the most prolific or influential in your field, so that you can try to persuade them to follow you (and potentially retweet your tweets to their thousands of followers).
- Look at who your followers, and those you follow, are following. (This information is displayed at the top of their profile. Just click Following.) Also look at @replies and click to view profiles of people with whom your followers/people you are following are connecting and conversing with.
- Journalists, bloggers and taste-makers. Use MuckRack.com to browse a Twitter directory of journalists.

To boost your credibility you'll want as many of those you follow as possible to follow you back. If you end up following 3050 people but only 65 follow you in return, others may choose not to follow you. So avoid following hundreds of people at once if you wish to have a valuable ratio.

Attracting people to follow you!

Make your connections count. Think *quality* over *quantity* in terms of connections. While it's important to broadcast your message far and wide, you should also be mindful of the quality and relevance of your connections. The more people who see your content, the faster your messages will be spread, but only if those people are *relevant*. The long-term impact of a hundred enthusiasts will outweigh 50,000 less interested followers. There's little point in having thousands of fans if only a small percentage of them are actually participating and interacting, while the rest are disinterested and failing to engage.

Your aim then is to find a hive of influencers; ideally a mix of business leaders influential in your field, with thousands of followers, and brand loyalists with a handful of followers. These are the people most likely to create a positive buzz about you and your business.

That is why it's so vital to set up your profile and start tweeting before connecting with people. They need something to look at when you follow them, and if they like the look of your profile, they may follow you back. The more followers you have, the more authority you gain, not only across yours and your followers' networks (if they retweet you) but also from the perspective of the all-important search engines. Google, and other search engines, analyse author authority to rank profile links in terms of quality. So, the more followers you have, the more authority (and higher rank) you will ultimately gain.

You are not obliged to follow everyone who follows you, but remember you can only send DMs (Direct Messages) to people who are following you and vice versa. To create quality connections who are genuinely interested in your content, ensure that both your audience and content are relevant. Only accept invitations that you deem to be meaningful. In order to evaluate that, it's worth knowing what your followers are about, so you can start conversations and build relationships.

Your Twitter following is your reach, so you want to attract as many relevant followers as you possibly can.

So how do you do that?

1 **Become a useful and much-needed resource**. If you provide value in your tweets, more people will want to follow you. So have something useful and meaningful to say. Don't merely promote your stuff: share your expert knowledge.

2 **Include Twitter Follow buttons on your website/blog**. This will enable visitors to follow you easily.

3 **Use Twitter widgets to display your tweets on your website or blog**. Get them by clicking on Edit Profile then selecting Widgets from the left-hand menu. You fill out the information and copy and paste the widget code that Twitter generates for you into your website.

4 **Collect positive tweets about your business to further boost your credibility**. Do this by using the Favourites feature. To mark a tweet as your favourite, hover over it to bring up the Reply/Retweet options and the Favourite option will come up. Click on the star for favourite and it'll turn yellow; that tweet will then be added to your favourites list. You can provide prospects with a link to your Favourites page as proof of how great you are.

5 **Give people who aren't yet following you back a reason to follow you**. Examine their tweets and reply to relevant ones. Engage them in conversation, provide praise, offer feedback.

And therein lies the key to Twitter mastery – you need to engage people. It's not just about broadcasting, it's about conversing, engaging and responding.

Engage and respond

Social media sites are interactive, and so must be viewed as places in which to have *conversations*. The better quality your relationships are, the more trusted, credible and well-perceived you will be; the more people will introduce you to others and refer business to you; and the more business you will generate. Make your conversations meaningful to build credibility: interact, don't just broadcast.

Your followers and fans have demonstrated they have a reason to connect with you by clicking the Like or Follow or Accept button. From that moment on, your job is to mobilize them beyond the 'like' by interacting and engaging with them.

ENGAGE IN CONVERSATIONS WITH SPECIFIC PEOPLE

You can tweet at specific people directly. If they follow you back you can send them a Direct Message. However, if they do not (and you want them to) you can reply to their tweets. There are two ways to do this: one way will make your tweet visible only to them, you and your followers; the other way will make your tweet visible to everyone (and thus increase visibility).

If you click 'reply', their @username will appear at the very beginning of your tweet and will therefore only be visible to them, you and your followers. Conversely, by adding their @username somewhere within the tweet but NOT at the beginning, your tweet will be universally visible to everyone. So avoid putting @username in the very beginning of your tweets, unless you want to reduce visibility.

If you want to send your followers a Direct Message, you can do so by clicking on the Direct Message link and then including your message. Here are a few tips on engaging with specific people:

- **Reply to Direct Messages and mentions.** Keep the conversations going. Demonstrate that you are listening by responding promptly to every question, comment, direct message and invitation. Remember, when your connections engage with you, your fan page or Twitter handle appears in their feed, so you can multiply the impact of your individual interactions. When you are invited to connect, don't merely click Accept and leave it there. Collecting connections means you are saying 'hello' and then ending the conversation. Send personalized messages and reply to connection requests or 'follows'.

- **Don't just tweet or post updates about your products and services.** And don't try to control the conversation; instead, be a part of it and join in.
- **DM your top fans/friends.** Enlist their help to share your news/tweets.
- **Show an interest in your fans/followers/prospective customers.** Comment on something interesting you find in someone's profile. Find some common ground and start a conversation. In order to build and maintain a good rapport with your connections, keep your eye on what they're doing. If they achieve something, send your congratulations.

ENGAGE IN CONVERSATION VIA TWITTER CHATS AND TWEETUPS

Twitter chats are a dynamic way of harnessing hashtags to create a live real-time discussion and share peer knowledge on Twitter. It works by gathering a group of Twitter users at a scheduled time to discuss a certain topic using a previously agreed hashtag, so that anyone searching for that hashtag can follow or join the conversation. You can either host your own Twitter chat or join one of the hundreds of regularly scheduled Twitter chats on specific topics.

- **Host a Twitter chat:** If you are an expert in a specific topic, say life coaching, it can be fruitful to host your own Twitter chat by answering questions or offering tips using a specific hashtag, such as #selfconfidencechat. You'd need to tweet the topic, date and time to your followers and supply the chosen hashtag. It's worth using a dashboard service such as Hootsuite or TweetDeck to schedule questions to be discussed at specific intervals to provide structure. You can then RT posts by others which use that hashtag and then promote a special relevant offer to those who take part, such as an eBook on improving self-confidence. To really pull in a crowd you could invite someone well-known from your industry as a high-calibre guest. It's important not to spam tweet chats with your offers as they should be friendly and welcoming discussions.

- **Hold a Tweetup.** If you are organizing an event or webinar, select a hashtag and tweet about it with a link to the event sign-up page. Whenever you promote the event, use the hashtag and ask those who are attending to do the same. Then, during the event, people can live-tweet about what's happening, resulting in an aggregated list of tweets in real-time about the event. This can be used to promote the next event or spark the curiosity of people who couldn't make the event but wish to engage in the conversation around it.

- **Hold a Twitter party or Twitathon.** For example, Innocent Drinks held a Twitter party where they invited mums and dads to contribute '140 lunchbox ideas in 140 characters'. They placed the resulting tips into a ten-page PDF file, complete with recipes, funny vegetable celebrities (Quince William and Peas Morgan anyone?) and jokes; only one page was devoted to their own lunchbox-specific product range. On the back page they thanked all the tweeters. They then linked to the downloadable document from their website, their Facebook page and other social media profiles.

ENGAGE JOURNALISTS IN CONVERSATION TO GENERATE MEDIA COVERAGE

One of the most powerful elements of Twitter is its capacity to connect you directly with the media in the shape of influential journalists, bloggers and taste-makers.

- Seek out relevant industry blogs using a blog search engine such as Technorati. Follow bloggers on Twitter.
- Use MuckRack to find journalists by publication (source) or topic (beat). Follow a good number of journalists.

- Get into the habit of following writers of content you read online. Schedule in some time to actively build a relationship with them. You might tweet about an article that you've enjoyed and offer your opinion.
- Look at #journorequest and try to find people who are 'looking for case studies' (you could just type that into the Twitter search bar).

TWEET ENGAGINGLY TO ENCOURAGE RETWEETS

Social media empowers people to spread the word through sharing or, in Twitter's case 'retweeting' what you have tweeted. Getting retweeted is therefore a key goal. But you will only get retweeted if you tweet useful, informative, engaging and/or entertaining tweets that compel your followers to hit the RT link.

- **Reveal your expertise.** Every single piece of content you add should evoke some form of reaction and engagement from users, whether that's laughing out loud, provoking a thought, clicking, sharing, liking or buying. So don't merely post random articles and blogs – everyone else does that. Instead establish your expertise as a valued resource and author authority. Only post content that your audience deems to be interactive and engaging.
- **Analyse your followers' interactions.** In doing so you can discover the content that sparks the most debate and interaction. Then post high-quality content in the most qualified places you can find and ask users directly 'do you like this?', and invite them to like, share and retweet.
- **Be useful.** Consider what you can do for your customers. For example, for the happybrideguide.co.uk we might tweet the question: 'How can we make your wedding even better?' and send a link to our website. Include links to a range of resources including lead-generating free guides or whitepapers on areas that you have expertise in.

Manage your twitter time: measure and adjust

Twitter can eat into your time. Therefore, to maximize effectiveness, you should schedule and monitor your tweets so you can automate some of the process and focus on tweeting the kind of tweets that generate the best response/results.

SCHEDULE YOUR TWEETS

Use a tool that will automatically publish at pre-set times a steady stream of tweets. Try the Buffer app, Hootsuite or Socialoomph. You can then monitor those tweets and use the information you glean to maximize your effectiveness (so you post tweets that are likely to get the best response rate). You will still need to check-in to Twitter to respond accordingly to tweets and retweets that are directed at or relevant to you.

MEASURE AND ADJUST

When it comes to monitoring and analysis, there are certain key metrics you should measure:

- **Reach** – the total number of followers to whom your tweets are distributed. Use tweetreach.com to measure how far your tweets travel.
- **Reach/follower growth by month** – to see if your tweets are helping you to extend your reach.
- **Response rate** – the number of people who respond to specific tweets, the number of @replies per tweet and the number of retweets.
- **Visibility (brand awareness)** – the number of times your brand gets a mention (search.twitter.com) and the number of times your shortened links get clicked (Bitly).
- **Grading** – the number of followers you have and how influential they are, via Tweet.Grader.com.
- **Sales funnel** – the number of visitors who arrive via Twitter (your Google Analytics package may show them as coming from 't.co'), i.e. people who have received

notification that you are following them and have then clicked your link. And, crucially, it shows the number of visitors who then convert into leads (e.g. who sign up to your newsletter) or customers. You can then calculate your Twitter Visitor to Lead Rate.

Perhaps the two most important pieces of data to measure are follower growth and sales funnel: from seeing your tweet to buying from you. TwitterCounter.com allows you to view your follower growth over a period of time, enabling you to see exactly how many new followers you have gained each day so that you can figure out how effective your daily Twitter activity has been.

As well as tracking your follower growth, it's vital to track the path a user takes from clicking a tweeted link, to visiting a web page, to completing a sign-up form on a landing page, and thus becoming a lead, with the ultimate goal of them then becoming a customer.

The best tool to use to view your traffic and where that traffic comes from is via your free Google Analytics package: make sure you have signed up to Google Analytics (www.google.com/analytics/), and have inserted the code into your site and submitted a sitemap. In fact, Google Analytics now even has a Social Reporting section (under Traffic) where you can view how much traffic you are generating from individual social sites and track the social flow.

However, if you want to know where traffic is coming from, you'll need to delve deeper and use a tool such as HubSpot or Hootesuite. You can also use Bitly, which enables you to shorten links to make them Twitter-friendly. Bitly also enables you to discover the number of clicks that a specific Bitly shortened link has generated.

At the lower end of the analytics tools, Hootesuite is free, or a minimal fee per month for the pro version. Alternatively, at the higher end, you can use HubSpot software which enables you to schedule multiple tweets at once.

You can view multiple accounts activity on the dashboard and create analytical Twitter Profile Stats reports using Hootesuite for free. However, if you want to add modules to your report, such as Daily Retweets, Mentions by Influencers, Compare Keywords or Follower Growth, you'll need to sign up to the pro version.

TweetDeck also enables you to arrange your feeds with customizable columns, schedule Tweets to suit your audience, monitor and manage unlimited accounts and stay up to date with notification alerts for new Tweets.

Importantly (and this is something that many people using tools such as TweetDeck don't do) you will need to add a tracking token to the end of links that you post in Twitter, so that Google Analytics knows that a visitor has come via that link in Twitter. This is because users sharing your link via TweetDeck or a similar programme may not show up in your analytics. Generally, a tracking token might look like this, /?utm_medium=social&utm_source=twitter, and you'd add this to the end of your link. But you should run some tests by adding a tracking token to your links to ensure that they work and using the help within your analytics software to investigate further.

Additionally, in order to choose the most promising hashtags, you can use tools such as Hashtracking and Hootesuite to see how many times a hashtag has been used, and gauge the popularity of hashtags for use in your next campaign.

Facebook

With over 1.5 billion people (one in seven people on Earth)[23] having accounts on Facebook and logging in with increasing regularity, it's an unrivalled platform for connection, collaboration and communication. Of course, making connections on Facebook is not limited to friends. Through both Facebook Pages and Facebook Groups, you can (as the Facebook blog says), 'Stay more connected with everything that matters in your life – from businesses and public figures to common interests and hobbies.'

Facebook Pages are visible to everyone on the internet by default and enable anyone to become a 'fan' by liking your page. They then receive your updates in their newsfeed and you are able to interact with them.

Facebook Groups enable communication between people who have something in common; for example, cookery, fashion, beauty, culture, startups, business, entrepreneurship, charity etc. You can set up your own groups around a topic that is relevant to your business and also post in relevant groups.

When you create a group, you can decide whether to make it publicly available for anyone to join, require administrator approval for members to join or keep it private and by invitation only. As with Pages, new posts by a group are included in the News Feeds of its members and members can interact and share with one another from the group.

Many people make the mistake of promoting their business through their profile. While the 'subscription' option, where users can 'subscribe' to anyone's profile makes it possible to grow thousands of subscribers rather than just hundreds of friends, this is still your personal profile. So we suggest you use your personal profile for friends and people you genuinely know well, and pages and groups for your business.

Ultimately, through Facebook, you can consistently increase traffic, gain visibility and exposure, gather market insights and generate leads. It's a level playing field for anyone to develop their own platform to grow their business. To get the most from Facebook you need to build a good presence through a page and/or group, engage with people who like/join and amplify that engagement to turn likers and group members into customers.

This takes time. Mobilizing people beyond the 'like' is not easy, but it is possible. That said, to extend your reach, engage with your 'fans' and achieve your goals you need to stand out and put a good amount of effort in. When your fans interact with you, it can appear on their friends' timeline. Just as the more you interact with someone, the more you'll see their posts in your newsfeed, the more fans interact with your content, the more they will see your content in their newsfeed. Often, that's the only way they'll see your content because, according to studies, the majority won't revisit your page; instead, they'll see your content in their newsfeeds and interact with it from there.

That's the good news: that your content appears in their newsfeeds which, ideally, enables their friends to see it too.

The bad news is that fewer people are seeing content as posts gets older, so you need to be proactive and post content on a regular basis. More later on how your content is 'ranked' in terms of visibility.

Optimize your page

With over 1.5 billion Facebook users, each with an average of 200 friends, your job is to try to get on as many of your fans' newsfeeds as possible, as you jostle for position among posts from their other friends and pages they are fans of. No mean feat.

You can choose to set up as a company or a brand. If location is important and you have a physical shop, you can find your business 'place' by searching for your business name in the Facebook search bar, or you can visit the location and create a 'place' via your mobile phone. When you find your business 'place', click on 'Is this your business' which appears at the bottom left. You'll then need to verify by phone or by sending documentation to prove that you are a verified representative. You can then administer that 'place' on Facebook.

To get the most from your business Facebook page and the effort you put into maintaining it, the key area to focus on is WHAT to post and WHEN in order to generate the best response which then produces more interaction, and so on. However, before we explore that, let's optimize your page, set some goals and evaluate your audience.

Spruce up your page:

- Add a compelling cover image. There are strict rules about your cover image. It should NOT include coupons, prices, discounts, purchase information or contact details, and should not include calls to action such as 'download today' or 'like' or 'share'. However, you CAN include any brand images you like and any imagery and wording to connect with your fans and inspire them. Use your custom tabs and posts as calls to action, and include contact details in the About section.

- Make sure you have a unique personalized page URL, which you are able to set up as long as you have 25 fans. Just go into Edit Page, Update Info and then see Username and change this to suit your business branding.
- Add milestones to highlight key events, whether that's launching a new product or website, reaching 1000 fans, featuring in a newspaper, appearing on TV or radio, and so on.
- Pin key content to the top by clicking on the 'pencil' icon and clicking Pin to Top. You can also highlight posts by clicking on the star icon to stretch a post across both columns to make it stand out. Also, if you forgot to add Monday's post and it's now Thursday, you just add the post, click the pencil icon and choose to Change Date.
- Make sure your web address appears in the FIRST SENTENCE of the About information to send more traffic to your website (many people fail to do this). Make each of the 165 words in the About section count.
- Get image sizes right. Wall post images work best if they are 404 × 404 pixels. Your profile picture should be 180 × 180 pixels; cover photo 851 × 315, app/tab thumbnails 111 × 74. Milestone images/highlighted content images are 843 × 403 pixels.
- Test. Try moving tabs around, updating your About copy, focusing on a specific type of content, etc.
- Create custom tabs to generate leads, showcase your web pages, offer competitions, display your newsletter, or invite people to follow you on Twitter/Pinterest. Try www.woobox.com for sweepstakes, coupons, static HTML iframe tabs (explained below) plus Twitter and Pinterest tabs, etc. Alternatively you can use a free tool (which also has a premium option) called ShortStack, or try out PageModo. There are many tabs/apps to choose

tabs/apps to choose from. You can add videos, shopping carts, and welcome pages, among others. One of the most useful is the iFrame tab which enables you to post a page link from your website to recreate it within the Facebook Page. You can do this using WooBox, ShortStack or by typing 'Static HTML' into the search box in Facebook and visiting one of the available apps (although often these will not enable you to add a URL but can be useful for creating bespoke welcome pages where you can add images). We recommend playing around with a few but not spending *too* much time on this area.

Custom tabs (or 'apps' as they are now called) are useful as they enable you to use forms or point towards your email signup to capture contact information in order to stay connected and build relationships outside of Facebook. However, if the research is accurate, and most fans only visit your page once and then interact with your content from their newsfeeds, they will only see your custom tabs once. Hence the importance of focusing on what you post, to whom and when.

Mobilize fans beyond the 'like'

A Facebook 'like' is the start, not the end of a relationship. To really mobilize fans beyond the 'like' you need to get to know them. The way to do this is to use Page Insights to find out demographics, content popularity, engagement figures and so on.

In the meantime, it's a good idea to be prepared.

- Create a weekly editorial calendar/schedule to define topic ideas, questions to ask, calls to action to include, photos/quotes/inspiration to offer – think value/relevance: what can you provide fans with that will genuinely help them achieve their own goals?
- Aim to include a mixture of engaging content within your editorial schedule from status updates and engaging questions to photos, polls and videos.

- Schedule in time to respond to messages and comments. Response is crucial to make sure fans know they are being heard and not ignored. When people post on your page wall or comment on your posts, respond. Show people that you are listening and validate their engagement by continuing the conversation.

What to post

Did you know that:

- only 16–20 per cent of your fans see your content (some studies reveal that it's closer to just 7 per cent)
- 98 per cent don't return to your page?

This is due in part to Edge Rank. While Page Rank is the way Google filters and ranks websites to determine their visibility on their search engine, Edge Rank is how Facebook filters your page content. Edge Rank is a 'newsfeed algorithm'; it gives each Facebook post a life-cycle and it determines your posts' visibility using three key criteria:

1 **Interaction level** (affinity) – the end-users relationship with you or your page in terms of how often they have interacted (liked/shared/commented) with your posts in the past.
2 **Rank** (weight) – the weighting that Facebook assigns to your content depending on the type of post it is (i.e. text, photo, video, link).
3 **Recency and relevance** – how recent and relevant the post is.

Facebook needs to rank posts because if each user has 200+ friends and likes a large number of pages, that's a lot of content to serve up. Edge Rank is a way of filtering that content.

To improve your newsfeed visibility/Edge Rank, you need to achieve a great balance between:

> **Entertainment and Education**
> **Inspiration and Information**

Because:

- The longer the thread the higher the Edge Rank.
- The higher the Edge Rank, the more likely you are to appear in your fans' newsfeeds.
- The more often you appear in your fans' newsfeeds, the more likely you are to appear on their friends' timeline.

With the average Facebook user having over 200 friends, boosting engagement and your Edge Rank is a vital strategy to focus on. To find out what percentage of fans you're reaching, you can try this: add up your reach for the past 30 days then divide that number by the number of your likes, and you should end up with the percentage of fans you're reaching.

Top Stories are also displayed based on the relationship of the content poster to the person whose newsfeed they are being displayed in, the engagement level (number of likes/comments) and the type of story.

To engage people and boost your Edge Rank you also need to:

- Post the right thing
- At the right time
- To the right people

Let's look at that in more detail.

Post the right thing

FACT: Fresh, Unique, Engaging Content is Still, and Will Always Be, King On The Web.

- **Keep posts succinct, i.e. short, simple and clear.** Buddy Media carried out a study which revealed that status updates on fan pages of fewer than 80 characters get an average of 27 per cent higher engagement rate.[24]
- **Avoid link shortening URLs on Facebook.** They are fine and expected for Twitter posts but studies have shown that you'll get more clicks by using a brand-specific URL

shortener. Fans (especially those on mobile phones) want to know where you're taking them.

- **Ask questions.** Offer multiple-choice answers to a question or simply end your post with a question as this results in 15 per cent higher engagement than questions placed at the beginning of a post. 'Would' generates the most likes/comments with 'Why' generating the least engagement. 'Should', 'When' and Where' questions also drive good engagement. Asking questions and requesting feedback generates answers, and answers (i.e. comments) boost your Edge Rank while also providing you with useful insights into what your target audience wants/needs most from you.
- **Respond to answers.** Tag those who've responded in your own response.
- **Post photos, videos and links.** Photos can be very effective: they get 120 per cent more engagement than standard posts, while videos get 100 per cent more. According to InfiniGraph, photos get from 5 to 20 times as much interaction as any type of Facebook post.[25] Even if all you want to say is a status update such as 'Is it the weekend yet?' or 'The weekend has arrived', add text to an image using www.picmonkey.com or caption images with www.memegenerator.net. Or create your own witty ecards using www.someecards.com/usercards/create. Photos and videos carry the most 'weight' in terms of Edge Rank. Links also impact the Edge Rank rating by creating a strong affinity level if those links are shared, and are, therefore, great for boosting visibility.
- **Post exclusive content only accessible to fans.**
- **Post invitations.** Invite people to promote themselves in some way (via a Like Ladder/posting their business goals and page, introducing themselves, etc.).
- **Ask people directly what you want them to do.** For example, 'Like this post if you agree', 'Share if you do too' or 'Tell us below'.

- **Use the right wording.** According to Buddy Media, 'like', 'submit', 'post', 'comment' and 'take', and other action words, are the most effective.[26] Posting instructions and directing your fans what to do generates responses in posts (but not in contests/promotions where softer words such as 'win' 'winning' work better than direct language such as 'coupon' 'contest' or 'promotion').
- **Post calls to action.** These should link to a landing page that can capture leads off Facebook – this is vital.

Top 20 Facebook post ideas

1 Ask questions with the six 'W's: What, When, Where, Who, Why and Would? Use simple answer formats, such as multiple choice, or 'true or false', to help users engage easily.
2 Acknowledge fans. They could even be rewarded with a discount coupon or prize.
3 Provide added value information such as stats, industry trends, news or facts. A study by Pew internet revealed that 71 per cent of social media users find out about news from social media.[27] If you want to become known as a resource for news and interesting relevant links, collect inspirational shareable content via sites such as StumbleUpon, Mashable and Trendsmap. Also use tools such as TweetDeck or Hootsuite to keep track of all your social media channels to find great links to share. Another way to find great post-worthy content to encourage shares, likes and comments is to set up Google alerts for targeted keywords, use Trackur, Regator, Inbound.org, Scoop.it and Bottlenose.
4 Post a thought-provoking relevant photo and invite captions. Turn it into a caption contest with a prize for the best one.
5 Provide a daily tip or quote.
6 Share a view or statement and ask your audience to 'like' if they agree or disagree.
7 Call people to take action.

8   Invite fans to share their plans/goals for the day/week and tag their own business pages.

9   Ask fans to share their top tips on a specific topic. Create a list of top 10 or 20 golden rules, either as a document or onto an image using PicMonkey, and encourage people to share it. Give credit to the top contributors by tagging them.

10 Harness the power of photography: invite fans to pick a favourite photo from an album and comment on why they've made that choice. Or invite fans to enter their own photos into a photo gallery competition.

11 Hold a Facebook Page party. Create an event and invite all your contacts, giving a good week or two's notice. Post items you'd like to introduce your fans to one after the other with a specific deal/discount and expiration date/time limited offer. Include games with prizes to encourage people to stay on your page for the duration of the party.

12 Create and post an infographic.

13 Share some must-visit websites.

14 Share 'Dos and Don'ts' relating to a specific topic. Invite contributions.

15 Post a link to your newsletter sign-up form with an incentive to sign up.

16 Show your other social media profiles, provide reasons why fans should connect with you and invite them to post their social media profiles in the comments box.

17 Share your best testimonial, then ask fans to share their best ones too.

18 Provide time-limited coupons or offers via ShortStack or by using Facebook offers (you need 400 fans or more in order to post offers).

19 Ask people what they want: 'What would you like to see more of on our page? Would you prefer motivational tips? Useful resources lists? Links to news? Quotes? Photos? Share your ideas here.'

20 Ask people to fill in the blank. Post 'Why I love...' and invite your fans to complete the statement.

Post at the right time

People can unlike you and 'hide' your posts. This often happens when you've joined a Like Ladder and have lots of new likers who aren't really that interested in what you have to say. Their newsfeeds get cluttered up with irrelevant posts and so they periodically go through and delete those which are not appealing to them. That's one of the problems with Like Ladders. They can be useful to hike up your likes, and some of those fans will be within your target audience and therefore relatively interested in what you are posting, but a good number won't be.

The way to avoid being hidden or unliked is to:

- avoid posting too frequently (over-posting)
- keep posts relevant
- understand the lifespan of your posts.

The way to avoid posting too frequently is to understand your engagement rate and if over-posting annoys fans enough to disengage. You need to understand the lifespan of your posts (averaging at three hours) so that you don't post a new post while an existing one is still 'alive' (i.e. when a post is still within a newsfeed). If you do, you run the risk of annoying and alienating fans. Generally, while you should create a flow of activity on your page, it's critical to leave a good four hours or so between posts to maximize Edge Rank and thus engagement.

So, when is the best time to post on Facebook?

As usual, research from differing sources conflicts, but here are the results of various research studies.

Bitly tracked links posted to see how viral they went.[28] They say that:

- Facebook's highest traffic takes place from 1pm–3pm EST (6pm–8pm GMT).
- Traffic begins to increase from 9am EST (2pm GMT).
- Peak traffic is on Wednesday at 3pm (8pm GMT).

Kiss Metrics revealed that:[29]

- The best day to share is on Saturday.
- The best times to share are noon and 7pm EST (5pm and midnight GMT).

Buddy Media examined 100 of the world's largest retail brands to discover that:[30]

- The best days to post are on Sunday and Wednesday.
- The best times to post are 7am and 8pm EST (noon and 1am GMT).

Other sources suggest that engagement rates are highest on Thursday and Friday as the weekend approaches. Across the board, midweek seems to work well, as do weekends.

You'll need to figure out when your optimum time to post is, and post then. Post regularly but don't over-do it. I find posting two to four times per day works well.

Post to the right people

You want to gain fans. You want as many people as possible, ideally a broad range who are most likely to want what you have to sell via your website, to like your page. We already know how to use the advertising tool to figure out the size of our target market and to use Insights to see what kind of people are liking our page. Now we need to grow our fanbase and get in front of as many of those people as we can.

You can enable people to 'subscribe' to your personal Facebook profile as well as 'liking' your business 'fan' page. Admittedly, you could lose a lot of genuine friends if you post regular business-related stuff, and you may not wish your business contacts to see your personal profile, but this can be a way to increase visibility. It is up to you.

So, apart from the organic approach to posting content, how else can you increase your visibility in users' newsfeeds and get your content in front of the right people?

Ten ways to get more fans

1 Use the Build Audience feature to invite your email contacts to your Facebook Page.
2 Invite your Facebook friends or share a link to the page on your personal profile timeline.
3 Promote your posts as you post them on the page.
4 Promote posts in adverts.
5 Advertise.
6 Run offers.
7 Use social plug-ins to populate your web presence to encourage those who visit your website/blog, etc to follow you on Facebook.
8 Link your social media accounts.
9 Try out Interest Lists.
10 Include a compelling reason to follow you on Facebook as a PS in your regular emails.

PAID PROMOTION/ADVERTISING

With promoted posts and advertising you can drill down quite specifically to reach your target audience.

If you promote posts directly from your page, they can only reach people who like your page and their connections (to increase the likelihood of more existing fans and their friends seeing your content). If you advertise or promote posts via sponsored stories you can select to only promote to a specific audience (e.g. people who live in the UK, parents, people who have indicated an interest in digital marketing).

For more information about promoted/paid-for posts, go to: https://www.facebook.com/help/promote.

RUN OFFERS

To run offers you will need more than 400 fans. You can also set up custom tabs, using WooBox and ShortStack, among others, to run promotions, or try apps such as Wyng (www.wyng.com). Through Wyng you can run viral promotions (and run a free trial campaign). So you fill out a short form to set up your campaign, use sample creative bits and pieces and Wyng will then automatically create Facebook tabs for your campaign. You can track metrics such as new fans, total visits, reach and virality, and so on.

Whatever promotions you run on Facebook make sure you abide by Facebook's Promotional Guidelines.

USE SOCIAL PLUG-INS

Social plug-ins let you see what your friends have liked, commented on or shared on sites across the web. From the point of view of a business wanting to get their web page content shared on Facebook, adding social plug-ins to your website enables the friends of those who like/share your web pages to see that interaction. Using them is another great way to provide your website users with the tools to promote you on Facebook.

Social plug-ins enable you to provide engaging social experiences for your users with just a line of HTML, without the need for the viewer to have signed into your site. Find out more here: https://developers.facebook.com/docs/plugins/.

For example, the Like Button lets users share pages from your site back to their Facebook profile with one click: https://developers.facebook.com/docs/reference/plugins/like/. You can also use a line of code to include Facebook badges on your website which point back to your Facebook page.

Also check out https://developers.facebook.com/docs/sharing which enables Facebook users to share content from your app or website with their friends. It's a little more technical than social plug-ins, which merely require the copying and pasting of code into your site.

LINK YOUR SOCIAL MEDIA ACCOUNTS

- Link your Facebook Page to Twitter so your Facebook fan page posts are tweeted: http://facebook.com/twitter.
- End tweets with #fb and this will post them to your fan page wall: http://facebook.com/selectivetwitter.

- Link your blog feed to your Facebook Page: http://facebook.com/networkedblog.
- Update new YouTube videos to your Video App tab.

TRY OUT THE INTEREST LISTS FEATURE

Interest Lists allow users to organize groups of friends and to find content based on their interests, and could be a great way to get your content in front of more people. However, pages within lists are often grouped together so there is still a risk of not getting on people's newsfeeds unless you're one of the most popular pages within the list. Many people won't bother looking at Interest Lists (after all they don't look at your page, so why should they?). Prominence of Interest Lists is also a potential issue. That said, if you are targeting savvy Facebook users who do use Interest Lists, then they are seeking exactly what you have to offer and will add your page to appropriate lists accordingly. As such, they could become 'super fans' and more likely to buy from you. Indeed Interest Lists can be a great way to separate updates from friends with updates from favourite pages.

Next to the Like Button on your page there is a drop down box. If your fans click on that, they will be presented with the option to Add to Interest List. See: https://www.facebook.com/bookmarks/interests. It may be worth asking your fans to Add us to your interest list. Here's how...' and give a brief explanation. You can see who has added your page to their interest list by accessing the New Likes section in your Admin Panel and selecting Subscribers.

Measure and adjust: harness the power of Insights

Facebook Insights is a tool which allows you to see how users are interacting with your page. Insights provides the following information:

- **Total likes** – provides a total of all the likes you have on social media.
- **Friends of fans** – shows the overall reach you'd have if every friend of your fans saw them 'like' one of your posts.

- **People talking about this** – reveals all fan activity and interaction including when anyone likes, shares, comments, tags you, your page, checks-in at your location or responds to an invitation.
- **Weekly total reach** – shows how many people have seen your content over the last seven days.
- **Posts** – the purple graph shows how many posts you've made per day including all Post Types, Snippets of Posts and so on.
- **Reach** – shows how many people have seen your post in the last 28 days, along with the source of that reach (i.e. viral, paid, organic).
- **Engaged users** – shows how many interactions and clicks you have generated.
- **Virality** – based on the reach and the engagement rate, this shows how many people (out of everyone who saw it) took action when they saw your post.

DIG DEEP INTO YOUR INSIGHTS TO IMPROVE YOUR CONTENT

Get to know your likers. Who are they? What do they do? What do they like most about your content? Which content is most engaging and popular?

- Look at the hot and cold areas of content: what gets shared/ignored/incites likes or unlikes?
- Track negative feedback. You may have missed these comments (or may not have any at all) but, if you click on Engaged Users in the Page Posts part of your Insights you can see if any posts have gained any negative feedback. This basically means that someone has clicked Hide or Unlike from their newsfeeds, because either they saw your post as irrelevant to them or you were posting too often that day to suit their personal preferences. It's worth tracking because you may find that overt sales calls to action incite more negative feedback than other types of post, so can keep them to a minimum or weave them into other non-promotional posts.

- Assess where your likes are coming from during any selected time period from by clicking likes. You'll see a demographic of the age range and location of your fans. But also, vitally you can see where they came from broken down into actual LIKE SOURCES. This can help you evaluate whether advertising is working and what kind of Facebook promotional activity is worth your while.

- Track your 'talking about this' number to see how engaging and viral specific pieces of content actually are. This data shows the recommendation and engagement rate of your posts and page. What's great here is that you can also COMPARE your rate with that of your competitors. To do this you divide the number of people who 'talk about this' by the total number of fans and then multiply the result by 100 to get a comparable ratio.

- Set up goals on Google Analytics and use the social referral tool to track how much traffic you are generating from social sites and how much of that traffic is actually getting to your 'thank you for ordering' page or sign up page (i.e. converting into a lead or customer). Track exit pages too so you can make appropriate tweaks where necessary.

- Use all the data you glean from Facebook Insights to inform your future posts. Which types of post worked best? What wording? Which offers? Which time of day? What days?

- Use Google Insights to analyse keywords/search terms to use in your social media posts, boards (Pinterest), hashtags and so on.

- Check reach to evaluate how many people saw what you posted and whether they were reached via paid, organic or viral posts. 'Organic' reach is the number of fans you reach through your posts. 'Viral' reach is the number of friends of fans you reach thanks to your fans' actions ('talking about this'). 'Paid' reach are the number of users you reach through Facebook ad campaigns.

- Check reach in terms of the number of users you reach for each post, how many are talking about it and the percentage virality of each post to help you measure the effectiveness of each individual post. This can be very helpful in deciding what format works best and what subject triggers the most interest among your fans. Some may reach more people but may not have as much virality/be talked about or engaged with as much.
- Check unique users by frequency – most people will come and look at your page once (hence the need to get on newsfeeds).
- Check reach by number of page views. As well as finding out who is looking at your content, how many page views, etc., you can also see how many views your 'tabs' get, including custom tabs.
- Check demographics. This is incredibly handy to see what age range people are, and what countries and cities your fans are from. You can determine whether or not you're reaching the target audience you were hoping to reach and whether you need to shift your focus towards a new demographic and post relevant content accordingly.
- Check out the competition; compare and contrast. You can assess how well your competitors are doing with their Facebook Page as underneath their name you will see how many likes they have and how many people are 'talking about this'.

You can even export all of this data into spreadsheet format to have a good old delve. Just select the data type, file format and date range and download.

Assess your likeability

Look at your Insights and see if you have any posts recently which have generated 'negative user feedback' – that is essentially someone opting to hide or unlike you. Dig deeper. On the day(s) when you had negative feedback, how often did you post? What did you post?

What type of post is being rejected? Why might that be? Use this analysis to determine your optimum frequency for posting, and also the types of things to post.

FIGURE OUT YOUR ENGAGEMENT RATE

Don't get too hung up on the volume of 'likes'. It's definitely about quality over quantity. While having a large number of fans does boost credibility and potential visibility, it's no good having thousands of fans and only a small number 'talking about this' (i.e. liking, commenting, sharing, @ tagging, or writing on your wall). That said, the more likes you have, the higher your visibility will be even if you have a low engagement rate; you'll just have to work harder (not only to get the likes but to get people taking action).

The average engagement rate even for big brands is just 2 per cent[31] – so for a big brand with 100,000 fans or more, that's 2000 talking about it. If you were able to achieve an engagement rate of 25 per cent, with 1000 fans (250 talking about you) that would be fantastic and, with that engagement rate, you'd need 8000 fans (instead of 100,000) to get the same number of people (2000) talking about you as are talking about some of the leading brands. 8000 fans seems like a lot, and it is, but if you aim high and focus on getting anything from 50–200 new fans per month, coupled with posting relevant content, you could see a real impact on your engagement rate and thus your lead generation/conversion rate.

See www.selfmadebook.uk for a list of useful Facebook resources.

Instagram

Instagram can be an effective tool to build your brand by sharing photographs and videos (with or without creative filters) with your followers. These photos can be shared, not only on Instagram, but also on social channels like Facebook and Twitter. So let's explore how to develop a relatable personality on Instagram that will fascinate your leads and get them taking the action you want them to.

What is Instagram?

It is an app, rather than a website and, given that a large proportion of web users now use their mobile phone to access the internet, with millions of photos posted and billions of daily likes, its user numbers are growing by the day.

Ultimately, Instagram is a kind of micro-blog that uses pictures rather than words; it gives your customers and prospects the chance to get to know the people behind the brand, and explore behind the scenes. While Facebook doesn't display your posts in all of your followers' feeds, Instagram does. Furthermore, in order to reach more people, you need to advertise on Facebook (which also has an 'advertise on Instagram' option, given that the former now owns the latter). There are no limitations to how many characters per post you can include, so you can add long messages/captions.

The first thing to do is to set up a profile (ideally with a consistent handle/name that ties in well with your Twitter handle and Facebook Page). You can then write your biography and include your web link, and link your Instagram account to your Twitter and Facebook accounts. It's advisable to post 6–10 pictures first before going out to get more followers. Six photos will show you have two rows of pictures which will be enough for potential followers to see and decide whether or not to follow you. So get posting.

What to post on Instagram?

This will depend on your business and your objectives so you should play around to see what suits you, but here are some suggestions:

- Show your creative process. Tell your story – from product sketches during your design phase to delivery of boxes showing your new stock arriving, and so on.
- Shots of you at work, work in progress, your studio or an activity that you do during your working day.
- Pictures of events you've attended.
- What you've seen on your walk that morning.
- Post graphics featuring quotes, useful tips or other text to boost engagement. You are not limited to only posting

photographs, but you should ensure they are relevant, so source quotes from pioneers of your industry or quotes relevant to your vision and values. Relevant quotes and photos of people doing the kind of activities that your brand holds in high regard. Allow your brand to express your brand values and share with the world what kind of world you want to live in and why.

- Show off sneak previews of your products.
- Tell the stories of the people behind the brand. Upload images of new recruits and people involved in your business.

Instagram is not for selling so you should post 80 per cent of images that are not intent on driving sales but, rather, showcase the person and lifestyle behind the brand, and just 20 per cent that aim to drive sales.

Photos should be good and you can spruce them up by using the tools that Instagram provides, from cropping and zooming to increasing brightness and contrast.

You can't link from individual photos (although you can include the web address, it just won't be clickable). However you can link people to your website from your profile. This makes it difficult to actually track visitors from Instagram, as they may type your URL into their web browser. This is why it's always good to ask customers how they found you and/or survey them to find out.

How to get more Instagram followers

- Follow people who you want to follow you and like/ comment on their posts. This will draw attention to your profile by triggering a notification when they login to Instagram. It will show them that you have followed, liked, commented on their posts and they are likely to check out your profile. If they like what they see, they may follow you (although you might need to repeat this a few times before they do so). Seek out those who follow your competitors and follow/like/comment.

- Use hashtags. They are as important on Instagram as they are on Twitter, because users click on hashtags to find similar photos (or tweets on Twitter). So hashtags help people find you and you can generate 10–20 or more followers per photo with the right hashtags. You can include up to 30 hashtags per post but it can be a good idea to use them in your comments instead, as you want to promote your posts to people other than existing followers, so this can be a good strategy to use.
- Seek out influencers on Instagram who have a lot of followers. How might you be able to encourage them to mention you on Instagram? Perhaps offering a free gift or something similar could encourage them to use or wear your product and share it on Instagram with a mention of where their users can get it, tagging you in the photo? That could result in a good number of new followers.
- Post regularly. Consistent use of any social media generates the best response so, if you have an active profile, people are more likely to follow you. You can track which days/times of day people tend to respond most to your posts and post more frequently then. Iconosquare can help you with that, or the inbuilt 'insights' analytics section that comes with a Instagram business account.
- Run a competition. People will often share a photo or comment if they have the opportunity to win something, so if you run a competition where you invite people to 'comment and repost' or 'tag a friend', this can work well.
- Spot trends and post accordingly. If you use a scheduling tool such as Hootsuite, you can download their trend spotting app to stay abreast of what is trending and post relevant images with relevant hashtags: http://appdirectory. hootsuite.com/62/trendspottr. However, please be aware that 'scheduling' for Instagram only truly means that the application will remind you to post and provide you with your previously created image and text. Instagram prohibits applications from posting on your behalf.

Turning followers into customers

It's important to focus first on growing your tribe of like-minded people rather than selling to them straight away. Over time people will begin to ask where they can buy what you offer. You should make it clear in the description of your product posts what the price is and provide a link and any other useful benefits. However, as many people don't read the descriptions, include vital information, such as price, words that create urgency, such as 'limited stock' and the web address, to the photo itself. Use PicMonkey or Canva.com to add text to your images.

Get your followers involved:

- Invite customers to include your @name when they take photos of themselves using your products so that you can build a customer community and visual showcase.
- Invite your users to contribute images to your Instagram feed by coming up with a theme and inviting them to post images with a specific hashtag in their posts.
- Invite customers to join a more focused Instagram tag team. After all, another way to build loyalty and encourage followers to visit your website, is to tell not only your story, but that of your employees too. Furthermore, you can also share your customers' stories. For example, The North Face outdoorwear firm has almost 1 million followers as its own Athlete Instagram Field Team post photos of themselves having adventures in remote parts of the world, from kayaking to mountain-climbing – the photos are engaging and represent their customers' stories and the values of the brand in one fell swoop.
- Encourage users to tag a friend. For example, 'tag a friend who is getting married soon', 'or tag a friend who will get this quote'.
- Ask users to 'comment below with…'. For example, 'comment below with your favourite outdoor activity'.

More Instagram tips

- Create an editorial calendar to plan your posts across the month and share your Instagram photos across Facebook and Twitter too to make good use of your time.
- Turn the headline of a blog post into a graphic and, if you do this regularly, update the link in your biography to link to your blog.
- Create calls to action in your images, such as 'Don't you want to succeed online?' or 'Have you mastered xyz yet?'
- Offer a discount code or flash sale that is exclusive to Instagram followers. This rewards them for following you on Instagram. However, remember to focus on posting more 'non-salesy' images than sales-related pictures in order to continue to build your tribe.
- Make the most of free tools available. Canva has pre-set layouts for free usage and squareready fits images into a square without cropping them. Other apps, such as Pic Stitch and Diptic make photo collages. It's important that your images are good quality, so it's worth playing around with some of these free graphics tools.

YouTube

Self-made people don't always think of YouTube as a key port of call when promoting their brand on social media, and yet it can be a really useful way to gain online exposure. This is because it is often easier to rank well in Google's search results with a YouTube video than with a regular website, as Google owns YouTube (making it the Google of video). Over 20 hours of video are uploaded every single minute though, so it's important that any videos you upload to this channel are of a good quality. They can also be rated with a 'thumbs up' or 'thumbs down' so you want to ensure that your upward pointing thumbs outweigh the downward pointing ones.

Billions of videos are viewed each day, and Google videos appear on search engine rankings so can be as important as text only pages. By creating videos to complement your blog posts and building backlinks from YouTube to your website, you can generate a higher Google ranking as you become more authoritative.

If your products target millennials then you should absolutely be using YouTube as a marketing platform. That said, YouTube is multi-generational so, if you target other age groups, it's worth investigating too.

Videos can be a great way to showcase your products, take your customers on a journey, give viewers a real insight into who you are as a company, what you do and why you do it. Instructional videos can be a wonderful way to position yourself as an expert in your field too. You can create a real buzz about a product or business launch with video and, if your videos are especially useful, you can build quite a following to your channel.

There are a lot of advantages to video marketing. However, it does take a lot of time to plan and execute a good quality video, plus you'll need a decent video camera. Furthermore, there is less opportunity for interaction than on other social media channels so, whilst viewers can rate your video and post their own comments which you can respond to, there's less of a two-way dialogue, so it can be more impersonal.

Also remember that people learn differently. Some prefer to read content, others like audio, so will subscribe to podcasts, whereas others are visual and opt to watch and learn from video content online. By creating videos you are serving that sector of the population.

What works best on YouTube?

It's important to create content rather than adverts. Even demonstration videos don't tend to engage or convert as well as videos that tell a story, and which are relevant and authentic. For that reason you need to keep it real and consistent. So, if you are the face of your videos, people are more likely to respond as they see you are real and relatable. Be transparent and share your story. Here are some content suggestions:

- Instructional educational videos. A series of 'how to' educational videos works well so that you can position yourself as an expert in your field. If you are planning a series, give viewers a teaser of what you are going to reveal/show/explain in your next video to encourage them to sign up to your mailing list or favourite your video, so that they can subscribe to your channel.
- Demonstrations of your products or tutorials about how to use your product. This is something that can be embedded into your website to boost sales. By seeing your product being used, a prospect is more likely to click to buy it. That said, demos are less popular than educational or entertaining videos.
- A 'day in the life of' video, where you set up a camera in a few areas around your workplace and showcase what happens there during a working day can work well. This can then be edited together and speeded up, although you may well need some help to do this. You can get help with video editing from local students or via sites such as Fiverr.
- 'On-the-road' pieces where you travel from location to location. These can inspire interest and give you the chance to do something a bit different. It's OK to use a camera phone for such shots but you need high resolution for more detailed information.
- Repurposed content. You can turn blog posts into podcasts or vlogs (video blogs) giving prospects different ways to enjoy your content.

Setting up your YouTube channel

First you need to set up your YouTube account which must be tied to a Google+ account. If you don't have the latter, a Google+ page for your brand will automatically be created when you create a You Tube account. If you do have one already, you can use that. Make sure your profile photo represents you and your brand well because your

YouTube Channel profile photo will default to the one you are using on your Google+ account.

Choose a YouTube Channel name that is associated with your brand name and domain name, so that Google can see that your YouTube channel is official.

Fill out the Home and About tabs in your YouTube Channel and enter a clear, concise and compelling description about your brand and the content that you aim to share via your channel. Link to your other social media profiles and then add any channel partners you wish to be associated with (otherwise leave the 'add channels' section blank).

Get accustomed to the YouTube Creator Studio. This is the central dashboard where you can manage your channel and create content. Use the video manager to manage your content, create playlists, live-stream live events and view all the videos that you've liked. You can also use your video manager to create playlists from uploads by marking those you want to add and clicking on the 'playlists' button.

Use the Channel section to add personality to your page and select whether or not you want to monetize your channel and earn revenue from your videos. This is worth doing if your videos are likely to attract a lot of views.

One of the benefits of using YouTube for your video marketing campaigns is that you can use its analytics package to find where traffic came from, what kind of devices people are using to view your videos, and analyse data such as audience demographics, retention and playback locations.

Attracting a fanbase

Post response videos on channels where you think their target audience might be interested in your channel.

In your email newsletters and your other social media posts, encourage people to embed your videos on their websites. The action of embedding acts as a vote for your video and your online authority, which is one of the key criteria used by Google to rank websites.

Another way to secure 'votes' is to persuade people to share your videos on their social media pages and profiles. This shows Google that you are producing valuable and relevant content and, given that Google take social media metrics into account when ranking pages, is vital.

Shout from the rooftops about your YouTube Channel once it is live. Post the link on your website, blogs, to your email lists and all over your social media platforms and then link to each new video you post. Also ensure that you have a YouTube button above the fold on your website.

Respond promptly to any comments posted and follow those commenters who have their own channel and comment where you can. It is possible to build relationships in this way.

Create a trailer for those who have yet to subscribe to your channel to showcase who you are and what your channel is all about. Invite viewers to subscribe to your channel.

YouTube know-how: top tips

1 Make sure the first shot is a good one because it is this that YouTube takes as the still image to represent the video within its listings.
2 Take either high- or low-resolution videos but not 'middle' resolution so that viewers know what to expect.
3 Film previews and exclusives to generate awareness and hype about your video before you put it out live. It's important to get your database excited about the forthcoming video, because YouTube rank your video based on the number of views it attracts within the first few days, so you want to generate interest in advance to maximize the number of views you'll get when the video goes live.
4 Make sure you share your videos with everyone rather than make them private (unless you are charging for video tutorials as part of an online course and need to ensure that they are only accessible to those who've bought the course).

5 Include captions and call to actions in your videos linking to content on your site, other videos and email autoresponder, and products that you are selling.

6 Link to your website in the first line of every video description, as you have limited space to profile your business here.

. . . .

Expert insight

Q&A with Jay Shetty, filmmaker and social media influencer

Q: *How did you become the social media influencer that you are today?*

A: At the age of 22 I decided I wanted to live my life in a way that would have an impact on other people around me, so I travelled to India and became a monk. Part of my time was spent on philanthropic ventures, such as food distribution programmes. And that's where I got this real buzz and taste for learning. When I eventually returned to London I had to decide what to do next, so I set up a coaching business, teaching the business community about mindfulness and meditation.

At the end of 2015 I decided I wanted to get my message out to a much bigger, global audience, and in 2016, I launched my first video. Within months it had gone viral, and now I'm an online host, producer, film maker as well as a coach and consultant.

Q: *To what do you attribute your success?*

A: A lot of it comes down to having confidence and learning as much as you can. Speak to as many entrepreneurs and influencers as possible, to gain an insight into what they do. And knock on as many doors as possible, to find someone to champion your cause. The *Huffington Post* liked what I was doing and decided to repurpose three of my videos and share them on their website. The videos went ridiculously viral and led to a close working relationship with the *Huffington Post*. In under 12 months we had 200 million views online, which is amazing. I believe that's down to originality and topical content.

Q: *Do you have any tips on how to get followers?*

A:

1 **Post regularly.** You need to have a social media 'machine' in the sense that people need to see you every day to take notice of you. If, for example, you're a food blogger, only posting one recipe a week, it's likely that no one is ever going to see you, no matter how good your recipe is, how good your picture is, or how good your video is. So, at the moment, I aim to post 6–12 times a day on my public figure page on Facebook, and a couple of times a day on Instagram. People want constant inspirational, motivational content; if you're not delivering it, then either they're not going to find you or they're going to go elsewhere. People need to see you every day, because that's how they consume social media.

2 **Build a social media machine.** If you can't create daily content, then consider sharing other people's. In this way, you've got fresh content every day that you haven't had to generate yourself, and you're promoting other people's content, which means they are more likely to help you out. Then you've got cross-posting, and collaboration. It also means that your audience is seeing you being active every day; you're showing them that you're actually interested in helping them. I had a strong presence on social media for two years before I launched my first video: I already had 10,000 followers on Twitter, 5000 people on Facebook, and about 5000 people on LinkedIn, so that first video went viral.

3 **Professional production is essential.** Make sure the first videos you put out are well produced. Snapchat, selfie and mobile videos are great for going viral once, but people still want to see content with high production values. This is particularly important that if you're trying to build a brand.

And, remember, you've only got about eight seconds to grab someone's attention in the video, and a video longer than two minutes is unlikely to be viewed.

4 **Analyse the 'science' behind the content.** Observe the science of good video: so, when you see a viral video, try to work out why it's so popular. When I see a video get over 10 million views, I watch it and ask, 'Why has this got 10 million views? Is it because the title has got a certain word in it? Is it because it's been filmed from a certain angle? Is it because the point is made really succinctly?' If you're only watching your own stuff, and not watching and analysing what other people have produced, then that's not going to help. I spend more time watching other people who I think are awesome online, than I do watching my own stuff.

Q: *What advice would you give to aspiring bloggers/vloggers and influencers?*

A:

1 **Understand the value of your story.** Really know your origin story: where you come from, your successes and failures, etc. – why you are the way you are.

2 **Understand your message.** If you want to be a blogger (or vlogger) you really have to understand what your message is all about and what your brand is about. Can you articulate it well enough so that you sound different from every other comedy or business blogger out there?

3 **Understand your 'Why?'.** What motivates you? Why should people follow you? You may think 'I want views. I want to be on camera. I want to be famous', but those are not reasons 'why', they're just outcomes. Nor should you do it just to prove someone wrong. It helps if you can work out why your message is different, why it's important, and how is your message true to you? I recommend that you read *Start With Why*, by Simon Sinek.

4 **Understand what works for you.** Find a vlogger whose style you like, in terms of editing and delivery, and say, 'What can I learn from them?' Not content-based: you don't want to steal their content, but you do want to know how they're editing to make their broadcasts work. You don't want to copy their delivery either – you need to find your own style – but you do need to analyse it. My own presenting style is to know the points that I want to make, but let them come out more naturally. One reason for this, I believe, is that today people want 'raw' content; they want people to be themselves and share how they feel.

5 **Promote shamelessly.** Send your videos out to everyone you know. Even if every tweet on your Twitter page says 'Please, watch my video', that's fine because that's what it takes. All you need is one person to turn around and say, 'You're right, I love your content', but that might take a hundred or a thousand tweets.

6 **Keep taking risks.** Don't rest on your laurels. People say to me, 'Oh, so now you've made it.' I haven't made anything, it's a continual journey. Know that if you take one risk in your lifetime, you're going to have to take another 1000. Don't think that one risk is enough, or that one time being broke is enough: you can end up back where you started. Don't think, 'I did that once, I'm an entrepreneur now.'

• •

As a self-made entrepreneur you will need to devote significant time to learning about these social media channels and testing them out to see which is likely to generate the best response. Once you have created good quality content and tested the channels, you can hire someone to manage these on your behalf. However, it's worth getting your hands dirty before you hand over to someone else, because people buy from people and they want to hear from YOU! Authenticity, relatability and integrity are crucial when it comes to building relationships, rapport and community via social media.

7

Fast-Track To Funding

An entrepreneur without funding is a musician without an instrument.

Robert A. Rice Jr.

Just as you need an instrument in order to be a musician, you need to spend money in order to make money, and that often means you may need to find some giants to 'stand on the shoulders of'. In business, the best time to raise funding is when you are making money, not when you are losing it or before you've made any. That may not bode so well for startups, but raising cash with a viable proof of concept is possible, even before traction has been established. Especially today.

In the past, entrepreneurs would spend hours on end pounding the streets with their business plan in hand, hoping to convince an investor that their idea would be the 'next big thing'. This approach was not only time-consuming, but also frequently yielded less-than-stellar results. Thankfully, at the moment, support for entrepreneurs, startups and small businesses is at an all-time high. Everyone from politicians to the stars of BBC television shows, *The Apprentice* and *Dragons' Den*, acknowledge that small businesses are the 'lifeblood' of the UK economy.

By investing in small businesses, we help to bolster that economy. As founders of a number of businesses ourselves, the million dollar question we are often asked is 'how did you start and fund your business?'; the answer is through a variety of methods because, more often than not, you will need alternatives to fall back on. Perhaps one source fails? For example, the bank will not increase your loan facility or the Government funding requirements suddenly change so you no longer qualify.

Whatever the case we have found 42 routes to funding! And this is not an exhaustive list. Indeed, sometimes you just need to get creative, especially when things aren't going your way.

For example, Jason Vale got creative when he needed to finance his retreat and spa venue in Portugal:

'When it came to building Juicy Oasis, nobody would lend me any money – nobody at all,' explains Jason. Even though Jason had created an amazing brand, when recession hit, potential investors and lenders became particularly risk-averse. So he had to follow his mantra and find 'another way' of sourcing the finance.

'I had to think on my feet and I had to think differently,' says Jason. He had found a derelict building by a river. 'It was my mum's dying wish for me to build it, so we decided to film a short video of the river and its surroundings with words that would sell the tranquil space as a beautiful place to come. I decided to sell places in advance and made up a number of platinum packages and titanium packages that included a lot of value. Platinum cost £5000 but included transfers, enabled members to come with someone else, and so on. I was even giving away one-to-one consultations as part of the membership packages: anything just to build this place. And we didn't know what we were going to say in the e-shots as there was no building yet, so we just did what came from the heart,' adds Jason.

'The response was astonishing! In four days we generated half a million, from something that didn't even exist yet! I suppose you could call it early crowdfunding, but that didn't exist back then. We had to ask "how" questions. We had to ask, "How can I generate some money to build this place when there isn't an investor?" ' Doing so has paid off. 'In the three years since we've opened, we've had a 100 per cent occupancy rate.'

Evidently, there are the traditional routes to funding, and there are the more creative methods, as Jason illustrates.

Furthermore, you need to decide early on how big you want to grow your business. Some people prefer to opt for organic growth, avoiding external finance and investing all profits back into the business. That's what Mark Hobbs did. New Leaf Distribution has 25 staff and, as Mark says, 'would have been much bigger if we had borrowed money'. But, crucially, you have to do what is right for you. Mark says:

'We've never borrowed any money, and we don't ever intend to. This was the right way for me and it's actually a pull for business owners to work their business on the basis of what is right for them.'

Six of the best

Here we shall describe six effective methods of business funding that we consider to be 'six of the best' – and outline their advantages, disadvantages and our stance on each, so that you can consider which funding options (if any) are right for you and your business.

Some entrepreneurs labour under the misguided impression that, outside of their immediate network, the only sources of capital available to them are banks, investors and venture capitalists. This is simply untrue! So let's explore the possibilities.

1 Loans

A loan is a form of credit. When you take out a loan, you make repayments over an agreed period of time. Loans tend to attract interest; therefore, in addition to repaying the loan amount, you will normally have to make interest payments so will end up repaying more than you borrowed, but you can do so via making small manageable repayments. The rate of interest varies and depends on the loan period, the amount you borrow, whether the loan is 'secured' (guaranteed by your home, for instance) and the Bank of England base rate. Interest rates may be 'fixed' (the same for the life of the loan which can be easier to manage) or 'variable' (subject to change over the life of the loan).

ADVANTAGES OF A LOAN

The main 'plus points' of a loan are:

- You are guaranteed the money for the term of the loan, which means it is not repayable on demand, and you do not have to give the lender a proportion of your profits or a share of your company – known as 'equity'.

- You can agree with the lender an amount that you can afford to pay back each week or month and, if opting for a fixed interest rate, can factor that amount into your cash flow forecasts for any given period.

DISADVANTAGES OF A LOAN

The main drawbacks of a loan are:

- If it is secured against your property, you could lose your home if you do not maintain repayments.
- Loans generally lack flexibility. For instance, the terms and conditions of your loan agreement may state that you will incur charges if you repay the loan early. This is called a penalty clause.
- Also, if your customers do not pay you on time, this could lead to difficulties in making monthly repayments.

2 Grants

A grant is money given to you with a specific project or purpose in mind, which you do not have to pay back. Ultimately, it is a 'conditional gift'. Grants are available from various sources, including local authorities and charitable organizations. However, in general, grants are only made for a proportion of your expenditure so you will be expected to stump up the rest of the cash needed.

ADVANTAGES OF A GRANT

- Free money. Since grants are non-repayable, you will not have to make any interest payments on them and you will not lose any control over your business.

DISADVANTAGES OF A GRANT

- Unsurprisingly, competition for grants is fierce!
- The application is detailed, protracted and time-consuming and you will have to find a grant that suits the particular needs of your project, which is not always possible.

- One major flaw of grants, which ordinarily provide partial funding, is that they are often only awarded to proposed projects – projects that have already started are not generally eligible.

3 Crowdfunding

'Crowdfunding' involves you connecting with a community of people willing to pool their financial contributions to enable you to reach your funding goal. This process is usually facilitated via a crowdfunding websites, such as Kickstarter or Crowdfunder.

The 'quid pro quo' is that money is invested, loaned or contributed to your project in return for recognition or rewards. For example, if you are selling t-shirts you can set up a crowdfunding campaign which provides a reward of a t-shirt or pack of t-shirts to those who invest, essentially reducing the risk of the venture by providing you with pre-orders and the capital needed to fulfil them. Educational and creative projects fare particularly well using this mechanism, so you would be well-advised to research the potential of this funding option.

Advantages of crowdfunding

- Access to capital. Rewards-centred crowdfunding enables entrepreneurs to raise money in exchange for gifts or products.
- Hedges risk. Funding aside, there are always expenses that are practically impossible for you to predict, challenges in market validation and other people who want a stake in your venture to help get it started. A crowdfunding strategy 'hedges', or reduces, these risks and allows you to secure market validation and retain the equity in your venture before going full throttle and taking the concept to market. You are essentially testing out your idea in front of an audience of potential customers. Those who fund your idea are validating it, which is gold for a startup.

- Marketing and PR. Crowdfunding is an easy and cost-effective means of introducing your venture to various channels, thus providing you with free PR! Social media-ready platforms make it simple to drive referral traffic to your website and improve the prospects of your venture 'going viral' on the internet when people share and spread the word of your enterprise to their network.
- Proof of concept. A successful crowdfunding campaign is a way of showing potential investors that your venture 'has legs', which instils confidence from the outset. It also provides you with an objective basis on which to forge ahead and see your venture to market.
- Brainstorming. It is nigh on impossible for you to cater for every single eventuality in your business venture – this is where other people come in. An effective crowdfunding strategy will engage the general public and solicit comments, feedback and ideas, which can be used to further develop and refine your offering.
- Prospective loyal customers. Research suggests that people who buy into a business venture, or the idea behind it, at an early stage, tend to be the ones who care most about the brand and its message. They are also the people most likely to be loyal customers (and evangelists) in the future.
- Ease of application. Unlike loans and other capital investments, which are traditionally the entrepreneur's bureaucratic nightmare, crowdfunding applications are easier and, perhaps more notably, more fun to process as they involve being creative. All you need to do is make contact with the crowdfunding platform that is appropriate for your theme and purpose, share your venture's message, create a video and outline some enticing rewards.
- Pre-sale opportunities. Crowdfunding allows you the option of pre-selling your product, service or concept even though you have not yet taken it to market. This can be financially lucrative and also provides you with a rich source of user feedback.

DISADVANTAGES OF CROWDFUNDING

In view of the considerable benefits of crowdfunding, some business gurus say that its disadvantages pale into insignificance. However, we still believe they are worthy of note.

- Although often preferable to the laborious form-filling involved in grant and loan applications, it can still take a good deal of effort to create a successful crowdfunding campaign, which will consist of a compelling video and persuasive story about why you are doing what you do and why investing an amount in exchange for a reward is a worthwhile thing to do.

- The prevalence of 'all-or-nothing' crowdfunding platforms means that you will only receive the funds raised if you reach 100 per cent (or more) of your funding target. If you fail to reach this goal, all money raised will be returned to investors. If you don't raise the amount you have stated that you need within the timescale selected (e.g. £25,000 in 60 days) then you don't get a penny. So, even if you raise £20,000, you won't get that capital because you didn't raise the full amount. For that reason, carefully considering how much to raise is worthwhile. Better to be overfunded than underfunded. Some websites now allow you to take the money without reaching your target – find the one that best suits you.

- If you have not obtained the necessary 'intellectual property' (i.e. copyright, trademark or patent protection) you leave your idea vulnerable to being copied, potentially by people who may be in a position to bring the concept to market faster than you can. The whole idea is to be the first person to get a commercially viable product to market. The first in time prevails.

- Crowdfunding is largely unregulated, although the Financial Conduct Authority has jurisdiction over loan and investment-based crowdfunding. If crowdfunding holds limited appeal due to its relative infancy in the funding market, the next source of funding may resonant with you due to its longevity.

4 Investment (equity) finance

Investment finance requires you to sell a portion of your business (in the form of equity/shares) to an investor who takes a share of any profits generated or losses suffered by your company. The BBC television series, *Dragons' Den* (*Shark Tank* in the USA), is probably the most popular example of this type of funding.

ADVANTAGES OF INVESTMENT FINANCE

- Investors often bring new skills, abilities, opportunities and (crucially) contacts to the table, which may serve to further the interests of your business.
- Equally, their presence means that you share the risks of the business with them.

DISADVANTAGES OF INVESTMENT FINANCE

Investment finance is a specialist funding opportunity, on which you should seek professional advice before pursuing.

- The application process can be extensive, costly and time-consuming.
- You will no longer own all of your business (although your share could be increased in the future if you have an agreement in place stating that, if you achieve certain profit targets, you will receive a certain percentage of shares back). This is called a 'ratchet deal'.
- In line with the apportioning of shares outside your business, some business decisions will no longer be your own – you may have to consult with your investors before making certain management manoeuvres.
- Significantly, this source of funding is unavailable to sole traders and people in partnership. Whilst they have 'interests,' they do not hold any 'shares' for sale.

5 Factoring

Factoring is essentially a financial mechanism to provide you with better cash flow in the business once you have clients. Simply stated, factoring involves an invoice financier who performs dual functions on your behalf.

Firstly, they manage your sales ledger and, secondly, they collect debts due from your customers. You effectively sell your invoices to the factoring firm who take a portion of the invoice and/or charge a fee.

ADVANTAGES OF FACTORING

- Factoring is a highly effective time-saver because the responsibility of handling the sales ledger now rests with an invoice financier.
- Use of factoring increases the probability of your dealing with solvent customers. This is because invoice financiers run a credit check on all potential customers.
- Increased cash flow. Instead of potentially waiting 60-90 days for a client to make payment, factoring provides you with percentage of the money almost immediately.

DISADVANTAGES OF FACTORING

- Your customers may not wish to liaise with an invoice financier – they may insist on dealing with you directly.
- Due to the use of a third party representative, factoring offers you limited control over how your 'brand' is projected and managed. If, for instance, an invoice financier acts out of turn with your customers, this can adversely affect how your customers perceive you, which could result in lost orders.

Most surveys of entrepreneurs reveal that the final source of funding is probably the most commonly used method to start a business – personal finance. Many a self-made entrepreneur started out in business this way ... including (to some degree) both of the authors of this book!

6 Personal finance (friends and family)

Sources of personal finance include (among other things) savings, credit cards, and friends and family. Existing business literature has thoroughly recounted the pros and cons of using savings and credit cards to fund business, so we have opted instead to focus on the little-discussed but often-used option of funding by family and friends.

Family and friends are the primary source of personal funds for very early-stage startups, and borrowing from them presents an interesting alternative to more traditional forms of financing.

Commitment commands credibility therefore, from an investor's perspective, if your family and friends do not believe in you enough to make an investment, why should anyone else?

ADVANTAGES OF PERSONAL FINANCE

- Location! Location! Location! One of the key advantages of raising money from friends and family is that they are easy to find, plus you already know them (and they know you) – warts and all.
- Another positive feature is low (or no) interest payments and no bank contracts.

DISADVANTAGES OF PERSONAL FINANCE

Three main disadvantages of friends and family financing come to mind.

- It violates the sacred principle of not mixing your business and personal lives.
- Family and friends are not likely to be as well-connected as 'angel' investors or venture capital firms.
- They may not be accredited investors, which could result in complications down the line.

The 'B' line: the bottom line

How you finance your business can make all the difference between it becoming a runaway success or a dismal failure. In business, all money may sound like 'good' money, but this is far from the case – it is very much situation-dependent. What works well for one business may not necessarily work for yours and vice versa.

The bottom line is: it generally makes more sense to tap into a variety of different business funding sources. This means it is vital to be responsible in your funding decisions; to do your homework. Understand the terms of the funding chosen and assess the risk on the basis of a worst-case scenario – if things don't work out and the business fails, will you be able to keep up with repayments?

A worthwhile exercise to complete is to write a list of what exactly you need capital for. What do you need to buy, from staff to software and supplies? And what would you like help with, from partners and industry contacts to marketing help? Next, consider your revenue options and assess each source of finance to find those which have the best fit for your needs.

Other funding options

The other 36 funding options are listed here. More information can be found on the resource page when you sign up on our website www.selfmadebook.uk:

7 Overdrafts
8 Community schemes
9 Sponsorship packages
10 Venture capitalists*
11 Business angels (e.g. Angels' Den, The Angels Society)*
12 Local authorities
13 Exchange of services (e.g. bartering)
14 Accelerator Academy (large corporates and accelerators)

---

* These both provide investment finance.

15 Arts Council (charities)
16 Borro (asset-based funding)
17 Community Development Finance Institutions (CDFIs)
18 Community Enterprise Funding, e.g. Big Society Capital (Social Enterprise)
19 Collider12 (large corporates and accelerators)
20 Community Business Loan, e.g. RBS Community Business Loan (social enterprise)
21 *Dragons' Den* (TV!)
22 Enterprise Finance Guarantee Scheme (Government)
23 Funding circle (working capital)
24 Growth accelerator (Government)
25 IBM Smartcamp (large corporates and accelerators)
26 Iwoca (working capital)
27 Microsoft BizSpark (large corporates and accelerators)
28 MITIE Millions (large corporates and accelerators)
29 Nesta (charities)
30 New Enterprise Allowance (Government)
31 Retail bond
32 Shell LiveWIRE (large corporates and accelerators)
33 Social Enterprise UK (social enterprise)
34 Seedcamp (large corporates and accelerators)
35 Springboard (large corporates and accelerators)
36 Startup Loans (Government)
37 The Prince's Trust (charities)
38 The Young Foundation (social enterprise)
39 Technology Strategy Board (Government)
40 UKTI, including Export Insight Visits and Tradeshow Access Programme (Government)
41 Wayra (large corporates and accelerators)
42 Wonga for Business (working capital)

Whichever sources of finance you strive to secure, it's crucial to do your homework before pitching to anyone – whether that's a relative, your bank manager, a deep-pocketed angel investor or the crowd of investors in a crowdfunding community.

Good luck!

• •

Expert insight

Q&A with Gordon Merrylees, Head of Entrepreneurship,
Royal Bank of Scotland, NatWest and Ulster Bank

Q: *Who are you and what do you do?*

A: My name is Gordon Merrylees and I am Head of Entrepreneurship for the Royal Bank of Scotland, NatWest and Ulster Bank. I do
say that I have the best job in the bank; I get so much satisfaction
seeing businesses grow from startup to getting their products and
ideas to market. I love the excitement and pace, and the passion these
people have is incredible, and I get to help them realize their dreams;
I feel like this is what I was always meant to do.

Q: *How has the RBS group been working with and supporting*
startups and small businesses?

A: We are the largest SME bank in the UK and in the last few years
we have become the biggest lender to SMEs, supporting their growth
and that of the UK economy. We have over 1 million small business
customers in the £0–£2million turnover bracket and we're committed to helping them start, grow and be successful.

I also run an award-winning team covering the whole of the UK
and we support entrepreneurs to grow their businesses and achieve
their ambitions through our entrepreneurship strategy. In partnership
with Entrepreneurial Spark we have opened 13 business accelerator
hubs throughout the UK. We offer free support to businesses that
come into our programme and help them to grow while providing free desk space. Our accelerator programme is now the world's
largest of its kind and we are striving to make it recognized as the
very best too. The key aspect here is we open up the collective reach,
networks, knowledge and expertise of our bank and harness this for
the benefit of the entrepreneurs we support every day. We connect
them to our existing customers and their supply chains that can lead

to investment. We nourish businesses to fulfil their full potential; the failure rate of new startup businesses in the UK is around 65 per cent in the critical first few years, whereas Entrepreneurial Spark businesses have a survival rate of 87 per cent.

We understand the challenges that contribute to the failure of businesses and we create programmes and events nationally to help steer businesses around potential pitfalls. We run events such as 'opportunity knocks' which brings together businesses, entrepreneurs, investors, business advisors and relationship managers and encourages connectivity, networking and collaboration while focusing on raising investments and building a team.

Funding, mentoring, access to influencers, skills and expertise are all key areas of focus for us at the bank.

Q: *What do you look for in potential business customers?*

A: As a bank we serve anyone who is interested in starting a business and our banking team can support any enquiry of this nature from a startup to a corporate business and everything in-between. Specifically the focus for my team is to support those entrepreneurs who have real growth and scale ambition. Our Entrepreneurial Spark accelerator programme, powered by the bank, is set up to do just that. We look for people who are passionate and believe in themselves and are looking to excel in their business. The best entrepreneurs continually look for value, creating opportunities for their company wherever they are and with whomever they talk to; they continually drive their company, team and product forward. Focus, passion and deep engagement to a vision are critical elements of effective innovation and company building.

Q: *How should new businesses approach the business banking relationship – what do they need to know, do or consider?*

A: My personal advice is to be transparent, honest and realistic, and ensure you have done the groundwork in validation to make sure you establish a customer for whatever it is you're selling.

Traditionally, though, as a bank (when considering funding) we like a business plan which includes projections and cash flow: know your break-even figures, have a USP, know your target market, and have a good CV or track record in the industry that you are going into. Also establish your five-year plans: for the first five years on how to grow your business, the next five on how to stabilize your business and, potentially, the last five years on an exit strategy.

One area of support that I've seen have real impact is the enablement process which Entrepreneurial Spark is famous for. Entrepreneurs are held accountable for achieving goals and making progress, to ensure that they are able to stick to the programme and build their business to its full potential. They are also taught the art of the 'Perfect Pitch', which is basically how to deliver a business plan verbally. We use a basic structure to teach entrepreneurs how to prepare for their audience, keep it simple and communicate the business clearly.

The structure of a 'Perfect Pitch':

● The Hook
● The Problem/Pain point
● The Solution and Innovation
● Market Size/Revenue Model
● Competition and Risk Awareness
● The Startup Team
● Traction
● The Ask

Q: *Which products/services would you recommend to a new business owner and why?*

A: A business bank account is key to ensure you are set up correctly from the outset. Running a businesses from a personal account can have implications at a later date and can be really destructive. Banks frown upon this practice as it breaks the terms and conditions of the account, and it takes time, money and sanity to separate out business transactions from personal ones.

Mobile banking apps – entrepreneurs can always be on the go and may predominantly work from their phone. Mobile apps and digital banking quite simply give entrepreneurs access from anywhere to run their business from the palm of their hand.

Ensuring the right cover is in place for you to run and operate your business is crucial in mitigating risks. We offer business insurance, public and products liability insurance, employer's liability insurance, business interruption and legal expenses.

Q: *Do you have any key messages for tomorrow's entrepreneurs?*

A: Starting up is not easy: you need to be brave and bold, and to achieve anything in life you must have the right mindset. If you have the determination and commitment you will be able to achieve anything, so be the person who thinks differently, who is a round peg in the square hole. Cash is the key reason businesses fail so be smart when starting out; don't jump into a scenario at the outset with large fixed costs like rent and staff if you don't have the confirmed income to pay them… oh and the main thing: focus, focus, focus.

Q: *In your experience of working with emerging entrepreneurs and business owners, what are your top tips on personal and business success?*

A: Validate, validate, validate!! Spend time upfront to confirm that what it is you are about to build is something people want and are actually willing to pay for.

Build a great team; no one can do it alone so always hire someone better than you. As Steve Jobs once said, 'A small team off A-Plus players can run circles around a giant team off B and C players.'

Lastly, come and join our Entrepreneurial Spark programme … it will change your life.

8

Sell! Sell! Sell!

How to sell – understand the need, create the solution

Through your marketing strategies you need to communicate your value to the right people at the right time. Through your sales strategies you need to demonstrate how your value proposition meets a prospective customer's needs in order to persuade them to become a customer. Then you need to deliver that value profitably, thus creating a win–win for you and your customer.

Many years ago, before Byron embarked on his own self-made journey, he had a sales job. It was here that Byron learned two key lessons: one – questions are good, but inflexible scripts are not; and two – you have two ears and one mouth for a reason, to listen rather than talk!

In order to solve problems you need to provide a solution. However, in order to understand clearly which problems need solving and ensure that you have the right solution to solve them, you need to LISTEN. You can't create or offer a solution if you don't fully understand the precise need. And, if you can satisfy your prospects' unmet needs, they are far more likely to buy from you.

So, during your valuable time with customers and prospects we suggest that you only open your mouth to ask questions and then LISTEN CAREFULLY TO THE ANSWERS. Your goal in asking questions is to identify the exact needs of your customer so you can then figure out how you can help fulfil those needs and solve the problems they are experiencing.

Another key component of problem solving is ensuring that your offering does solve problems. One way to do this is to ask your current satisfied customers what problems your product or service has solved for them and communicate this via testimonials, website copy and when you pitch your offering to customers (AFTER you have listened closely to what they have to say).

If you assume your customer wants to buy an umbrella to shelter them from the rain when, in fact, they want it to shade them from the sun, you may lose the sale because you aren't listening and are instead trying to sell them a different type of brolly. And that just won't wash.

Of course we've all made the mistake of being so keen to demonstrate how our solution is the absolute best product in the world that we do all the talking. As someone with something to sell, it's all too easy to start talking about yourself and just pitch without asking your customers what their needs are and what they are focusing on at the moment. When I first started my business I concentrated on what I could do rather than what people wanted, but I soon learned from this mistake.

'Now we always find out the needs of the customer first before we even talk about our offering,' says Byron, who has become an expert at asking the right key questions about those needs. 'We find out the short-term goals, long-term goals and their aspirations and then align our offering with what they have told us. That's the way we sell. We look at the need first before we look at how our offering fits the need.'

Salespeople who don't listen to their prospects find themselves leaving empty handed. No deal done. Maybe the customer didn't want the expensive radio you tried to sell them, because all they really needed was a new battery for the old one and, had you provided the solution to their problem, they might be more likely to return when they DO need a new radio.

Plus, you want to become known as the 'go to' expert in your field who gives the best advice. Yet, you can only dish out that advice if you actually listen to the customers' questions and then provide the precise advice they are seeking.

Once you have listened, you know what customers want. This means you are in a far better position to explain WHAT'S IN IT FOR THEM, i.e. to define the value, because this is the only reason they will buy from you. You can use the knowledge you have gained by listening to your customers, to focus on the benefits that your product or service provides and ensure that these are well aligned with their needs.

Through listening, you get to figure out what your value proposition is and gain a reputation for delivering it. For example, Byron's property company became known for providing a reliable service to landlords. His value proposition was that, if you needed a safe pair of hands, you'd go to Byron, and he and his team would deliver. For a landlord, exceptional service at a fair price is a top priority, which is how Byron was able to grow his business so swiftly. Given that most people – both business customers and individual consumers – want to be less stressed, if you have a product or service which makes their lives easier, you can build a strong value proposition on that.

I've learned that people come to The Be Group to improve themselves, so our mantra has become 'BE YOU, ONLY BETTER'. However, it was only through listening to the needs of our prospects and customers which enabled us to work out that, in helping them to be the best and most authentic version of themselves, we can help them to stand out from the rest.

LISTEN CAREFULLY + ASK QUESTIONS + LISTEN
CAREFULLY + DEMONSTRATE VALUE = SALE

Bianca and Byron's selling dos and don'ts

- DO your homework. Preparation is important. We use questionnaires in our companies, which allow us to find out the customers' needs without having to think on the spot. Importantly, a questionnaire is not a set script, just a list of questions relevant to the customer. Once the customer has completed the questionnaire and you have ascertained that they need and can afford what you have to offer, and that what you have to offer is of sufficient VALUE to them, you are well placed to make the sale.

- DO listen to what they have to say about their needs and objectives first and then respond in a way that clearly illustrates how you might help them to achieve those objectives. Only open your mouth to ask questions that tell you more about their needs. You can't provide a solution to their problem unless you hear directly from each individual what that problem is and what it is they are looking for.

- DO have your 'elevator pitch' polished and prepared. You never know when you might need it and when it could lead to a sale. For example, I was at a college in South London for a project meeting. I happened to be in the lift with the Principal, and he told me they had a graduation event coming up soon and he wanted to get Lord Sugar to give the keynote speech. I said, 'That's nice, but why would you need Lord Sugar, when you're in the lift with me?' He laughed, told me that was a good point and took my card. Shortly afterwards he booked me to make the speech, which was a lucrative gig. It's vital to be prepared and to be willing to seize the day, as you never know when an opportunity will present itself.

- DO what you say you will do. Be a person of your word. If you say you're going to email them in the morning, email them in the morning. If you say you're going to pass them a referral, pass them a referral. If you can't deliver for whatever reason, inform them. This will help you to build a reputation for reliability.

- DO limit availability if you can. Jason Vale did exactly this when he filmed a documentary at his retreat. 'We could afford to give a whole month over to 50 people and foot the bill. This meant we could use them as guinea pigs. We closed the retreat to the public the following month to discuss what did and didn't work. When we opened it up (having already sold our founding memberships) people were saying, "How did you get in, they are full for the next ten weeks, nobody can get in? You just can't get in this place." But, that creates urgency and demand and makes it the "in" place to go; the celebrity retreat of choice.'

- DON'T go for the hard sell. Pushy isn't effective. Bombarding the person with lots of information and statistics about you and your organization will overwhelm them.

- DON'T talk about price too early. Often people tell you the price quite early in the conversation without ascertaining the need, i.e. working out why it's going to be valuable and positive to the customer. What I find with my clients is that, although the price is relevant, it's not as relevant as what you have to offer. If you have what the client needs then they can often find the money.

- DON'T be afraid to be yourself and add individuality to your sales pitches. 'A company I once worked for had a strict script which took the personality out of sales. You had to follow the cue sheet and couldn't ask any other questions in any other sequence. So, when the customer entered the building you had to say "Picked a nice day for it?" laughs Byron. 'Robots don't make good salespeople.'

- DON'T assume that 'no' now means 'no, never'. For example, Byron approached the blog platform, SMEInsider to suggest that I blog for them. At the time, they said no, they didn't have any opportunities. However, through remaining open and approachable, and asking questions like 'How can we collaborate in the future?', they came back to us with a better proposal. Initially, this involved blogging each week about *The Apprentice*, which led to my becoming the UK ambassador for Nominet's .uk domain, and doing keynote speeches at The Business Show at Excel and making guest appearances to represent the brand. 'That was about being open and having dialogue with open questions about how the relationship might develop over time,' adds Byron.

The deal isn't the end – it's just the beginning

As you close the deal, think about this 'closing' process not as an ending but as a beginning, not as a closing but as an opening, in terms of opening the customer to their long-term journey with you. Let them know what to do if they have any additional questions, inform them about promotions, upgrade dates and what happens next.

Sales is a lot about relationship building. That's why it's a good idea to try to meet people face to face. Once you've met in person, it makes it easier to pick up the phone and follow up. If something comes up where you can help each other and you have a mutually beneficial relationship, it's easier to develop the relationship from there. For example, I recently met a PR expert who is top of her field. Editors get hundreds of emails a day and they don't have time to open many of them, yet they always open emails from her, because she has made the effort to get to know them individually and develop a relationship with them. As a result she knows how and when they prefer to be contacted, so they recognize her emails when they come in, open them and act on them when they can.

Anything that you can do to build on that first contact to develop a relationship is time well spent. It is well known in business that it is much easier and cheaper to sell to existing customers than it is to attract and sell to new ones, because you've already started a relationship with them. So dazzle your customers with your products and your service, treat them well, and they are more likely to come back to you time and time again, and bring along their friends.

Customer loyalty is so valuable. Such customer retention saves you time and money investing in acquiring new customers. Plus, if you can analyse which 20 per cent of your customers give you the most business, this will help you to figure out which demographics to target with which (best-selling) products, as well as allowing you to target existing customers with products/services that fit their needs on an ongoing basis.

Good customer service

Good customer service is a crucial part of the sales process. Everyone has a customer service horror story about being kept on hold for hours, or about promises made but not kept. And, because of the negative bias people tend to have, we are likely to share our negative experiences with more people than we do our positive experiences. As a self-made entrepreneur, you want people to shout from the rooftops about how fabulous your company is, not how terrible. So it's critical to consider every touch point that you have with your customer, from when they are a prospect interested in your wares, to long after they buy from you.

In fact, it's now more important than ever before to get a good reputation for excellent customer service. Why? Because today, when your customers slam or praise your business, they do so more publicly than ever before: tweeting complaints, posting bad reviews on TripAdvisor, or sharing their views on Facebook. Not only that, but people now tend to have larger personal networks than they had pre-internet. So, whilst this can work in your favour as happy customers recommend you to that large network of prospects, it can equally harm your business if an unsatisfied customer shares their disappointment with their contacts. Therefore, it's worth doing all that you can not merely to satisfy your customers but to exceed their expectations at every opportunity.

Word of mouth has many more ways to travel and everybody's personal reach extends much further, so make sure those words are good, positive ones. From handwritten thank-yous on your invoices, to free badges and notebooks; from texting customers to let them know that something is on its way, to checking on the recovery of a client from an illness; from giving your coaching clients a free audio book to listen to *en route* to your practice or hiring a car valet company to wash your customers' cars whilst they shop with you; from delivering early rather than 'on time' or simply smiling every time you see them: there are all kinds of ways to go the extra mile and make a long-lasting impression. As well as simply treating your customers as you would like to be treated, pay attention to detail to make buying from you as rewarding and enjoyable an experience as possible. Assess the customer's journey from first becoming aware of you to buying from you and consider ways that you might pleasantly surprise them at each contact point.

Byron's luxury chauffeuring company VIP Chauffeur Car Hire, for instance, asks what the customer's colour scheme is for their wedding, so the colour of the ribbons on the car can be matched to it, to add a personal touch. 'We also ask customers what their favourite song/artist is,' explains Byron. 'And, on the wedding day, we play those songs in the car for them. Our customers appreciate that little extra, which costs us next to nothing.'

Also, despite being busy, it's important to give people your time. For example, although I don't see myself as a celebrity, because I've been on TV people sometimes ask to have their picture taken with me. I'm more than willing to do so, although I've been to events where the speaker dashes off or refuses to talk to us 'ordinary' people. There's no price on being nice. In fact, my philosophy is, it's nice to be important but it's more important to be nice.

Ultimately, aim to shine in all that you do, but you are only human, so on occasions where you do slip up, make sure it's easy for customers to send their complaints directly to you, and respond to them quickly and with courtesy. Ideally, go the extra mile to turn complainants into your biggest fans.

I believe that exceeding the expectations of customers, rather than just satisfying them, is one of the core actions that has enabled Byron and I to build successful enterprises. Happy customers are incredibly valuable. In fact, if you ask any successful business owner what has made them successful, exceptional customer service will rank very highly. Jason Vale agrees:

'Your number one priority in business should be to understand your guests, clients or customers, beyond how much they are going to spend with you. Because what you want to create are not just customers, you want raving fans. All of your customers should be your fans: you want them talking about you everywhere, so they are saying, "Oh my word! Have you been here? Have you tried this?" They are your own marketers essentially.'

Indeed, so, whether you are exceeding expectations from the outset or after a mistake, the bottom line is this: customers who feel valued create value. So delight them and they will delight you in return. Here's how…

How to get your customers selling for you

You can optimize the value of your best customers, not just from the custom they give you, but through the custom they generate for you through other methods. For instance, some might be influential within their own communities, both offline and online and could create a buzz on your behalf; others might be happy to provide you with case studies, testimonials and/or referrals. As such, they can essentially become an extension of your sales team.

Obviously, you need to provide wonderful products and services that people are keen to share. But you also need to be savvy when it comes to helping your customers to work for you.

Here is a range of ways in which you can get your customers to sell for you:

- Ask for referrals. 'Referrals are huge in everything we do,' says Byron. 'Not everyone asks their customers for referrals but we always do this. It's as simple as saying, 'If I do a good job for you, are you happy to recommend me to other people?' or 'If I give you this reduced price are you happy to give me one or two referrals in exchange?' And then reminding them after you've delivered and inviting them to keep their part of the bargain.'
- Offer commission. You can set up an affiliate marketing programme, where people can earn a commission from sales made directly via an affiliate link (with a specific tracking code that is unique to them) from their website, or you can simply offer commission to anyone who sends you a lead which turns into a sale. This works both ways. Byron often refers people and 'matchmakes' to generate additional income for his own businesses. We've recently set up an

affiliate programme for Bianca Miller London whereby a blogger or anyone who has a good network can push the product out to their contacts and get paid for any sales that result. People like to have multiple revenue streams now and earn passive income, and this method gives influential people who share your target market a great opportunity to do so, whilst you benefit from sales that you wouldn't have gained otherwise – another win–win sales solution.

- Focus on giving. By doing things that help advance other people you can build up very strong relationships with them. As a result they feel incentivized to go out of their way to help you in return. I think that is a large part of the sales process.
- Ask everyone you do business with if they could give you a testimonial. When people buy, they like to read real statements of recommendation from people who've already bought. A testimonial is a referral from a stranger rather than from an acquaintance, but it can still be rather persuasive in overcoming any objections and reassuring people that they are in safe hands. I try to get a testimonial from every client: the types of clients I work with in the corporate sector like to see that other clients have given me a seal of approval. If you can say you've worked with such and such a company and also have a recommendation from them on your website, the prospective client is more likely to think, 'If you're good enough to work with them, you must be worth the money you're asking for.' The feedback you get from a testimonial helps you to better understand precisely what the value is that you've provided and then documenting that to boost credibility.
- Ask if a client is willing to go one step further and provide a video testimonial. Byron says, 'At VIP Chauffeur Car Hire, we often have prom guests or married couples who have hired our cars for their big day providing video testimonials. We find the videos go one step further in providing an insight into what the big day could be like for the potential customer and is fantastic for social media

marketing purposes.' These videos show the happily married couple next to, or in, the car, for example, and show other couples what is possible. Videos and pictures certainly help to bring a testimonial to life and assert its authenticity.

- Invite testimonial providers to be part of a case study for your website. Those customers who offer especially glowing testimonials might be happy to go one step further and share their story online about how you helped them to solve a specific problem. They will get a link from your site to theirs and, the bigger you become, the more awareness they will derive from it. For you, a case study is a fantastic opportunity to showcase how you helped someone in the same boat as your prospect, illustrating what challenges they faced and what benefits they gained as a result of being your customer. Now that's persuasive!

- Get your products into the hands of influencers. There will be a number of people within your industry who have the capacity to create a buzz and spread your messages out virally. These well-connected influencers (bloggers, celebrities, networkers) will have what is known as a high SNP (Social Networking Potential). This essentially means that they have a large network and, due to being well-respected within that network, have influence over the people within it. As well as sending trial products to taste-makers (celebrities and journalists with a high SNP), also send to other media such as influential bloggers in your industry. For example, Alesha Dixon has posted about Bianca Miller London on her Instagram account, Cheryl Tweedy has liked some of our posts and Lord Sugar tweeted about our launch. We've found that one good way to get products into the hands of celebrities is through their glam teams (make up, hair and fashion stylists). Remember though, celebrities are not the only influencers; bloggers are influential too, and they are often perceived as a more trusted source of information.

Perfecting your value proposition by listening to customer feedback

Just as feedback is useful to show where you are doing things right, via testimonials and the like, it is also useful when you haven't done something right, so you can improve areas where you could have done something better.

For example, I delivered two training sessions for Accenture via my business. The feedback I received about my personal branding session was that it was spot on and to keep doing it the way I was doing it. From that I was able to get a testimonial. The feedback about my 'powerful presenting' training session was equally valuable. The company suggested it'd be helpful to include more information about breathing techniques and where to put your arms when you're on stage, so to have a focus on body language. Consequently, we added that and I delivered the session the following time. Accenture were pleased that I had listened to them and given them exactly what they needed. By listening to the customer I secured the next training session, and have continued to be their chosen provider for the last few years. Evidently, being open to receiving feedback and tweaking accordingly is absolutely paramount in business, so keep those communication channels wide open.

What's more, trends, opportunities and challenges shift, so it's important to keep your ear to the ground to gain as much insight as you can. Listening doesn't just get you the sale, it helps you to perfect your value proposition and go with the times to propel growth even further.

Valued customers can create additional value by becoming value proposition advisors. They can test products, be part of a pilot scheme, give you feedback on price, packaging, designs and functionality. They feel valued when you give them a voice and you can reward them for being part of your 'inner circle' too. Whether you offer lifetime discounts or another type of incentive, these customers are in the best position to give you insights into whether your products or services are right, and what improvements could be made.

So get your products and services out there into the hands of real people and collect their responses. Keep doing this as you update your products and services over time. Set up focus groups and user clubs, and uncover problems so that you can work on solutions. Correct mistakes and improve continually.

As well as gathering feedback about your products and services, you could also ask your customer club, or community, for their feedback on your marketing materials. Whether it's the title for your next book, the heading for your next mailshot or the benefits that they rank the highest, continue dialogue to gain feedback on an ongoing basis. Social media, such as Facebook groups and Twitter, are a great way to do this.

When it comes to your sales strategy, your ears are your greatest tool. Listening before and after you make a sale will help you to gain custom and retain it. Listening will also enable you to delight your customers and give them real value and, in so doing, increase the likelihood of them giving you more value over time.

Part 3: The Reaction

This part of the book is not only about growing your business, it's about growing with your business. We'll focus on how personal development, including mentoring and setting achievable goals, can have important benefits for your business. Having the right mindset – including a positive outlook and self-belief – can make all the difference to your level of success. We'll also explore analysing risk, with a view to expanding your operation.

9

Personal Development

If you want to be wealthy and happy, learn to work harder on yourself
than you do on your job.

Earl Shoaff, entrepreneur and motivational speaker

Becoming your best self

It has been said that 'What you become in life is infinitely more important than anything you might get,'[32] and that is why it is as important
to develop yourself as it is to develop your business. With self-growth
comes mastery and with mastery comes ability. When we equip ourselves as people, we equip ourselves as business people at the same time.

Enterprises, like people, should be constantly evolving. The need
to continuously improve generally happens as a result of either inspiration or desperation but, as far as personal development is concerned,
it is a life-long commitment.

No matter how well you think you're doing, you still need to be
open to learning. Byron and I still go to conferences, still go to hear
expert speakers, and continue to read books by personal development
gurus, from Brian Tracy to Simon Sinek. Learning from the best in
the business adds value to your own and you can always learn something new. There is always an opportunity to gain new knowledge.

As you work on your business, your primary question will be the
same one that your customers ask themselves before they buy from
you: 'What's in it for me?' You focus on what you are going to get
from doing a deal, whether that is profit, a useful contact, a platform
on which to grow, a partnership, an introduction into a new market,
a sale, and so on and so forth.

When you work on yourself, your primary question will be: 'What am I becoming?' This will help you to grow as a person, and to focus on purposeful learning and tasks that allow you to become the best version of yourself. This has the magical effect of better enabling you to get what you want, because as you become the best version of yourself you attract the best outcomes, both in life and in business. Plus you have more to offer to others – whether that's staff, customers or family members. A win–win if ever there was one.

> To have more than you've got, become more than you are.
>
> *Jim Rohn, entrepreneur and motivational speaker*

Changing and/or improving our daily habits, and setting and achieving personal goals are all important ways to grow as individuals. As such, it's important to invest time into this personal growth, just as we invest in our business growth.

As Mark Hobbs of New Leaf Distribution says, 'Success is the realization of a worthy idea.' And, in order to bring ideas to fruition you need to set goals. Mark has set up his own website with a '12-Part Goal Matrix' at www.12pgm.com: the idea is to set goals on both personal and business improvement, and break them down into short-term, medium-term and long-term.

Mark is also an advocate of cultivating a mindset of self-belief whilst continuing to work hard on yourself and your business. Mark says:

'The reason people may struggle is because they don't believe in what they do, but you've got to believe in what you do, no matter what happens. You need the capacity to take rejection; if you don't have that, it's going to be tough.'

Running your own business is certainly a roller-coaster ride of ups and downs, so you need to ride the waves and go with the flow, learning as you go.

'I think everyone in business knows it goes up and down,' says Alesha Dixon. 'Sometimes you have to hit a low before you hit your high. And that's a really strong lesson. Then you can have faith in the unknown because actually, everything doesn't happen immediately, you have to be okay with the lows. With my career, when I've had moments where things have dipped, I have now found peace with that because I've realized, those low moments are when I've learned the biggest lessons, which have propelled me to the place I am now.'

For that reason Alesha has found she now worries less about the future. When we asked Alesha what she might say to her younger self, she replied instantly. 'Don't worry so much!'

She says, 'I think I spent a lot of time and energy wasted worrying about what could be or what might not be, and it was unnecessary energy, because you cannot change certain things. Some things are just out of your hands, so you've got to allow things to happen organically and they tend to work out.'

Alesha admits to being insecure and fearful about the world as a teenager. 'My fear has held me back in certain situations, and that's something I'm trying to work on within myself. So much so that I've told myself to "grow a pair"; to not be afraid to call up the CEO of that company. Don't be afraid to have the meeting with the big boss. Don't be afraid to put yourself out there,' she says.

'I believe the universe is very good at presenting us with opportunities: when we don't get the message the first time, it arrives in another shape or form. We're all on this journey of self-discovery.'

To help us on our journey, Alesha believes we have certain tools and owe it to ourselves to do what we love. 'You have to just follow your gut instinct, do what feels right, do what makes you happy, so that you wake up in the morning and absolutely love what you do, because then you will execute it to the highest level that you can. That's all you can do; the rest takes care of itself and, sometimes, it's okay for things to not always pan out.'

Certainly, Byron and I have found that the deepest learning takes place when things don't work out and you have another roll of the dice, but this time with more clarity, knowledge and experience. In growing, you have to take the rough with the smooth, but do what you can on your personal journey of self-discovery to improve.

For some entrepreneurs, personal growth *is* their business. For example, Jason Vale used to be addicted to smoking, alcohol and junk food and was a chronic sufferer of psoriasis, eczema and hayfever. He began juicing to improve his own health and consequently lost weight; he also gave up smoking and drinking, and stopped eating junk food by changing his mindset surrounding his addictions.

'I was smoking 60 cigarettes and drinking 14 pints and suffering from psoriasis but had the mindset that I'd rather die young and eat McDonald's and have a happy life than eat broccoli and be bored out of my skull. But I got sicker and sicker and, because there was something about the green stuff that made me want to vomit, I wondered how else I could get it in me,' explains Jason who realized he needed to work on himself if he was going to get well. 'I discovered this little American book on juicing, at a time when juicing wasn't widespread in the UK.' Jason started to experiment, drank juice for three months and, 'After some experimentation, people started to notice that I looked better and asked me what I was doing. Alongside juicing, I began studying addiction psychology and writing about it all.'

He knew what his weaknesses and motivations were, and knew that sufficient change would require a big shift in mindset. He knew he had to commit to investing in himself, so he devoted time to learning about juicing and addiction psychology. He read a lot of books. The final part of the personal development pie was believing that he could achieve his goals.

Indeed, if you explore the life of anyone who has evolved personally, you will find some common denominators. This is because such personal growth involves these common traits:

1 **Self-awareness.** Knowing your strengths, motivations and weaknesses is important in understanding how to get the best out of yourself.

2 **Self-commitment.** Successful self-made people always stay open to learning. They commit to investing in themselves; they read a lot, stay up to date with knowledge that makes them the go-to person in their industry and devote time to continual improvement. They put in the hours so they can become amazing at what they do.

3 **Self-belief.** When you are on a journey to being self made you need to believe in yourself. If you don't who else will? So when people who have never tried tell a self-made person that they can't, a self-made person will show them that they can, and will. They will also believe that where they are now isn't where they are going to stay; that they have what it takes to achieve their goals, and they work incredibly hard in order to bring their vision to fruition.

In order to grow your business and grow your self, you need to have a 'can do' attitude in order to find a way around obstacles. Because, obstacles crop up all the time, in business as they do in life.

Without this 'can do' attitude, Jason Vale wouldn't have achieved what he has.

'I said to my mum "I'm going to write a book" and she encouraged me, even though she knew I couldn't spell or write,' smiles Jason, who is now a best-selling author. 'I left school at 15 with no real education at all. But I just wanted to write, so I started writing about juicing and how I got into it. I wrote about addiction psychology, which was what I was studying. I write the way that I speak, because, who says you can't? When people tell themselves, "I can't do this, I can't do that," it's a struggle. But a mantra I live by is "no rules". Who says you can't write a book? My philosophy is, there's always another way.'

Jason has proved this time and time again. When he was told he couldn't write a book, he went and wrote a manuscript. When he was told he would never get published if he didn't have an agent, or if he didn't send in the three chapters and synopsis, he secured a publishing deal without an agent and by sending in the whole manuscript. When he was told he couldn't write a second book, he got creative and created the demand by approaching juicing companies and doing a deal that would lead to them purchasing thousands of books. He found another way to grow. Jason says:

'There is always another way. You've just got to believe in yourself. For example, if I wanted to get a hold of the CEO of a company today, I would send him/her a fax because no one else does it. There is always another way to get somebody's attention or achieve your goals.'

Jason says that his advisors are people who have been there and done it themselves: 'Sir Richard Branson is my advisor through his autobiographies. When you read Peter Jones' autobiography, or Duncan Bannatyne's, you learn and grow. If you want to study health, you study healthy people; if you want to study finance, you study financiers; and that's the best way forward. Branson once said, "Have fun and the money will come." There's a huge difference between achieving to be happy and happily achieving. Tony Robbins is also one of my huge mentors. And you put up a visualization: for 20 years I went, "Ah, wouldn't it be nice to speak on the same stage as him." In October 2016, I spoke with Tony at a major event.'

So who says you can't? With enough drive, with the right 'can do' attitude and self-belief, and with enough time invested into learning, you can develop your self and your business beyond what anyone else might think possible. A lot of it comes down to mindset.

Mastering your mind

Successful people often share this 'can do' attitude and growth mindset, and understand that there is no such thing as failure only feedback (as mistakes are useful learning tools which reveal how not to do things next time); however, personal development goals differ from person to person and are set individually. We each have our own strengths to develop, talents to top up and skills to learn.

We also each have our own unique set of beliefs, some of which might be limiting ones that prevent us from moving forward, and others which may serve us well and help us to achieve what we set out to. Often, personal development and self-growth involves working through any limiting beliefs that we may have and reframing how we think about an event, adversity or opportunity, so that we may replace those limiting beliefs with empowering ones.

There are many methods of doing this. From using Cognitive Behavioural Therapy (CBT) to practising mindfulness, from considering the mental mind chatter that you tell yourself and questioning negative thoughts, to incorporating meditation into your life. Just as, if you needed to become better at negotiating, you might read a book on negotiation, if you need to shift your beliefs to better serve you, you might read a book on any of the aforementioned strategies and practices. Because knowledge is power, whether it relates to how you run your business or how you live your life.

Another upside of personal development is that, through learning how to develop yourself, you will likely learn how to better manage stress and anxiety (a useful tool to have in your toolbox if you are juggling all that is involved in working for yourself). So, by committing to personal development and the stress management side of personal growth, you will carve out a healthier state of mind that will help you to run your business and make decisions. When we worry we are less able to make good decisions, so learning how to reduce anxiety is a skill worth investing in as a self-made entrepreneur.

Everyone has a different way of learning. Byron likes to listen, whether that's to an audio book in the car or to a specialist in their field: 'I travelled to Sweden recently to see leadership expert Brian

Tracy speak, in order to advance myself. I don't absorb it as much from the internet, so for me it's about meeting people, learning from the experts – the best in the business – and listening to audio books.' I also love listening to people and to audio books, but I find I absorb information better by watching videos or reading.

As you start and grow your business, set aside some time and money to invest in personal development books, attending workshops and conferences, and listening to other people who have been there, learned the lessons and are well placed to share those lessons with you.

So, a word of advice from Jason Vale:

'You can't sacrifice your nutrition and your exercise. You can't say "I was working late so I had a pot noodle again." You need to find balance. If you want your car to drive at its optimum then you need the right fuel, especially when you're building your business. So, when you are building a business, go for almost zero tolerance with alcohol, because you need to be razor sharp. You can't afford to celebrate every half kind of achievement. Don't celebrate the opening of your shop, because you haven't sold anything yet. Opening the shop isn't enough to make you go and get drunk and not come in the next day to serve the people who are going to pay for the shop. Have a glass of champagne to wet the baby's head, but you can't afford to not be clear-headed or to sacrifice your health. So take care of yourself with good nutrition and exercise.'

Mentoring

Experience is the name every one gives to their mistakes.

Oscar Wilde, writer and wit

Being self made can be a lonely existence if you bury your head in your business. At times, it can feel like nobody understands and that you have the whole world on your shoulders. But you are never alone. There are coaches and mentors who can help by being a sounding board for you to bounce ideas off, a shoulder to cry on, or a sympathetic ear and/or guiding voice. It can be comforting to have someone you can be open and honest with who isn't going to laugh at or patronize you but is there to listen to your good/bad/ugly stories. Jason Vale recalls:

'My biggest advisor was my mum. Her main advice to me from the age of six was never to moan, but instead to "turn your lemons into lemonade". And funnily enough, that's what we ended up doing: literally turning lemons into lemonade.'

As well as taking words of encouragement from your friends and family, you can and should build your own network. I have a network that I can go to and ask for help with this, and their opinions on that. It's a wide range of people with different skills, strengths and knowledge in a variety of industries. I'm still in contact with a few of the other contestants from *The Apprentice*. We keep in touch and support each other's businesses. Whilst filming they're not your friends, they're your competitors, but now we're not in a competitive environment, we can be friends and support each other. In business it's important to maintain relationships, because you never know when those people are going to be in a position to help you and you them.

In addition to your network, having a mentor can really help you to grow as a person and as a business. Both Byron and I mentor people, advising them and getting them thinking about their businesses. We also share insights from our own experiences, and introduce mentees to people who we think they would benefit from connecting with.

Indeed, we would encourage people to have one or two mentors, because as well as being a source of advice or learning, they will also have their own networks. So once you have a mentor you are opening up another network that allows you to benefit from a broader range of experiences.

Mentors also prevent you from making the mistakes that they made. They provide the valuable lessons that come from making mistakes, without your having to make the mistakes yourself.

From building confidence and helping to secure finance to providing key business contacts, business mentors can harness their wealth of experience to help you avoid mistakes, improve decision-making skills and develop the right mindset. Fundamentally a mentor should be seen as an essential asset to a self-made person.

Author of *The Motivated Mind*, Dr Raj Persaud even suggests that those with mentors are frequently 'more resilient to obstacles, willing to take risks, have greater self-belief, and are more aware of their own strengths and weaknesses.'[33]

Furthermore, a 2011 Startup Genome Report study[34] by Marmer, Herrmann and Berman of 650 startup firms in Silicon Valley found that mentors had a significant impact on firms' ability to raise money. Startup entrepreneurs without mentors, in contrast, 'almost always failed to raise funding'. The study concludes that 'the right mentors significantly influence a company's performance and ability to raise money'. They can do this by providing a trusted and credible 'face' and guidance through the process of applying for Government loan schemes. They may even be able to attend critical investor meetings and presentations, adding weight to your capital-sourcing cause.

The value of experience

The role of a mentor is not always to give advice though. Rather, a mentor should shadow and walk alongside their mentee, provide anecdotal evidence from their own experience and encourage the mentee to find their own solutions.

Mentoring is about finding someone you can trust who has been there before, walked that road and is willing to impart their knowledge and experience. It's a one-to-one relationship and two-way process to enable business owners to reach their full potential. The mentoring relationship should be a solid and trusting one which helps the mentee to think through for themselves how they would prefer to run their business, by occasionally leaning on someone who has already learned (perhaps the hard way) how to get things right. Mentors have faced and overcome all manner of obstacles and challenges. They've made mistakes and learned from them. As such, mentors can help you to avoid repeating those mistakes by suggesting tips and techniques based on specific questions, decisions and situations.

So what precisely should a good mentor do?

As well as being approachable, easy-to-contact, engaging, experienced, and knowledgeable; a good mentor will:

- Share professional wisdom, make strategic suggestions and warn of dangers and how to avoid mistakes.
- Inspire you to realize your potential and build your confidence, empowering you to reach your goals.
- Supply contacts and networks to further personal and business development
- Listen, question and gain an understanding of the business and the challenges it needs to overcome, and what is needed then to assist you, the business owner, to adapt to new skills, practise new behaviours and improve business performance.
- Facilitate decision-making by suggesting alternatives based on personal experience.

How to get the most from your mentor

1 **Plan.** It's important to map out how strategic goals will be achieved, monitored and measured.
2 **Define clear expectations.** Expectations from mentor and mentee should be addressed in terms of available time

allocated, tasks to complete, when to review and check-in with each other and sustain the two-way communication. How exactly will the relationship work? Will contacts be available? Create a perfect mentor profile regarding what you expect from your mentor and share it with them. The exact model utilized will depend on who the mentor is, whether they are backed by a mentoring organization, how formal the arrangement is, and so on. It's vital to understand exactly what your mentor will provide before entering into a contract to ensure your expectations will be met.

3 **Listen.** Mentors/mentees must both actively listen to each other.

4 **Go with your instincts.** 'Owning a business is very personal. It reflects our personality, drive and values and choosing a mentor that you trust, respect and get on with is critical,' advises entrepreneur, Penny Power. 'Many mentors have learned from their mistakes, not just their successes. Humility, openness and the desire to unconditionally help you to achieve your dreams should be obvious very early in the relationship between a mentor and their mentee.'

5 **Be patient.** Mentoring is a long-distance relationship rather than a quick sprint.

6 **Try reverse mentoring.** Mentoring isn't just about young people seeking advice from older, experienced people. Ask a tech-savvy member of Generation Y to mentor you on everything from tweeting to maximizing the capabilities of a smartphone.

7 **Use peer-to-peer networks.** These are invaluable to gain and give advice. Try a Mastermind group (Mastermind groups are designed to help you navigate through challenges using the collective intelligence of others), or attend local networking groups to find experienced people to talk to.

As a starting point in finding a mentor, visit www.selfmadebook.uk for an up-to-date list of online resources.

10

Taking Calculated Risks and Scaling Up

Growing a successful and sustainable business is a balancing act. And, as a self-made person, you will soon realize how much there is to balance: risk with reward; focus with flexibility; short-term targets with long-term strategies. You must balance what you spend with what you bring in, balance profitability and growth and even balance the internal insight you gain over time with external support from your mentor and network. Additionally, you'll need to balance optimistic and pessimistic financial assumptions to project your most-likely cash flow scenarios and continually be aware of the strengths and weaknesses, opportunities and threats, which apply to your business at any given time.

Balancing all of this as you grow is not an easy task. However, balancing is made easier by regularly reviewing, measuring and tracking results as you go. Assessing and evaluating what is working and what isn't, consistently reviewing what is going on in the marketplace and analysing risk on a monthly or quarterly basis is vital if you want to scale up successfully.

The good news is, you are small. This means you have agility and flexibility to adapt quickly whenever you need to.

In this chapter we'll explore the next level – growth. We've already looked at having a business idea and validating it, commercializing what you do by getting clear on your value proposition and go-to-market strategy, and then going about marketing and selling, and gaining and retaining customers. The next two phases in the life-cycle of a business are 'Scale' and 'Exit'.

If you are on track towards your ultimate destination, that is. For example if, following your plan defined in Chapter 1, you have built up a database of customers in the period of time you intended to, are generating a good level of custom and bolstering your network of contacts as each week passes, then you have proven your business model. There are a few main ways, therefore, in which you can grow:

- You can sell more of what you already sell to your existing customers.
- You can sell more of what you already sell to new customers
- You can increase the price of what you already sell.
- You can add more products/services to your offering.

However, you should only diversify with new products or services once your core areas of expertise are sound and secure. It's important not to move outside of your field too early. Doing so can be detrimental to your core business. Remember, your advantage is what you do uncommonly well, so you should continue to do that, always. However, you can add value to your offering by listening to your customers and to the competition, and keeping abreast of trends so that you may maximize any opportunities that come your way.

If you develop a habit of regular assessment, of doing a regular SWOT analysis, where you analyse your Strengths and Weaknesses (internal factors) alongside your Opportunities and Threats (external factors), you will be well placed to adapt where necessary, take calculated risks to seize opportunities and minimize threats and, by developing your strengths, you can counter your weaknesses.

It's crucial to work on the areas of your business that reap the best rewards and, in order to identify which products and customers those are, you need to review regularly. Otherwise you may end up being 'a busy fool'. That's something my dad used to advise me against. But often, when we start up in business, we become just that – a busy fool. I know I did. When I started my business and was trying to build the brand, I probably wasn't charging enough; financially it wasn't working out as I had expected, but I WAS busy. So I was thinking 'Yay! I'm busy' in one moment and then 'But is there any money? No, in the next. I realized I was being a busy fool. I wasn't running a charity, so I needed to do something about it. And I did: I limited what I did for free and upped my prices to reflect my value. And do you know what? People paid.

Risky business – analyse and assess risk

There are many pros and cons of being your own boss: perhaps one of the biggest cons is being completely responsible for making all the decisions. With that responsibility comes fear and overcoming that fear is one of the biggest challenges you will face as an entrepreneur. It's worth reading the best-selling book by Susan Jeffers, *Feel The Fear And Do It Anyway*.[35] The good news is, as you embrace the fear, step out of your comfort zone, take a risk and move forward with a decision, the fear lessens.

Making a decision means making progress instead of staying still and stagnating. You will either fail and learn from it, or you will succeed – either way, making that decision and taking that risk is moving forward.

Sometimes you just need to ask yourself what the worst-case scenario might be, then consider what the more likely scenario is. And remind yourself of all the stuff you've done that has been tough, the hardships you've faced, the obstacles you've overcome. You're still here. Proof that you can handle it.

That said, I tend to be quite risk-averse in terms of being very certain about an opportunity before I go ahead. I have to do the research. I need to feel that it is a solid proposition and that I'm definitely going to be ok, and I will only tend to take a risk if it is moving towards where I want to get to and I feel reassured by my research. Byron is the opposite. He'll look at the risk and assess it and then he'll just do it anyway. He will analyse the risk and find a less worrisome, more reassuring perspective. Even with staffing we have opposing approaches.

Byron explains: 'Let's say we have a product to sell, and a new salesperson is going to cost £18k. Instead of seeing it as £18k worth of risk for a new member of staff, I would now see that as £1500 per month. And if it doesn't work, what am I going to lose in three months? £4500 – does that mean they're not going to sell anything? No, they're surely going to sell something. So my estimate is that they're going to sell at least £700 worth which further reduces the risks. That's how I break down my decisions. It makes it less daunting. Furthermore, today there are a lot of freelancers and people you can hire per hour, so I would consider that as a plan B option. Anything is possible.'

It's helpful if you have someone to play devil's advocate and someone who is more of a risk taker. Sometimes, as a self-made person, you are both of those people and the battle goes on in your head.

I remember that happening when I took the risk to apply for *The Apprentice*. If I was edited badly or didn't represent myself adequately, I could end up ruining my reputation. Given that personal branding is my 'thing' I needed to ensure that, if I got on the programme, I led with integrity and showcased who I am.

Ultimately, for me, going on *The Apprentice* was scary, because there was so much to lose, but there was also so much to gain. That tends to be the case when it comes to risk. The higher the risk the more you have to lose. I could have done badly and been fired in week one, and some of my clients might not have wanted me to come back and deliver personal branding training. What would that have said about me? So it was a huge risk. And yet, 80,000 people apply, and I managed to be one of the people chosen. I could have won £250k and a business partnership with Lord Sugar. The risk was worth taking.

I remember receiving the call to say I was on the show. I was two years into running my own business and nobody knew I'd applied. (I thought there was no point sharing that until I knew whether or not I was going to be on the show.) The open-plan office isn't great for private calls, so I went into the toilet to take the call there. 'Bianca,' said the voice on the phone, 'We thought you were great, we'd love you to be on the show.' Even then I wasn't sure if they meant I was actually on the show or perhaps I would just be a stand in. They told me I was on the show.

At that moment the fear crept in. What if I messed up, got fired, or did something embarrassing. And then I realized what was more frightening than any of that – not trying in the first place, not grabbing this opportunity with both hands: passing it up and regretting doing so. And so on the show I went and came second. I presented myself well and impressed Karren Brady sufficiently that she said she was not surprised I was in personal branding as I had my own personal brand sorted out. That was a wonderful testimonial and, since the show, my personal branding business has continued to go from strength to strength.

If I'd let fear stop me from taking that opportunity, I would have missed out on a lot of subsequent opportunities. So now I feel the fear and do it anyway. Because that's how you move forward. You've got to invest in yourself and take risks in order to grow. As a self-made person you need to speculate to accumulate. That's a rule.

Byron has always seized opportunities and invited people in his network to join him. Those who are fearful of risk often see from the sidelines how, had they seized the opportunities he's offered to them, they might have been on their way to being millionaires by now.

'I'm now offering consultancy and a business in a box for my chauffeuring company and we're looking to franchise it,' explains Byron. 'Someone I've known for ten years called me but, as he doesn't take risks, he's not sure he wants to get involved in this so he wanted to talk it through. I explained to him that, if you are not willing to take risks, don't get into business. If you are completely risk-averse, I advise you to stay in your job, because you simply can't be in business and not take a risk every now and again. Being in business is a risk in itself.'

Byron reminded his risk-averse friend of an opportunity he'd not taken many years ago. 'I reminded him about a property I had available, just before the credit crunch in 2007. The property was in Purley and was selling for £200k which was quite pricey, at the luxury end of the market. He chose not to buy it because he didn't want to take the risk. He wanted to play it safe. Now it's worth around £450k. If he had taken that risk, he'd be £250k richer.'

Ultimately, the concept of business is that you speculate to accumulate. You speculate on where you think the business is going to accumulate income. Of course, it may not work out, but you have to speculate in order to accumulate and you don't start a business if you're not trying to accumulate wealth or change your life. As such, each day you're taking risks and trying something new – be it trying out a new sales campaign or a new member of staff... so you're constantly speculating.

If Byron hadn't taken the risk to buy a car and get into chauffeuring, he wouldn't be in the position he's in now – owner of a fleet of luxury vehicles and about to franchise his operation.

Byron spotted the opportunity when he was buying his own Range Rover. 'The guy I was buying it from had a number of luxury cars sitting in his driveway. The entrepreneurial spirit in me got curious about why he was not doing something with those cars.'

So Byron figured out that the only way he could persuade this guy to work with him was to prove that the concept worked. 'I invested in some marketing and the relevant insurances so I could demonstrate that this proposition worked. And four years later the company had progressed to owning a fleet of eight vehicles including two Rolls Royces. We also now have access to just short of a hundred vehicles. All from speculating, taking a calculated risk and seizing the moment.'

Jason Vale wouldn't be where he is today without having taken some risks. He sold places at his retreat and funded the construction before he had even built it, by taking a risk.

When he was 30 years old, Jason had what he called his 'sliding doors' moment. Writing a book had been outside of his comfort zone and, instead of just writing a few sample chapters, he bit the bullet and send the whole manuscript to a senior editor at Harper Collins. Within days, she rang him.

'When she told me she had my manuscript, I said, "Please read it… I know I probably should have done such and such but…" and she just said, "Shut up Jason. The reason I'm calling is because I was having a coffee and wondered what this big package was, so thought I'd just read the first four lines, and that was it, I was in. That hasn't happened to me in years. This is the best thing I've read on this subject in 25 years. You have to come in."'

Most people would agree there and then and scramble to get in to the publishers as quickly as possible, but Jason took a risk.

'I was trying to be cool, so I said to her "Oh that's really good, but Random House are interested," which of course they weren't, I hadn't sent it to anybody else. She said "Can we see you first? We'll make you an offer, please come in. What are you doing tomorrow?" And the rest, as they say, is history.'

Jason was made an offer and has published many more books since that first one. He seized the opportunity to take a risk. Since then he's gone on to sign long-term contracts to hire venues for retreats, when there is no guarantee he'll be able to fill them but, again, the risk has paid off and he maintains almost full occupancy.

Of course, sometimes you make mistakes, but you learn from them. Jason says:

'The biggest mistake I ever made was not keeping ownership of the special sale with the Moulinex deal, and sharing it with the publisher. But all mistakes are beneficial as they help you to learn.'

'Business is like a game of snakes and ladders. You just need to make sure there are more ladders than snakes and you win; that's it,' he adds. 'Because there are going to be snakes you're going to fall down, but you don't panic, you just realize that a snake is smaller than the ladder, find the next ladder and back up you go. You can't aim for perfection, because there is no such thing. You allow for your setbacks, because they're what makes you grow. You never know what a good day is without a bad day; therefore you can never know what a bad deal is if you've constantly had good deals, they just shape whoever you are.'

'You've got to know that you'll handle the worst situations. Even my girlfriend and I have got what we call our "beach hut jacket potato exit scenario". If everything went wrong and we lost everything and we ended up on beach eating a couple of jacket potatoes, we know we would be okay with that. So as you go along, it's important to try to stay grounded as to why you're doing it. Take risks, find out what's working, and, if it's not working, find the ladder: change your approach, that's the key.'

You may have heard the phrase 'Outside of your comfort zone is where the magic happens', and this is true. If you've invested in your own personal development (see Chapter 9) you will likely improve your ability to step out of your comfort zone. This can have a huge positive impact on your business.

Jason has stepped out of his comfort zone multiple times and found the magic. And, if he's made mistakes, he's always learned from them and taken a different approach.

You've got one life, one chance; is it worth NOT taking the risk?

Alesha Dixon too has had the courage to shake things up, rather than rest on her laurels. Stepping out of your comfort zone, while risky, can generate great rewards. Alesha says:

'When I made the choice to leave *Strictly Come Dancing* as a judge, it wasn't because I didn't love the show, I absolutely love the show, and still do. Something instinctively told me, three years is a really respectable amount of time to do that show. Don't pigeonhole yourself into that box, it's time to try new things, spread your wings, open up more opportunities and new ventures, so I made a very difficult decision. But it felt like the right thing to do was to move on.'

And so it was. Alesha moved onwards and upwards to become a guest judge on *Britain's Got Talent* and branch out into fashion, whilst continuing her music career too. Alesha explains:

'What it does is it freshens your brand. Every now and then you have to throw something into the mix that a) surprises people, b) creates a talking point, c) shows a different side of you, and d) helps you grow as an individual, otherwise you become stagnant in what you're doing.'

'It was the same when I left Mis-teeq. That was one of the most difficult decisions I've ever made in my life, but it just felt right,' she says. 'So, I always use the analogy of a chessboard, and I listen to this voice within me that I'm connecting to that says, "Right, time to make your next move. Time to move on".'

'I use my instinct a lot. Essentially, my theory is, regardless of whether the decision is right or not, it probably always will be right, because you made it and, if it wasn't for you, there was a lesson to be learned that will help you with your next venture or your next business decision to better understand: What can I change? What can I now do better?'

Stepping out of your comfort zone enables you to feel more comfortable with risk-taking and, if your business gets into difficulties, you are more likely to make some bold power moves in order to save it.

Power moves

Power moves are about changing the way you do things, especially if your current methods aren't working. It's all about being as effective as possible. If you are ever faced with potentially closing your business or letting staff members go, you can end up making really interesting decisions you may not have made had you not been in that desperate situation. Those decisions may end up saving your business or pushing it forward in a big way. Any successful business owner will have made a power move or two during their career and, once they've done it once they may realize that this is something they should be doing in their business every single day (instead of waiting for the bad stuff to hit the fan).

'Fundamentally, a power move is about making effective decisions that are going to benefit your business today, tomorrow and for months to come,' explains Byron. 'Decisions that will have the greatest positive impact.'

A power move involves stepping away from your desk and emails, and out of the comfort zone of your normal day-to-day process. This means being ambitious and doing something out of the ordinary, such as approaching a celebrity for an endorsement. It means doing something that could have a massive impact on your business.

The problem is, people often wait until things aren't going well before taking action and making power moves. But if you are constantly asking: 'What do I need to do to enhance my business and make my business better?' (which isn't sitting there answering emails or phone calls by the way), you will reap greater rewards.

It's important to constantly assess what is working well and what isn't. Remember, if you keep turning the same handle, you'll get the same result.

So, from time to time, you'll need to address some difficult questions. For example:

- How could your product be improved? This doesn't mean changing it for the sake of it, if it's selling like hot cakes. There's no point fixing what isn't broken; however, it's important to seek ways in which it could be improved, as genuine enhancements can bolster sales.
- Is your pricing competitive?
- Are you making an acceptable margin?
- Is there a demonstrable need and sufficient demand?
- Do you have loyal and reliable customers?
- Does anything need to change?
- Where are the gaps that need filling?

By assessing and analysing your current position, key themes and opportunities should become clear. What is your competitive advantage? Do you have sufficient resources to capitalize on this opportunity? What about your online strategy? Is anything missing?

'People get so bogged down in the day to day,' adds Byron. 'If you list ten things that you do normally on a typical day, nine of those probably don't generate income. Power moves are actions and decisions that amplify your value and focus on the one thing that brings in money. Rate everything you do, based on how much it will impact your business, from one to ten. Anything lower than a nine, don't do it on a power move day. Instead focus on the tens.

It's all about prioritizing based on what activities will have the most positive effect on your business.

Business growth: understand and listen to your customers and the market

One of the best ways to figure out which activities are going to have the most impact on your profit is to have an open dialogue with your customers and suppliers. The insight you gain from those who are already buying from and working with you is so valuable.

When it comes to selling more of what you already sell, increasing prices and adding more products/services to your existing offering – the main ways to scale your business up – customer insight is critical. In finding out exactly what your customers want, you can fill the gaps in your existing offerings. In finding out how you can improve what you offer, you can tweak it and subsequently sell more and charge more. Furthermore, this insider information will help you to sell more of what you currently sell to new customers. By understanding the benefits and language that produce the best customer response, you can roll these out in your communications with potential new customers.

Working out how you can best serve your customers is your route to scalability. It could be that you need to collaborate with someone else who already offers what your customer is asking you for, perhaps by entering into a joint venture, or you may be able to source whatever they want and sell directly to them. The other bonus of branching out, once your core business is stable and growing, is that you aren't putting all of your eggs in one basket.

Through addressing underserved market sectors and identifying any unmet needs that your customers have in this space, you can create a winning strategy for growth. If you can satisfy demand, exceed customer expectations, do something better, cheaper, faster or safer than the next business, you'll be in pole position for growth. Figuring out improved value propositions will really enable you to gain competitive advantage.

Growth via collaboration

Partnerships often pave the way on the road to growth. In fact, most super successful enterprises don't operate without one kind of alliance or another. It all comes down to leverage. Another company may have access to a market that you wish to gain a foothold in, and you may have some core competencies that this other company could benefit from. Together you can pull on each other's strengths to overcome your weaknesses and promote your mutual growth. It is in this way that collaborative partnerships fuel growth and enable enterprises to get into markets where they had no previous presence, fill gaps where there is demonstrable demand and pool resources to test new markets and extend reach. By contributing strengths and resources to a collaborative project, you can share the risk and skyrocket past the competition as you reach more of your target audience.

According to Accenture, most Fortune 500 companies have an average of 50–70 alliances each.[36] No wonder, given that collaboration is a tried-and-tested way to maximize opportunity whilst minimizing risk and investment.

By being more open to sharing resources you gain access to more talent, more customers and more ideas. Having conversations with other enterprises for mutual benefit is a strong strategy that is worth pursuing. There are all kinds of ways to enter into a strategic alliance with another business. You can form a revenue-share partnership where you each take an even slice of the rewards of your collaborative efforts. This is also how a joint venture works, although this involves setting up a new business or project where you share the risk and cost, and pool resources together in order to achieve a mutually beneficial objective. Other ways to reach a wider market could involve some form of licensing partnership where you give each other permission to distribute each other's material, and also a franchising model, where people pay you to run their own franchise of your business.

Whichever strategic alliance you opt for, there needs to be a clear and fair win–win for each party. If the other business has a wider reach and bigger audience, what can you bring to the table that is equally beneficial to them? Perhaps you have the technology or the product? Maybe you have the market intelligence and they have the office infrastructure? Either way, it must be clear from the outset how the value is shared and the relationship is equal and fair. If one company is set to gain at the expense of the other, the commitment and effort won't be aligned and the collaborative partnership could break down.

Jason Vale knew instinctively that a powerful way to boost his book sales would be to partner up with a juicer manufacturer. After all, his advocacy of juicing had helped grow the market for juicers and people were buying Breville and Moulinex products as a result, yet he wasn't receiving anything from them. In order to establish such a partnership, he had to hustle. Jason recalls:

'Moulinex, that's the first juicer I ever used, so I called their head of marketing. I said, "I'm the Juice Master." He said, "Sorry, who are you, what are you talking about?" I told him I'd sold loads of juicers for him, thanks to my book and told him I had a new book coming out. (I didn't).'

Jason told him that the first one has done so well that the publisher was asking him to write another one immediately. 'I was economical with the truth for greater good,' admits Jason. 'But that's hustling for a good purpose – to help improve people's health – so I don't see it as lying,' he smiles.

Jason told the marketing executive that his next call would be to Breville and was invited in for a meeting to show them his plans. When he realized that he felt like he was pitching to them (and subsequently losing them) he realized he needed to pull something out of the bag. And so he did.

'I'm putting my name on the juicer,' Jason told them. 'I've got two other companies that are crying for me to put my name on their juicer; the book's coming out with one of the biggest publishers in the world and its going to be translated into umpteen lanugages. They wouldn't let me leave the room and suggested we sit down and work something out.'

Some time later, the phone rang and it was Moulinex asking what he was looking for. Despite feeling out of his depth and making it all up as he went along, Jason piped up, 'Signing on fee, obviously.'

'I said, "I want my book in with the juicer, I'm happy to put it in free of charge. You pay the publisher for the book. I want

£30,000 signing on fee, and I'm going to need an advance obviously and I want 3 per cent of every unit sold." '

An hour later, Jason received the call which informed him he'd get £20k plus 2 per cent of every juicer sold, plus his name on the juicers, which would go into the Argos catalogue.

This collaboration then gave him huge leverage with publishers who were more than happy to commission his next book. This was the first step towards turning Jason into a household name – a real collaborative POWER MOVE!

TOP TIPS TO COLLABORATE EFFECTIVELY

1 Find windows of opportunity by identifying gaps you might fill for others and gaps in your own offering that others might fill. Do your homework to source potential partners.

2 Find the mutual bridge. Research to find companies with customers in the target market you wish to gain traction in and, from their point of view, consider how you might become the bridge for them to reach your target market.

3 Ask your customers to become match-makers. Can they introduce you to potential partners? Explain your goals and see if they can help.

4 Match values. Check that prospective partner companies share your values and are the kind of people that you fit well with.

5 Define objectives and rules from the outset to ensure the partnership is mutually beneficial. Be clear about what you expect from the partnership and how effort and shared results should be equal.

6 Understand the win–win motivations within the partner-ship and consider constantly how you can help them to suc-ceed in achieving their objectives. 'You shouldn't be scared of people in your category,' advises Jason Vale. 'In fact, the ones in your category are the ones that you should collabo-rate with, not be nervous of.'

7 Share your vision. Be honest and open about your SWOT (Strengths, Weaknesses, Opportunities and Threats) and encourage them to do the same.
8 Keep it legal. Have a written agreement in place which defines objectives, duration of the venture, expected commitment of each party, intellectual property ownership and defines how, if disputes arise, they would be resolved (e.g. via a mutually agreed mediator).

Knowing when to grow, when to hire people, when to partner with people in a collaborative way and whether to outsource or retain control can be a tough decision.

However, outsourcing and/or collaborating can be a really healthy way to grow organically at a pace that suits you. You may have reached a point where you can no longer do everything yourself but you may not have the space or money to expand your business. In those circumstances, you may need to seek out partners and outsource to those who are of a similar type and reputation. Outsourcing can be key in growth cycles and, once you get to a certain level and it is financially viable to do things inhouse again – with a larger team and more resources – you can stop outsourcing.

For example, Byron's chauffeuring company is now firmly established, and he has started moving from outsourcing in order to maintain a fleet to buying more cars. In this way, he is able to retain more control. Byron explains: 'We own a small fleet and we hire the rest; however, by outsourcing we have less control of what is available to book and how much to charge. As such I've taken a risk and bought another vehicle, as this means we have a greater degree of control over the fleet. This has allowed the company to bring things back inhouse and grow more quickly, but there isn't one answer to knowing when is the right time to grow.' Some say you should be bursting at the seams before you commit to growth; others say you should speculate to accumulate earlier than you might think and take the risk to enable rapid growth. There isn't a right answer – it depends on the business.

We've done the same thing with staffing sometimes, where we didn't want to take the risk and have hired freelancers. Then, once we are able to, we employ a full-time member of staff. Using freelancers until we are financially able to bring that service inhouse has worked really well for us.

Essentially it all comes back round to balance – finding the right balance between the position you are in and the position you are striving for, and outsourcing and partnering collaboratively until you have the necessary resources to scale up.

Part 4: The Evolution

As an entrepreneur, it's important that you are able to strike a healthy balance between running your company and taking the time to enjoy the benefits. In Part 4, we'll look at how to achieve that balance and how to manage your time. At this point, it's also a good idea to check on your progress — is the business going well or are there improvements to be made? If you have intellectual property, we'll advise you on how to protect it, and we'll hear from trademark expert Oliver Oguz. Finally, at the end of the business cycle, we'll discuss when and how to sell up and move on.

11

Reality Check As Challenges Arise

Finding balance

Within a few weeks of being your own boss, it will dawn on you: everything takes longer and costs more than you thought it would. You'll also realize that it is very difficult to switch off at the end of a working day. You may have more flexibility and freedom than ever before, but that comes at a price. Now that you have escaped the nine-to-five rat race and are back in control of your own working life, you care more. And that means you don't tend to stop at 5pm, because this is YOUR business and your life. So you'll find yourself checking your emails at midnight, working on writing a piece of website copy at 10pm and generally thinking about your business constantly. That is the reality of being self made – like your life, your business is what you make it, so you need to be devoted and it is difficult to be anything less.

Finding balance can be a challenge. That said, you DO have the freedom to move periods of working time around so, let's say you have the opportunity to see a play on a Wednesday afternoon, or maybe the sun is shining and friends are meeting for lunch; you get to do these things – you get to do whatever you like – but you will need to make up the time (because your time is money) later on. That's why working in the evenings isn't so bad, because you may have downed tools at 3pm to collect your child from school and are starting back up once they are in bed – giving you and them the best of both worlds.

So what are the other challenges and obstacles that you will face on your journey to becoming self made and successful?

The price is right (or wrong?)

Pricing is a key challenge for most small business owners. Knowing what to charge can be really tough. In fact, most entrepreneurs have a tendency to undercharge at first. It's difficult to know what customers will be willing to pay or how much they value what you're providing them with. With uncertainty, comes fear and lack of confidence. And then you find yourself in the loop of desperation where you think 'I'd rather secure this amount than nothing' and so you agree to do the work for less than you know you are worth, or price a product for less than you know it's worth.

When you start out, you think you need every single customer in order to survive. This fear results in your being too afraid to ask for too much, in case the customer says 'too expensive' and you end up with nothing. The fear of pricing yourself out of the market leads to undervaluation of what you offer and a price lower than your customers would actually be happy to pay.

Ultimately, if you are providing a service or product that is useful – has real value – to someone, undercharging gives off the signal that it is not that valuable. You need to set an appropriate price which reflects the true value of your offering. Quality costs. Many people demand top quality at top speed for a low price, but you need to explain to them that something has to give: they can either have something fast, but it won't be as good quality or they can wait a little longer to get something top quality. This helps people see the value in a quality provision.

Again, it's all about balance. You don't want to charge people less than they are willing to pay and you don't want to charge them way more than they can afford. But you should never assume what someone can afford. Instead focus on your value, on the value of what you are providing, how it will positively impact the customer and how valuable it is to them.

The right price is one which is competitive enough that your prospect won't go elsewhere, but with enough profit margin to help you to grow your business. It should reflect the true market value (and value to the customer) of what you are providing in terms of quality and quantity.

When someone says 'that's too expensive' (and they will), instead of immediately dropping the price, explain why you charge what you charge. You may end up compromising, depending on how much you want or need the business, but you may not have to.

Sometimes, when you have check your actual income and realize that your projected turnover was way too optimistic, it's easy to make the assumption that you've got your pricing wrong. But that isn't always the reason.

Says Lisa Barber, a marketing coach who runs 'kitchen table' workshops for small business owners:

'When customers aren't buying, many people find themselves assuming that price is the big issue. They start offering on-the-spot discounts, maybe they take their prices off their website or begin luring clients in with freebies, only to find they can't sustain a viable business this way. However, if you're offering a valuable service, something people already know that they want and need, whether or not you're too expensive isn't usually your biggest barrier. Instead, you need to focus on lowering the risk for people taking the next step.'

And therein lies the key – it's about removing the risk for the customer, some of which will have nothing to do with price.

'They might be worried about whether they'd fit in at your retreat, or they might worry about not getting the results you promise on your website,' adds Lisa.

So the barrier to buying often comes from something else. If they are worried about risking their money and being unsure about the results they'll get, a 'money-back guarantee' may be enough to reassure them.

They may also simply need to know a bit more about you – to understand your 'why', and get a feel about where you are coming from. So be transparent about your story and also about your prices.

Fundamentally, we shouldn't assume what our customers can or cannot afford, or assume that the reason they aren't buying is purely down to pricing our products or services too high.

So before reducing prices (and profits), it's important to consider how you might reduce the risk and make it safer for people to move forward and buy from you. We've already discussed using testimonials from existing customers to reassure prospective customers and allay their concerns. Writing a blog is another way to become more relatable and convey how your audience would fit right in with you.

Lisa also recommends honesty about who you don't wish to serve:

'Be very transparent about who you *won't* be a fit for. People will admire your integrity and appreciate the honest approach. Incorporate video blogs into your marketing – this helps people gauge whether there is likely to be a connection and makes it safer for them to contact you for support. This is especially relevant if you are asking people to commit to paying you for something before they've actually met you in person.'

'Another technique to de-risk buying from you is to provide something really valuable for free that potential clients can download,' adds Lisa. 'That gives them a really genuine taste of who you are and how you work.'

Jason Vale agrees:

'Smart marketing includes that old adage "speculate to accumulate", so give something for free. You do this when you say "How can I add value?". For example, when asked what fee I would charge to do a talk with Tony Robbins, I said, "I'll do this work for free." They replied, "Seriously?" And I told them I am selective about my talks and I'd be honoured to share the stage with Tony Robbins. The only condition was that I could give everybody a free book. They could see I was adding value. Now, with 3000 people attending, it would cost me £6000 to do this talk, but that's smart marketing. Because, all of a sudden, I'm my own best sales tool. I'll be on stage in front of 3000 people and give them a book. I won't sell anything from the stage. I won't tell them about the retreat. I will just give them value on stage. If they choose to read the book, which includes details of our app and retreat, there's a high chance they'll book or download or buy something else from me. Jason adds: 'I don't think people like a hard sell, but they do like value.'

The bottom line is, there's no single surefire way to price your products perfectly. There's a lot to think about: you need to know your own costs (materials, labour, operating expenses, debt service costs, salaries, and so on) and add a percentage on top, and you need to talk to target customers and consider their demographics and buying choices (i.e. are they budget hunters or premium purchasers for whom status and longevity are more critical?). You also need to track what competitors are charging, and understand what the market is willing to pay, and you must understand your own revenue targets and perception of your brand in that market. Finally, you have to consider quality level and how quickly you can get your product into customers' hands.

That said, it's generally better to overprice than underprice, because at least then you can bring your prices down if you find out that they really are too high.

Other people

Delegation can be a huge challenge to the sole trader who has, until now, performed every single task themselves. You want everything to be done well, and yet, in order to grow, you need to let go.

Therefore it's important for you, as a self-made person, to think of recruiting others as a way to fill in the gaps in your own skillset; to create a jigsaw of pieces that fit well together (because of their shared values) but which each have different talents.

People will soon be your greatest asset and it is the retention of these people that enables a smooth journey towards your vision, reduces the associated staff turnover costs of re-recruiting and retraining and ultimately assures the current and future value of your company.

The human factor creates far more value than processes or procedures because, put simply, valued people deliver value. Good staff take care of your customers who take care of your business. It's as simple as that.

There are two fundamental rules when it comes to other people and your business:

1 You need to find the right people.
2 You need to hold on to them.

Your staff will help you to make things happen and reach your destination. They represent your brand and create value. Conversely, people who don't fit into your organization, who don't put in the effort and who don't represent your brand well, are expensive.

Good staff enable you to step back from the operational side so that you can devote more time to working ON the business instead of just IN the business. This means you get to plan, explore strategy, set up partnerships and commit to growing the business rather than simply delivering the goods.

Taking on people to join you in your entrepreneurial quest can be one of the biggest challenges. Indeed, finding and retaining good people, is never easy.

As Jason Vale points out:

'Laying the foundations of a building often takes longer than putting up the building itself. The same is true of business. The magical part of business, for me, is when the business no longer owns you, you own it. The biggest challenge in getting to that point is climbing the first few rungs of the business ladder. Once you've done that, you gain momentum and everything seems to fall into place.'

'The biggest hurdle is making the transition from being a sole trader, where you're doing all the roles yourself, to being an employer. Having the confidence to move to the next stage, when you employ your first member of staff, is hard. You may be thinking "I can't afford to take them on", but actually, can you afford *not* to take them on? Because, if that person generates at least 20 per cent more than they cost you, they are worthwhile. You need to take that leap of faith, because employing staff actually frees you up to do what you need to do.'

However, employing the right people is just one part of the challenge, and retaining them is also tricky, but the hardest part of all is if you hire the wrong person.

'That's quite easy to do, because during interviews, candidates often present what I call an "Instagrammed" version of themselves,' smiles Jason.

So how do you deal with that as a new business owner who needs good people around you?

'I always say to somebody when I am interviewing them, "You look great on paper, you sound good in front of me, but if you're about to leave your job and you've been there for five years, don't blame me in a month's time if I get rid of you. Because, if you're everything that you say you are, you are the only person who can get you fired".'

As such it's important to ask people what mistakes they've made in the past and how they've learned from them. Encourage honesty as much as you can. Try to get to know the real person.

Mark Hobbs of New Leaf Distribution Ltd agrees that employing people is the biggest, yet most worthwhile risk that you can take in your journey to becoming self made. Mark says:

'If you're going to be a sole self-employed person, then you'll be working on your own forever and that's like walking through treacle. That transformation between a self-employed guy or girl and a business owner is about being brave enough to make the best recruitment happen, because, if you wait until you can afford it, you'll never do it.'

Sometimes, as Mark reveals, you need someone to tell you to hire that first person. Maybe, if you don't have someone close by, you've got us, through the pages of this book suggesting you do so. And maybe Mark's story will encourage you too:

'I was sharing an office with seven different businesses; that's how I started, having a corner of this office. I was working seven days a week with this semi-retired guy called Tony. One day, he pulled me to one side and said, "Mark, this has got to stop. If you don't sort yourself out and start delegating, you're going to die. You're alone and you will not make it." He told me that he had overheard me talking about recruiting a head of sales, or at least a trainer, for my business. I told him that I couldn't really afford to. That's when he replied, "Look, if you don't you're finished, so do it. Pick up the phone and recruit someone now." I protested, "I can't afford it," to which he replied, "You can't afford not to. You will work yourself out." In that moment, because of his experience, I embraced him and did what he said; I took on a member of staff, and you know what? The business took off. Because the moment you let go of things you're not so good at and you delegate things away to people who are awesome, things start to happen and flourish and grow. It's the other people who make all the difference.'

But how do you recruit the right people in the right role at the right time?

- Think balance and diversity. Your team should consist of people who can cover all the key competencies and functions required throughout the growth phase and beyond. Which areas of expertise do you need to take your business to the next level? It is wise to hire with your aspirations in mind so, if you want to take your business into foreign markets, employ someone who has experience of doing so. It is also wise to hire a diverse team of people from different backgrounds with different perspectives, so they can bring a range of approaches to the table.

- Be clear about your values and seek people who share them. This will help you to create a positive culture and a team of people who enjoy coming to work.
- Don't hire people who are just like you. Whilst it is helpful to have some commonalities in terms of shared values and vision, you need people who complement your skillset rather than duplicate what you and your existing team can already do.
- Consider different types of staff depending on how constant the work is, how long it will last and the number of working hours required. For example, as well as full- and part-time permanent staff, you might also hire temporary staff, self-employed freelancers and people on zero-hours contracts. The latter aren't obliged to accept work just as you are not obliged to offer it, but they can come in useful if you have seasonal busy points but don't wish to commit to regular hours.
- Define each role with absolute clarity so that you can match people with the positions you have available. A clear job description and person specification will help you to streamline the recruitment process by attracting only suitable applicants with the right skills and attitudes.
- Showcase the business personality in the job description too. As well as the job title, hours, location, salary, a clear summary of what responsibilities the role entails, and the key objectives, expectations and milestones, also include your company's values and mission statement. By highlighting your 'why' for being in business, you can relate to applicants' own personal motivations.
- Ask contacts to recommend people and look on LinkedIn for suitable applicants. You can advertise jobs on LinkedIn and on job sites. You can also search online databases of CVs and post your ad on relevant websites. Alternatively, you can use a recruitment or headhunting agency, and you can find low-cost freelancers on peopleperhour.com and elance.com.
- Choose wisely. When deciding whether or not to hire someone, review their track record and experiences as well as their abilities and skills.

- Ask questions about what motivates your candidates? Is it money, independence, teamwork, responsibility, recognition, security? What results have they achieved personally and how have they overcome obstacles or corrected mistakes in the past?
- Consider using psychometric testing to define candidates' personality types.

Once you've found the right people you want to ensure that they stay with you for as long as possible. So how exactly do you do that? The simple answer is that you keep them happy, you keep them secure and you reward them sufficiently. It's important to consider all the needs of your employees, not just their financial compensation.

Generally, talent retention comes down to cultivation, inclusion and motivation.

- **Talent cultivation and inclusion.** Develop potential by providing the right tools and an energizing environment that encourages ideas and innovation. Nurture talent by listening to people, valuing them and including them. The way that Byron and I see it is that people are like plants. If you want to cultivate them and help them to flourish, you need to water the shoots of their ideas, encourage their growth with the right support and provide the right environment to enable them to reach their potential. If you do that, they are likely to stay with you and grow with you and, in doing so, help your business to flourish too. So listen to your staff's ideas, engage them in conversation, create an open-plan environment where you, as their leader, are approachable, and communicate regularly to see which areas of their talent they are keen to develop further, then give them the opportunities to do so.
- **Talent motivation.** Find out what makes each person tick and then motivate them with suitable incentives and rewards. Well-treated staff treat customers well and work better for the business (and stay working for the business). Furthermore, according to recent studies, the level of interest from management in an individual's well-being is

said to be the most engaging and motivating factor of all, even above pay or career development. As well as motivating staff, showing that you care about their well-being can decrease the number of sick days taken, reducing downtime and sick pay. You also need to know what motivating factors staff will respond best to. Is it peer recognition? Is it level of responsibility? Or is it being provided with room and opportunities to grow? Understanding whether it is the nature of the work (level of interest and communication, culture and environment) that motivates them, or whether your staff are driven by financial security, recognition, appreciation and awards, or personal achievement and development, will help you to incentivize them accordingly.

Where does the time go?

Lack of time is constantly cited as a major barrier to business success. Indeed, not having enough hours in the day is a persistent problem for small business owners. And yet, to run your business effectively, you need time and energy. Without large teams to delegate tasks to and no PA to help with scheduling and prioritizing (at least at first), it can be tough to make the optimum use of our time, enabling us to take time out to recharge our batteries.

> Time is the coin of your life. It is the only coin you have, and only you can determine how it will be spent. Be careful lest you let other people spend it for you.
>
> *Carl Sandburg, poet*

Fundamentally, when it comes to running your own small business, time is money. Yet, as all business owners will know, everything generally ends up taking longer than you think it will. We are, by the very nature of running a small business, jugglers: juggling time, tasks and priorities.

That's why good time management is so important for a self-made person who has so much to do and so little time. Yet, before we can look at how to manage our time, we need to understand that two types of time exist for us all.

First, there's clock-based time where there are 60 seconds in one minute, 60 minutes in one hour and 24 hours in one day, and so on and so forth. Then there's relative time, which is all about perception. We've all had that experience where time seems to fly because we've been so engaged in our tasks that we haven't noticed a whole day has passed. On the hand, waiting to pay a cheque in at a bank, when you are in a hurry, can often feel like you've been standing in the queue for half an hour rather than only five minutes. So time can drag or it can fly by, depending on what we're doing. Most time management strategies focus on clock-time rather than relative time − how we experience time. We have no control over clock-time, but we can alter our perceptions of time: feeling that we don't have enough of it, or now is not the right time to do this or that. As a self-made person, your mindset really matters, from having that 'can-do' attitude, to changing how you think about time and seizing the moment. Because the time to achieve is now. *Carpe diem*!

And, as a self-made person, although you may need to be reactive to interruptions from time to time, you should be as proactive as possible in order to carve out enough time to do all that you need to do.

Mark Hobbs of New Leaf Distribution believes that time is our most valuable asset and should be cherished. And yet, he realizes that when you start out on your route to becoming self made, you sacrifice time that you would normally spend with others to work on your business and, given that time is your biggest asset, you need to do that at first. However, these days Mark teaches the notion of merge theory in relation to compartmentalization. Mark says:

'Most people have to use compartmentalization in their business, i.e. very distinct finite time zones for what they do, whereas I merge everything into my life. For example, I like motorbikes and going to the theatre, so I'll combine a business trip with my love of both. I'll always ride my motorbike anyway if I can, and I'll take my wife and go to the theatre while I'm in a place doing business. The trick is to merge it all in.'

The time is now: make the most of it

1 Keep a time diary in which you monitor where your time goes each day and week. Assess how much time you spend generating actual results and how much time you spend on conversations, actions and thoughts that don't serve you so well.

2 Prioritize what is the most important. Focus on the tasks that have the most impact. Trim down your to-do list to include between three to five top priority tasks to complete each day, using the Pareto Principle, aka the 80/20 rule. An economist, Pareto observed that 80 per cent of land in Italy was owned by 20 per cent of the population; the Pareto Principle suggests that it is 20 per cent of our efforts which brings in 80 per cent of our rewards, so 20 per cent of our customers bring in 80 per cent of our income. So:

- Schedule in time for highest-priority highest-impact power move actions, conversations and thoughts. (You do need to give yourself time to think as an entrepreneur. Often, this can be mixed together with time to walk and move around, as your cognitive ability improves with exercise.)

- Examine which 20 per cent of your customers are bringing in the most revenue by looking back over your annual sales figures. It could be specific customers or specific customer groups (e.g. hairdressers or parents of children under the age of four, or people based in a certain location). You then know who to focus your promotional activities on and who to contact to see if they are ready to buy from you again or refer business your way.

- Furthermore, you can look at which of your activities are generating the most income or highest ROI (return on investment), whether that's networking, gaining PR coverage, making follow-up calls or updating your website. Prioritize your tasks based on which will result in the most positive impact for you and your business. Eliminate tasks which bring little monetary benefit to the business.

- Preparation is everything. Use mind maps to jot down your key projects and most effective actions and tasks, then plot that information into an annual and daily planner. By investing time in planning your day/week/month/year, you will be able to use your time more efficiently. Aim to devote at least half of each day to proactive actions, conversations and thoughts that are likely to generate the best results.

3 Focus by allocating bursts of time for certain tasks. Work on your prioritized tasks for at least 45–60 minutes at a time and get rid of other distractions while you concentrate on completing each of the three top priority tasks on your list. Switch off your Skype and instant messaging, step away from Facebook and close your email account, or any other distractions during that set time. If you really must, once that 45–60-minute period is up, go and check your social media/emails. Then get back into the zone and focus for another chunk of time.

4 Schedule in certain tasks each day to avoid them interfering with your prioritized ones. So, for example, plan your social media activity at the most effective times of day. According to Bitly the best times to post on social media sites are generally first thing in the morning and then from 6–8pm GMT. Find out your most responsive time to post based on the engagement your posts generate and, if it's from 8–10am and 6–8pm, avoid going on Facebook in between those times. The same applies with emails. Schedule in time to check and respond to your emails in the morning, at lunch time and again at the end of the day, not continuously hitting the send/receive button as most people generally do.

5 Use technology to track where you might be losing time. For example, www.rescuetime.com informs you which websites or programmes you spend the most time on, so that you can address any time-wasting. There is also a tool which restricts the time you spend on Facebook: www.facebooklimiter.com. Try www.evernote.com to jot down whatever is on your mind and create online notebooks for different topics. You can even clip together articles you find to read later.

6 Reduce unproductive time. Cut back on face-to-face meetings that may be unnecessary and improve your scheduling. Have meetings online using gotomeeting.com or Skype rather than spending time getting to a meeting, parking the car, having the meeting and returning to your workplace.

7 Declutter, plan and get organized. Reduce the amount of time you spend looking for files, searching for paperwork, hunting for your keys/wallet/bag. Dedicate an hour this week to organizing your computer files into relevant folders, deleting emails and saving important ones in relevant folders, filing paperwork in specific folders and creating a dedicated space for your keys and wallet where you always put them without fail. Know where things are.

- List your key objectives before you make each call or perform each task. This will keep you focused on what you aim to attain.
- Dedicate time to emails and messages rather than responding immediately to every message. Only give people your immediate attention when it is business critical.

Time is money, and people are your most valuable assets, but so are the products of your creativity. Therefore, just as you should do what you can to protect your time and look after your staff, it's important to also protect your business and the creative assets that you build up over time.

Protecting your business

Once expressed, our creations – every single product that is conceived – become our intellectual property. Ideas or concepts aren't protected, but the expression of those ideas or concepts is. So, products, technical solutions and new inventions are protected by patents and design rights; literary, artistic, dramatic and musical works are protected by copyright; and brand names, words, sounds and even smells are protected by trademarks (a Danish perfume company has trademarked 'the smell of freshly cut grass' for its tennis ball spray product).

This means that your own designs, logo, software, brand, and packaging should be protected. These 'outputs of creativity' can become tangible commodities, the rights of which can be sold, traded, licensed, divided or retained.

And, with digitization reducing duplication and distribution costs and making it easier for other people to copy and distribute your work as their own, it's more important than ever before to protect your creative output. If you fail to protect it, there is nothing stopping a larger company with more resources from commercializing your idea themselves.

As well as protecting what is yours to prevent copycats from stealing your ideas, securing your intellectual property rights has the added benefit of bolstering your company's value and making your business more attractive to outside investors. Intellectual property is seen as a valuable asset which can be sold or licensed if necessary, therefore reducing the risk of purchasing a business.

There are a number of different types of intellectual property:

- **Patent.** This is essentially a legal document that grants the owner total rights (a monopoly) to produce, use or sell the patented product, and prevents anyone else from using their innovation or invention. The document also describes in detail the full technical workings of the invention. This means that a patent protects ownership and usage, but not privacy. Protection lasts for 20 years from the date the patent application was filed, after which time it enters the public domain and becomes available for others to commercially exploit. It is expensive to register a patent and it can be denied for a number of reasons. It also takes a long time for a decision to be made. While you wait for an application to proceed, the patent is known as 'patent pending'.
- **Trademark.** This applies to logos, brand names, slogans and other 'badges of origin', and can consist of words, letters, numbers, drawings, images, symbols, smells, sounds or a combination of these. ™ is the symbol for an unregistered trademark. It shows that you are using this trademark and own it but have not officially applied for it to be registered

(or have applied but have had your application refused). ®
is the symbol for a registered trademark. In order to qualify
for registration, your mark needs to abide by certain criteria.
So it needs to be distinctive and not similar or identical
to any other registered trademark in the same category of
goods or services as the mark you are registering. Trademark
registration is renewable every ten years. Owning a
trademark gives you the exclusive right to use your mark or
to authorize somebody else to use it. Registered trademark
owners can use trademark law to enforce their rights,
whereas unregistered trademark owners cannot.

- **Copyright.** This covers all creative works from books,
website copy and paintings to films, music, computer code,
software, graphics and all kinds of other digital media. It
essentially provides creators with exclusive rights to use, or
authorize others to use, their work. It's important to know
that the author, freelancer or employer owns the copyright,
rather than the publisher or employee, unless agreed
otherwise. (And copyright protection gives the owners rights
to prevent copying, publication, broadcasting, distribution or
hiring). You don't actually need to register your copyright,
as it exists automatically once you've created the work itself.
This means, as soon as you write or upload a piece of work,
it is protected by copyright. It is still vital though that you
prove this by time-stamping your work with a © symbol
and the date of creation. Copyright lasts between 50 and
70 years.

- **Design rights.** If you design anything in 2D or 3D, you
can protect it with unregistered or registered design rights.
These don't actually protect what the designed product
does (the functionality) – you'd need a patent for that – but
it does protect the design in terms of appearance. In order
to register a design it must have individual character and be
novel. Registered design rights last for 25 years, renewable
every five years. Unregistered design rights actually exist
automatically, as is the case with copyright, and this lasts for
15 years, as long as it is not a commonplace design.

So, as a self-made person with a lot of creative output, it's important for you to identify any intellectual property that you own. The best thing to do is to make a list of all your creative assets, from logo and brand name to packaging design, software and products. If they are new and original, they should be protected in some way, either by adding the © or ™ symbol, or by applying to register a patent, registered trademark or registered design right. This is the first way to assert your rights, by making sure you show yourself to be the creator and to give the year of creation. To register trademarks, designs, and patents visit www.ipo.gov.uk.

You should also ensure that you have agreements in place with manufacturers and the like, from confidentiality agreements to manufacturing agreements.

Additionally, it's advisable to keep good records that are dated. So put a date on and scan any paper notes/sketches and diagrams, and retain email communications. Work in progress should be able to communicate your creative story with dates.

Another tip is to put your domain name and IP renewal dates in your diary.

Finally, if you are planning to generate an additional revenue stream from your designs or from your software or other creative outputs, look into licensing your products either exclusively or non-exclusively. You can charge a licensing fee and/or earn a royalty each time your product is purchased via the licensor. You can license reproduction or distribution rights, rental or lending rights. Generally, royalty payments vary between 4 and 14 per cent, depending on the industry.

Business can have a ruthless side, and it's worth understanding the challenges and realities that small business owners face so that you can prepare and protect as you grow. From the challenges of finding the right balance, the right people and the right prices to protecting all that you own, keeping it real and in check is critical in order to grow without compounding any mistakes along the way. As you scale the business up, you get closer to your ultimate destination and the time will come when you need to decide whether to keep running the business or to exit and sell it.

....

Expert insight

Q&A with Oliver Oguz, director and trademark lawyer at Trademark Wizards

Q: *Who are you and what do you do?*

A: My name is Oliver Oguz and I am a Registered Trademark Attorney. Essentially, I help businesses and individuals protect and enforce their intellectual property rights. This typically includes brand names, logos and slogans, the design and appearance of packaging or products, any copyright protected works (such as literary and artistic works) and any other things that businesses use to make themselves stand out from the crowd. (Even jingles!)

Q: *How have you been working with startups and small businesses?*

A: One of the first questions that every entrepreneur asks themselves before setting up their business is: 'What is my brand name going to be?' A large portion of my time is spent helping entrepreneurs answer that question. I often work alongside startups, helping them to protect their intellectual property rights before they launch their businesses. This involves carrying out clearance searches to ensure that their chosen brand names and slogans are available for use and registration (and will not conflict with existing business names). I then help them protect those brand names and slogans by devising and implementing protection and filing strategies.

Furthermore, since the design of a product should be protected before it is made available to the public, I spend a lot of my time helping startups protect the design and appearance of their products before they are launched.

Q: *What industry-specific tools should entrepreneurs be using to benefit their business or to make business decisions?*

A: The UK Intellectual Property Office's search function,[37] the EU Intellectual Property Office's search function,[38] and World Intellectual Property Organization's search function.[39] These websites provide users with the ability to search to see whether their chosen trademark (brand name) has been registered in certain jurisdictions. There are many more online search facilities out there for specific individual territories. Some online search tools even use clever algorithms to find earlier trademarks that are visually and phonetically similar to the chosen mark.

There are also various tools available for searching designs, which we use on a regular basis, although conducting such searches can be very tricky.[40]

Q: *What four products would you recommend a business owner to purchase and why?*

A: First, I would protect the plain word version of your parent brand with a registered trademark, as this provides the broadest protection for the brand. This is usually the company name. Second, I would register a trademark for your logo, as this will be useful to protect the graphical stylized elements of your branding. Third, I would ensure that the company name is registered, which will usually be the same as the parent brand. Lastly, I would ensure that all of the domain names relating to the business are protected. If the business name is more than one word, buy the domain names with hyphens between the words.

Q: *What is your insight into fast-track personal and business success and the benefits brought to startups?*

As soon as you create the brand, don't just protect it for the goods and services that you intend to provide. Protect it broadly for related and complementary goods and services. This will not only prevent your brand from getting hijacked, but it will provide you with opportunities to license your brand into areas in which you would not have considered exploiting the brand yourself. This creates a rapid expansion of the brand into other markets, fully under your control, and ensuring that the goodwill and reputation generated by your licensees belongs to your company. You also have additional income streams from all of the royalties generated from the licensing revenue. The cost of the broad protection is only a matter of £200–£400 more than the basic protection.

If you see someone using your brand name without your permission, take strong action immediately. Don't let your brand become diluted and common, both on the trademark register and in the marketplace. What you usually find is that enforcing the trademark is a good way of finding licensees. Sometime the people infringing your mark are actually nice people and have a good quality service. You might want to accept them under your wing rather than stop them trading, for a fee of course.

Q: *Do you have any key messages for tomorrow's entrepreneurs?*

A: Exclusivity is key. Once you have thought of a brand name, you should always check to see whether it has been protected by someone else, or worse, is being used by someone else, before you invest money developing the brand. If it is not already protected or in use, you should ensure that you register it before anyone else has a chance to. The same goes for all aspects of your branding, whether that be your packaging, the shape, design or appearance of your products and your inventions. Everything that you apply your ingenuity and creativity to could become a very valuable asset. However, it will lose all its value if it is not protected and becomes generic or public knowledge.

Q: *Are there any emerging technologies that you are providing/nvolved in that business owners should look out for?*

A: Unfortunately, the emerging technologies that we are involved in are still patent pending, and therefore a closely guarded secret.

Q: *What question should every newly 'self-made' person ask someone in your industry before investing in their product/service?*

A: Can I protect any of the features of my product/service?

As far as products are concerned: can I protect my product's functional features (via a patent), its aesthetic appearance (via a design) or its brand name and get-up (via a trademark)?

As far as services are concerned: can I protect my business methods, ideas and client lists (via the law of confidential information), my marketing materials and business documents (via copyright) or my brand names and slogans (via a trademark)?

As far as software is concerned: can I protect the source code (via copyright), the Graphical User Interface (via copyright and designs) or my brand names and slogans (via a trademark)?

Q: *What are your two top tips?*

A:

1 Don't be deterred from seeking the advice of consultants for fear of cost. Many of those consultants will have very competitive fees specifically targeted to startups.
2 Try to make sure your company names, domain names and trademarks are all uniform and owned by you.

12
Selling Your Business

At the very start of this book we explored how a clear vision of where you are heading on your business journey is imperative. You need a destination in mind so that you can plot your route accordingly. Beginning with the end in mind, with a vision of what you are striving to achieve is, therefore, critical in business.

That destination might be to sell your business. Exit is the final chance to be rewarded for all of your efforts, to bring your vision to fruition, to potentially prosper and earn your fortune. As such it will often be the most important financial transaction of your life as an entrepreneur. Selling your business is the epitome of being self made – building a business from scratch and selling it for a good price – that's the self-made dream.

Of course this does ramp up the pressure, because your goal will ultimately be to maximize value from the sale of your business, with minimal disruption. One way to ensure this is to be as prepared as you possibly can.

Having the end in mind also applies in terms of how you record everything as you run your business. It's important to have processes in place so that your business is easy to assess and audit at any given moment because, when you're selling a business, different prospective buyers have different ideas about what it should look like. This means you need to capture all of that as you go along. The business needs to be structured from the beginning in a format that is easy to audit. That way, if someone walks in tomorrow, they can see everything, from how many minutes you spend on the phone to statistics on your website to the results you've gained from networking and where each and every order has come from. Being able to produce that paper trail is critical when you are packaging a business up for sale. Of course, all of this data is useful to have whether you aim to sell your business in a few years' time or not, because it helps you to understand where specific orders came from so you can determine how best to spend your time.

You will also need to decide in advance whether you wish to retain a small stake or non-executive role, or whether you'd rather sell all of your shares and leave the business behind in order to start a new one, or live a life of luxury off the proceeds. It depends on how attached you are to your business.

For example take Mike and Carol Clare, co-founders of bed retailer Dreams. They sold their 180-strong chain of stores in 2008, 22 years after founding it, for over £200 million.[41] Their children were far too young to take on the business, and Mike was keen to explore a new challenge. So Mike stepped down as chairman/CEO, but retained both a small shareholder stake and a non-executive role as president.

This decision came about because the business remained his passion and he was keen to stay involved, albeit in 'a small advisory way.' 'Selling was an emotional experience, but staying connected helped,' says Mike.

The exit plan

Just as it's important to have a plan when you start your business, it's equally important to have a plan in place when you sell it. Without an exit plan, shareholder value and credibility in capital markets can be adversely affected. Your exit plan will depend on who you are aiming to sell to and whether, as owner/manager of a business being sold, you are planning to stay on in another capacity or leave the business entirely.

In order to achieve your preferred outcome during the exit phase of a business, it makes sense to know who your prospective buyers are and tailor your business for exit to suit their strategic needs. Sure, needs change and strategies shift, but it is still important to address what your favoured exit route would be, consider how you will optimize the value of your company and have ideal potential acquirers and/or successors in mind from day one.

However, just because you are within touching distance of the final deal – the sale of your business – it does not mean that you'll actually reach your destination. Many deals fall through at the final stage, especially if you have strong emotional ties to a business that you have founded and run for many years. It's tough passing 'your baby' over to someone else.

So, there are a number of considerations to address. For example, owner dependency can kill an exit deal. When you pass your business on it should function independently of you. Businesses wholly dependent on the activities and performance of their owners are unlikely to attract a significant capital value on a sale. At the point of sale, the business should be able to run without the involvement of you, the owner, unless you have more of a line management role, which could be filled through normal recruitment.

Another important consideration is what exactly is for sale. For example, something we've learned with the benefit of hindsight is that, if you've got three strands to your business, you need to maintain them as separate entities before inviting prospective buyers to examine your business. Each business project should have its own telephone number and accounts. Of course, often, when you're starting you don't think of this end game and the necessity to keep different facets of the business separate: you just want to save money. However, as soon as you can afford to do so, we advise that you start sectioning off your business strands. Ultimately, someone may come in who has no interest in one of them but wants to buy another and the longer you've left all the money in one pot, the harder it is to isolate it, which can be tricky when it comes to due diligence.

Evidently, selling at the right time to the right buyers to achieve the right price is no easy task. Importantly then, it's worth looking at hiring an external advisor for this vital final phase. Additionally, there are certain questions that need to be answered and boxes ticked before implementing an exit strategy.

Here are some questions that you should ask yourself as you prepare for a sale:

- Is now a good time to sell the business?
- Will the business stand up to detailed due diligence?
- Can you demonstrate the growth prospects for the business?
- Are your financial expectations realistic?

- Is your business still owner-dependent?
- What will you do after you have sold your business?

Timing: selling at the right time

Timing a sale to maximize value for shareholders and creditors is one part of the challenge. The business must be ready, the marketplace must be hungry and buyers must be buying. It's no good selling when you're ready to sell if the marketplace is not ready to buy.

Therefore business owners should:

- **Assess market dynamics and conditions.** Evaluate where you are in the economic cycle and keep your eye on what's going on in the marketplace in terms of M&A (mergers and acquisitions) activity within your sector. Where you are will determine whether it is a buyer's or seller's market.
- **Sell at the highest peak of the cycle.** In other words, at or near the top of a rising market when a valuation is at an appealing level to generate a decent return. Some industries have their time when they do really well. Nursing homes were selling strategically for high prices at one time, while recruitment agencies are generally the first out of a recession and therefore become more valuable at a specific point in an economic cycle. Other businesses rarely show a decline in demand because, for example, the world will always need hairdressers, just as it will always need childcare options.
- **Consider why you are selling now. What's driving the sale of the business?** Because, the best time to sell a business is when you don't need to. So, if you are frequently approached about selling, consider doing so to avoid missing your window of opportunity; or, if the business is performing particularly well and you have decided to retire or relocate, the timing may be right. Conversely, if the business is not doing so well, the timing will be wrong. That is, whilst you may not have a problem selling it, you are likely to receive a much lower price for it.

Good preparation

As well as ensuring the business is profitable and deemed valuable, there will be a variety of loose ends you will need to tie up prior to marketing it for sale. Essentially, the more planning that has gone into the exit strategy preceding the sale, the less likely it is that a potential deal will collapse.

- **Plan way ahead of the sale.** It will undoubtedly take you longer that you think to sell a business. It can take between one and three years from deciding to sell to completing the sale.
- **Know your potential acquirer(s) and their strategic needs, then tailor the business to suit them.** If you know how acquiring your business might help a prospective buyer to achieve their strategic objectives, you'll be in a strong position to understand how valuable owning your company will be to them. So consider what might be the key reason for someone to buy your business. Revenue? Profit? Extending their geographical reach? Do your homework on them to establish where they are now, where they are heading and any areas in which they're experiencing difficulties too, as this could be where buying your business may benefit them.
- **Gather case studies and testimonials.** Choose ones which reflect customer satisfaction levels and the strength of your value proposition from a customer's perspective.
- **Focus on PR and on building up stories in the press.** That will get you on potential buyers' radar.
- **Allow for a lot of time and effort.** Selling a business can take up a lot of your time and you need to continue to run the business effectively whilst you are in the process of selling it. So consider how you are going to do this, ensuring that you continue to trade well and hit targets. You don't want prospective buyers to think your business is in decline when it isn't.

- **Prepare properly.** Start gathering data and getting paperwork in order early on. Transparency is vital. You need to make it as easy as possible for the buyer to do their due diligence. Pull everything together: from staff and customer contracts, to leases, business plans, accounts and case studies. You could place it all into a Dropbox and have it ready to send out to interested parties whenever requested.
- **Outline what is important to you from the sale of the business.** Are you most interested in getting a clean and fast exit? Getting a good price? The continuity of the business and long-term security from a staff perspective?
- **Check how you will maximize value.** Refer to the checklist below to help with this.

If someone is buying your business for financial reasons they will want to see a strong balance sheet and proof of sustainable profitability. A trade buyer may be more interested in the size of your customer base and the market share they are essentially buying. Others will be less interested in the historic profitability of the business and more concerned with the company's potential for future profitability and growth. They will also have in mind precisely how they can add value by investing their own money, energy, customer base, and product line into the business to further bolster its scalability and competitive advantage. As such there are many criteria that should be considered when preparing a business for sale to maximize its value, many of which have little to do with how much money it is making or has made in the past.

Checklist

Does the business have:

- **A strong management team?** This is critical. It's important to many people when buying a business that there is a strong management team in place, driving it forward. This will give buyers confidence that the company has people worth backing. That said, they may wish to bring in their own management team. However, you won't know that until you are selling, so it's worth having good people in place anyway.

- **A scalable business model with a strong list of active clients generating regular income?** Scalability can command a good valuation because it's revealing the huge potential of the business to continue to grow, reducing the risks of the purchase from a buyer's point of view. As well as growing in the regular sense, scalability is also about making more money for less input by selling either: more existing products to existing customers, more existing products to new customers, more new products to existing customers, or more new products to new customers. If you can show how you are currently focusing on these four variations you will demonstrate potential and scalability.
- **Profitability and stability?** Ideally a business should prove it has improved profits historically. However, future profitability is often more relevant to buyers so...
- **Realistic future potential and prospects within a sector that has growth potential?** There must be room for growth.
- **A strong brand and market position with good PR and clear value proposition?** If you can show buyers why customers choose you rather than your competitors, you'll be in a strong position, hence the need to collect testimonials from customers.
- **Paperwork all in order?** If you don't have your accounts and taxes in order, this will slow down the sale process and could put a potential buyer off.
- **Competing offers?** If you have interest from more than one party, this can drive the value up.
- **Good advisors?** Advisors can help you to find a buyer but also help you to get the best price and the best terms.

Typically, if you have created value, you are likely to attract buyers rather than having to go out looking for them because you'll already be on their radar. The best buyer may be a trade buyer who will value your business higher due to what it can offer them (such as an entry into a certain industry), whereas a financial buyer will be buying for a straightforward return on their investment. If a large company from Europe wants to buy your business to gain a foothold in the UK, you can probably get a high valuation. Whatever type of buyer you attract, you may still need to promote your business as 'for sale'. This can be tricky because you don't want to announce to all and sundry that your business is an acquisition target; this can create uncertainty. That said, it can also stimulate interest. Often, the best thing to do is to have a corporate finance advisor contact potential acquirers discreetly on your behalf.

Understand what your business is worth

There is going to be some negotiation here because, whilst you want to get the best and highest price, your potential buyer will seek to get as low a price as they can. Some advisors suggest that transparency helps build trust. Due diligence means that you cannot hide your weaknesses, so it is sometimes worth revealing weaknesses as well as strengths when you present your business for sale opportunity. This means any offer you get will take everything, warts and all, into consideration. However, if you leave it until the last minute to show how rundown your offices are, the offer could be suddenly reduced. But if you mention instead that you have recently secured a lucrative long-term contract, the price should reflect this and a higher offer be made. So, rather than sweeping weaknesses under the carpet, which provides buyers with ammunition to push the price down, reveal key strengths in order to negotiate the price up.

Also, all buyers know that there is no such thing as a perfect business and buyers often like to know there is room for growth, an opportunity for them to bring something to the table and add value to the business going forward. They will want to improve on the business, so revealing where that might be possible can prove fruitful.

There are brokers available to help you sell your business if you are willing to pay them a commission. They're the middlemen and they ask the hard questions. So if you're not good at structuring the business for sale, or actually selling it, we'd advise you to use an agent. They can manage the sale process and agree a strategy for sale, including who to approach, when and how. They will also help you determine a fair valuation.

One of the biggest challenges that we've found is to understand the value of your business because, ultimately, it is worth what someone is willing to pay for it. Byron says, 'You can work on different ratios (e.g. four times revenue) depending on the type of business, but it's still really challenging to know where to pitch it. You don't want to put someone off by valuing the business too high or miss out by valuing it lower than they would have paid.'

That said, it's important to have a good idea of what you want to get for the business before you begin to negotiate. When you're estimating value, consider future value as much as current worth. While you'll be offered a price based on what the company is worth today, try to push the price up based on tomorrow's value as well, if you can.

Always ask the purchaser to make you an offer rather than telling them what you are selling for. It's important to have them reveal their hand first because as soon as you reveal your price, they'll see that valuation as a ceiling rather than a floor, and they'll negotiate down rather than up. Do all you can to persuade them to make you an offer rather than keeping their cards close to their chest. Then ask them the right questions to help you establish their reasons for buying your business, and the value that it will bring to their existing operations.

Find out what they are planning to do with the business. If it is going to give them an entry into a whole new market, or will increase their market share and extend their geographical reach, the business will be incredibly valuable to them. It's about being bold enough. That said, you should ensure that your top price is a win–win for all parties. Whilst it's important to negotiate hard to get as high a price as you can, don't be greedy and risk losing the deal as a result. You'll need to be rational when it comes to negotiations and know when to walk away from a deal.

A final word

Whatever you do next, the mistakes you make and successes you have during your business journey will smooth your path and improve your decision-making. In building and growing your own business, in becoming well and truly SELF MADE, you will contribute not only to the national economy but also to your own wealth of experience. Whatever ambitions you pursue and challenges you face in the future, you will benefit from all that you learn.

So, we wish you the best of luck on your journey, be that as an entrepreneur or intrapreneur. The journey to becoming self made can be tough but we assure you it is also extremely rewarding. We look forward to hearing all about the steps you have taken in starting your business or project; please keep us updated via the website www.selfmadebook.uk, via social media using the handle @selfmadebookuk, or email us at office@selfmadebook.uk !

Notes

1 http://money.cnn.com/2015/04/05/technology/bill-gates-email-microsoft-40-anniversary/

2 http://www.businessinsider.com.au/larry-page-tried-to-sell-google-for-16-million-358-billion-less-than-its-worth-today-2014-4

3 https://www.harpercollins.co.uk/9780007390274/the-juice-master

4 https://en.wikipedia.org/wiki/E_Jerome_McCarthy

5 https://www.ft.com/content/15c8eca2-4968-11df-9060-00144feab49a

6 https://www.starbucks.com/about-us/company-information

7 http://uk.businessinsider.com/how-twitter-was-founded-2011-4?r=US&IR=T

8 Osterwalder, Alexander (2004). *The Business Model Ontology – A Proposition In A Design Science Approach*. PhD thesis University of Lausanne.

9 https://www.psychologicalscience.org/observer/how-many-seconds-to-a-first-impression

10 http://www.simine.com/docs/Naumann_et_al_PSPB_2009.pdf

11 Olivola, Christopher Y., Todorov, Alexander. 'Fooled by first impressions? Re-examining the diagnostic value of appearance-based inferences'. *Journal of Experimental Social Psychology*. 46 (2): 315–324. doi:10.1016/j.jesp.2009.12.002.

12 http://guykawasaki.com/the_art_of_bran/

13 Clifton, Rita, Ahmad, Sameena, *et al.* (2009). *Brands and Branding* (The Economist), p. 116

14 Sinek, Simon (2009). *Start With Why: How Great Leaders Inspire Everyone* (Penguin)

15 http://realbusiness.co.uk/sales-and-marketing/2015/04/29/brits-spent-a-record-16-5bn-via-deal-websites-in-2014/

16 3GEM Research, November 2016

17 Insight Engineers, Annual Trust and Awareness Research, August 2016

18 Rigby, G, *Supply Chain and Partnership Management for Entrepreneurs: An Instant Guide*, p. 4

19 https://www.entrepreneur.com/article/233444

20 LinkedIn had 147 million members in 2012, https://www.slideshare.net/amover/linkedin-demographics-statistics-jan-2012/2-EXECUTIVE_SUMMARY_ulliLinkedIns_members_have

21 http://blog.hubspot.com/blog/tabid/6307/bid/30030/LinkedIn-277-More-Effective-for-Lead-Generation-Than-Facebook-Twitter-New-Data.aspx#sm.0001mwr68by83dp3wki1lpmwylujs

22 Hubspot: 'Learn How To Attract Customers With Twitter', https://cdn2.hubspot.net/hub/231527/file-228573414-pdf/docs/attract-customers-with-twitter.pdf?t=1489163806876

23 https://zephoria.com/top-15-valuable-facebook-statistics/

24 'The Proven Ideal Length of Every Tweet, Facebook Post, and Headline Online', July 2014, https://www.fastcompany.com/3028656/the-proven-ideal-length-of-every-tweet-facebook-post-and-headline-online via Twitter Business Basics https://business.twitter.com/en/basics.html

25 Carter, Brian (October 2012), '5 Ways to Improve Your Facebook News Feed Exposure', http://www.socialmediaexaminer.com/master-facebook-edgerank/

26 Carter, Brian (October 2012), '5 Ways to Improve Your Facebook News Feed Exposure', http://www.socialmediaexaminer.com/master-facebook-edgerank/

27 Social Media Factsheet, January 2017, http://www.pewinternet.org/fact-sheet/social-media/

28 'Time is on your side', https://bitly.com/blog/time-is-on-your-side) via Forbes What Are The Best Times To Share On Facebook and Twitter?', Bruce Upbin, May 2012,

https://www.forbes.com/sites/bruceupbin/2012/05/09/
when-to-make-stuff-go-viral-online/#30622b433ee2

29 'The Science of Social Timing', https://blog.kissmetrics.
com/science-of-social-timing-1/

30 Cooper, Belle Beth (August 2013), 'A Scientific Guide to
Posting Tweets, Facebook Posts, Emails, and Blog Posts at the
Best Time', https://blog.bufferapp.com/best-time-to-tweet-
post-to-facebook-send-emails-publish-blogposts

31 http://uk.businessinsider.com/instagram-engagement-
rates-up-to-50-times-higher-than-twitter-socialbakers-
finds-2014-12

32 http://www.inc.com/travis-wright/why-personal-develop-
ment-is-critical-for-entrepreneurs.html

33 Persaud, Raj (2005). *The Motivated Mind* (Bantam Press)

34 https://s3.amazonaws.com/startupcompass-public/
StartupGenomeReport1_Why_Startups_Succeed_v2.pdf

35 Jeffers, Susan (1987). *Feel the Fear and Do It Anyway* (San
Diego: Harcourt Brace Jovanovich)

36 http://www.economist.com/node/14301470

37 https://www.gov.uk/search-for-trademark

38 https://euipo.europa.eu/eSearch/#advanced/trademarks

39 http://www.wipo.int/romarin/search.xhtml

40 https://www.tmdn.org/tmdsview-web/welcome and
https://euipo.europa.eu/eSearch/#advanced/designs

41 http://southernentrepreneurs.uk.com/meet-mike-clare-
best-known-as-the-entrepreneurial-founder-of-leading-brit-
ish-bed-and-mattress-retailer-dreams/

Contributors' details

Lex Sterling Solicitors

Lex Sterling Solicitors provides fixed-fee court attendance and a range of legal services across England and Wales. Our agency model is centred on staying nimble to our clients' needs. We represent your business as an extension of your internal team, working in a way that fits with your company's culture and requirements.

Most of our advocates have been with us for several years and have the expertise, integrity and professionalism you expect of a lawyer, at a fraction of the usual cost. As well as extensive knowledge of legal and court procedure, you will find our advocates and internal teams friendly and easy to deal with throughout the process.

One way we invest in our people is through providing accredited CPD training to ensure our teams stay on top of the latest legislation, policies and regulation.

Our commitment to you

We are passionate about providing successful outcomes for our clients. Our promise to all our clients is to offer the very best legal advice and to consistently exceed your expectations.

We know that every legal matter is unique and customise our service to meet your specific needs.

Point of Contact: Trevor Japal
T: +44 (0)20 8668 8175
E: reception@lexsterling.com
W: www.lexsterling.com

Nominet

Nominet is an internet company and trusted guardian of the UK namespace – one of the world's largest country code registries. In the UK, Nominet exclusively operates the .uk country code registry, as well as the Welsh domains .cymru, .wales and 35 other branded and generic top level domains, including .bbc and .london. Nominet has offices in Oxford and London.

In addition to operating the registry database which lists who has which domain name, Nominet also provides the technical infrastructure which allows a computer on the internet to link to the correct website when a URL is typed into a browser, or which directs an email to the correct recipient.

We are also a company committed to delivering public benefit and tackling social challenges. Since 2008 we have donated over £44m to the Nominet Trust, an independent charitable foundation. The Trust is the UK's leading funder for 'social tech' projects and to date has benefited over 10 million people.

Nominet has operated the UK domain for over 20 years.
T: +44 (0)1865 332244
E: nominet@nominet.uk
W: www.nominet.uk

Royal Bank of Scotland

The Royal Bank of Scotland offers startup packages to businesses that have been running for less than a year and with an annual turnover of under £1 million. The bank also runs Entrepreneurial Spark, a free programme aimed at helping new businesses to grow.

UK: 0345 600 2230

W: www.business.rbs.co.uk

Trade Mark Wizards Ltd

Trade Mark Wizards is a firm of established and experienced trademark practitioners who are experts in all aspects of brand protection including trademarks, designs, copyright, domain names and cyber law.

Once your brand has been perfected and refined, our expert team can help you protect your trademark, carrying out comprehensive clearance searches, filing trademark applications and defending and prosecuting these through to registration and monitoring the market for third-party infringements. Post-registration, we can help you enforce your intellectual property rights, taking appropriate action to put a stop to infringements in a quick and cost-effective way.

Point of Contact: Oliver Oguz

T: + 44 (0)208 907 9110

E: info@trademarkwizards.co.uk

W: www.trademarkwizards.co.uk

Index